LAW

Robert Spicer

An environmentally friendly book printed and bound in England by
www.printondemand-worldwide.com

Mixed Sources
Product group from well-managed forests, and other controlled sources
www.fsc.org Cert no. TT-COC-002641
© 1996 Forest Stewardship Council
FSC

PEFC Certified
This product is from sustainably managed forests and controlled sources
www.pefc.org
PEFC
PEFC/16-33-415

This book is made entirely of chain-of-custody materials

FastPrint
Publishing

www.fast-print.net/store.php

Law – A Critical Look at the English Legal System

A catalogue record for this book is available from the British Library

ISBN 978-178456-088-1

First published 2014 by
FASTPRINT PUBLISHING
Peterborough, England.

Second edition prepared with the assistance of Polly Lord, Associate, Frederick Place Chambers, who updated the text and compiled the glossary.

Production editor: Dylan Spicer

Thanks to Iain Jacobs, Lin Spicer and the librarians at the Law Library, Unversity of Bristol.

The man
Of virtuous soul commands not nor obeys.
Power like a desolating pestilence
Pollutes whate'er it touches: and obedience,
Bane of all genius, virtue, freedom, truth,
Makes slaves of men, and of the human frame
A mechanised automaton.
(Shelley, Queen Mab)

For Jasmine and Amber in the hope that things may get better ….

CONTENTS

INTRODUCTION

He saw a lawyer killing a viper
On a dunghill hard by his own stable;
and the Devil smiled, for it put him in mind
of Cain and his brother, Abel
(Coleridge, The Devil's Thoughts)

This book is written for non-lawyers and lawyers. It has the following aims:

- In general, to communicate a highly critical analysis of the current state of English law and lawyers.
- To continue to emphasise the overwhelming importance of the illegality of the Iraq war.
- To expose, explain and illustrate the central role of money in the English legal system.
- To argue, on behalf of non-lawyers, for the simplification, demystification and clarification of English legal rules.
- To examine the growing involvement of charity in the English legal system.
- To analyse English law and lawyers from the perspective of class justice.
- To restate and to publicise neglected voices of dissent on law and lawyers.
- To discuss the concept of human rights.
- To illustrate, with recent examples, the significance of health and safety law in the English legal system.
- To put forward realistic suggestions for alternative legal practice.

- To discuss the meaning and significance of dissent in the context of legal practice.
- To challenge existing preconceptions and accepted wisdom about the role of English law and lawyers.
- To discuss the effect, in a historical context, of revolutionary changes in society on law and lawyers.
- To raise public awareness and stimulate discussion of the key current issues in English law.

Chapter 1 looks at Money. It puts forward the argument that money is the key which unlocks the meaning of English law. It discusses the relationship between poverty and the enforcement of legal rights. No win no fee arrangements and legal aid are critically analysed. The Chapter also considers lawyers' earnings, law as business and the scandal of miners' compensation. It also examines the cost of becoming a lawyer and discusses the dubious history of Claims Direct.

Chapter 2 concerns Class. It defines and discusses the concept of class justice. The Chapter discusses the Crimewatch television programme as an exemplar of the spectacle of class justice and goes on to provide examples of class justice in practice. These examples include alcohol prohibition in the United States and the English system of Crown immunity. The current role of the English judiciary is considered. The Chapter also looks at examples of revolutionary legal systems including the Paris Commune and Cuba.

Chapter 3 deals with Dissent. It sets out rarely-published views of law. These include statements on the legal system from voices including the Levellers, William Godwin, American radical lawyers, Jessica Mitford, Nelson Mandela, Albie Sachs, E.P. Thompson, Tolstoy, Kropotkin, Emma Goldman and the French Illegalists. The importance of the McLibel case is also considered. Material from the Haldane Society and the Up Against the Law collective is included.

Chapter 4 looks at Rights. It deals with the relationship between individual and collective human rights, examines the torture "debate" and sets out material dealing with human rights in Cuba and in the post-apartheid Constitution of South Africa.

Chapter 5 deals with war, specifically the Iraq War. It argues that the legality of the Iraq War is the most important issue which currently faces English lawyers. It examines the legal issues arising from the War and considers English case law connected with the War. The Chapter analyses the effect of the Iraq War on the relationship between law and morality. It discusses the Nuremburg principles and examines the death penalty as illustrated by the "squalid lynching" of Saddam Hussein. It concludes with a critical comparative analysis of health and safety in a war context.

Chapter 6 – Mystery – attempts to unravel the mysteries of English law. It sets out a list of words and phrases in common use by lawyers which form a sort of secret code. The Chapter considers the reasons for obscure legal language, discusses legal Latin and sets out examples of clarity in the law. Examples of extreme mystery are also considered. Aspects of employment law are analysed in detail as illustrations of unnecessary mystification. Recent examples of judicial comments on demystification are set out.

Chapter 7 discusses current legal practice. It considers the advocacy monopoly and suggests methods of alternative practice. The Chapter examines the apparent contradictions between the public perception of lawyers and the image which the profession aims to project. The Queen's Counsel system is analysed. Barristers' public access rules are examined. The Chapter continues with a consideration of the nature of advocacy, the position of unrepresented litigants and the process by which lawyers qualify.

The book concludes with a list of further reading, a glossary of technical words and phrases, a list of cases and a detailed index.

Footnotes are deliberately excluded from the material. The main reason for this is that the author has struggled through too many books with more footnotes than text to be able to follow the thread of the material, and aims to avoid these diversionary fragmentations. Full case references, further reading and a detailed index are provided for those readers who may wish to follow up references in the text.

The material is subdivided throughout into a number of levels of headings and frequent use is made of bullet points. The aim of these devices is to make the text more accessible to the reader than conventional legal textbooks.

Some lawyers who have made a reasonable living from the practice of English law have not embraced the legal system as a saviour or a benefactor. They have always been critical. They aim to continue to be critical. They will not forget the circumstances in which their families struggled to survive and the role of English law in the preservation of a social and economic system which condemned their parents and grandparents to lives of unceasing toil and hardship.

Some lawyers do not love the law. They do not find it particularly fascinating. They do not like putting on fancy dress or enjoying the sound of their own voices.They do feel passionate about the denial of justice to the poor.

These lawyers do not find themselves under any obligation to put forward positive suggestions for the reform of the system other than to call for a national network of properly-funded Law Centres. Those who did not create the English legal system have no responsibility for its rescue.

Law reformers are thick on the ground in England, beavering away for years in committees which produce vast reports which are then often forgotten, or sweating over their chances of academic promotion by producing books and articles advocating the reform of specific areas of law.

When law reform is carried through, more often than not it creates more complexities and obscurities than it resolves. The conditional fee system, for example, imported from America despite decades of principled opposition from those who reacted with revulsion against ambulance chasing, sounds deceptively simple. Some claimants have an almost childlike faith in "no win no fee", which on the face of it is a clear concept. The reality is different.

The conditional fee system is overlaid with a mass of detail related to insurance. Insurance companies have profited massively since the evisceration of legal aid.
The system of conditional and/or contingency fees is so complex that it has become a new area of specialism. It may soon be a specialist subject in its own right, on law degree syllabuses. Non-experts have very little chance of understanding, let alone explaining, its bewildering complexities. There is plenty of money to be made from specialising in conditional fee law without ever taking on a no win no fee client.The reality is that lawyers will not generally take on no win no fee cases unless they are virtually unloseable.

Another example of a failed reform was the introduction of the employment dispute regulations. This reform was money-based with the overall intention of cutting down the number of employment tribunal claims. The new regulations were generally accepted to be disastrous and have now been repealed. This is fully discussed in Chapter 6 (Mystery).

The key point to be made in summarising the current state of the English legal system is that poor people can't afford justice.

In the interests of fairness and balance, what is good, in summary, about the English legal system?

- The independence of the judiciary.
- The incorruptibility of the judiciary in the sense of financial bribery. The English judiciary, unlike the legislature, has never been the subject of financial scandal.
- The jury system, as the only democratic element in the system, which is constantly under attack.
- The Human Rights Act 1998.
- A general adherence to the rule of law.
- A highly developed and sophisticated system of legal education.
- The permitted scope for individualism in the legal profession, which results in a small number of highly committed progressive lawyers.
- Law Centres.
- The Legal Action Group and its publications.
- The remnants of legal aid.
- Health and safety law and some aspects of employment law.
- The common law dealing with workplace stress.

- Some other areas of substantive law, for example road traffic, food hygiene, environmental law and common law negligence. These areas are not generally concerned with commerce, property or money.
- Progressive organisations, for example Liberty, the Haldane Society, Reprieve, Amnesty International and the Legal Action Group.
- Resistance by the judiciary to the increasing power of the executive.
- The intellectual achievements of the senior judiciary.

Before 2003 it seemed to be clear that the most important issue facing English law was the denial of justice to the poor. But the Iraq War has emerged as more significant than the buying and selling of justice, for the following reasons:

- The application of English law has been seen to be partly responsible for a wholly avoidable humanitarian disaster.
- Senior members of the former British government are regularly accused, in the press, of war crimes.
- Any claims which the British government might have had to moral ascendancy have been swept aside. The moral high ground has been lost, and English law is implicated in this debacle.
- English lawyers have not, in general, spoken out or acted against the first major illegal international act

of the twenty-first century. Individual lawyers and judges have protested but professional associations have, to their shame, been largely silent.

The Iraq War is fully examined in Chapter 5.

Recent developments

When my book on conspiracy law was published in 1981, it concluded, in summary, that conspiracy was the only criminal offence consistently used and developed to deal with political dissidents in the nineteenth century which retained an active role in the present political system and which had been recently applied in a similar context to that of the great Victorian trials. Conspiracy was a political law fashioned to meet the demands of the Victorian capitalists and still used to serve the needs of the modern capitalist state. This law was almost entirely judge-made.

What has changed in more than 30 years in England and Wales since those conclusions were reached?

- The most dramatic development has been that judges are now seen as the defenders of rights against the government. Judges are in almost continuous conflict with the executive. This has been described as the replacement of Parliament by the judiciary as the defender of citizens' rights. This raises the question of whether there has been a real change in the relationship between the English state and the judiciary. This is fully considered in Chapter 2 (Class).
- Radical legal opinion has virtually disappeared.

Legal journals are now almost exclusively concerned with black-letter law and money. They occasionally discuss "controversial" issues but these are well within the boundaries of liberal legal discussion and do not challenge fundamental concepts of law and lawyers. There are exceptions: Liberty and Amnesty International campaign for human rights without a profit motive. The Legal Action Group publishes a monthly journal and textbooks which are relatively inexpensive, practical and written in plain English. The Haldane Society puts forward a socialist analysis of current legal issues and publishes Socialist Lawyer.

- The virtual disappearance of legal aid in civil cases.
- A reduction in the number and funding of law centres.
- Reforms of the legal profession towards the free market. For example, barristers are now allowed direct access to their clients in accordance with the neoliberal agenda of the Office of Fair Trading.
- A massive increase in the number of lawyers, especially barristers, following the American model.
- An apparent increase in money worship and materialism.
- The apparent spread of American cultural, military and commercial imperialism including the introduction of the conditional fee system from America.
- Globalisation, for example the absorption of independent law publishers by multinational media corporations.
- An increase in government power.

Reform proposals

In 1986 Lord Gifford QC published proposals for the reform of the justice system, described as a realisable manifesto for a complete overhaul of the legal system. This included the following:

- The position of Queen's Counsel to be abolished. It is better, in Gifford's opinion, for lawyers to be assessed by their talents and reputation rather than by the secret bestowal of honours by the state.
- Wigs and gowns no longer to be worn. The wig and gown are intended to convey a message: that we, judges and barristers, are different and superior; that we have more in common with each other than with you, the litigants; that we practice a craft which you can never understand.
- Judges to be appointed from a wide range of people, including younger people, solicitors and academics.
- Magistrates to be selected from across the whole community.
- Extension of the right to trial by jury.
- Court procedures to be reformed to meet the needs of the public.
- Extension of the legal aid scheme.
- The creation and proper funding of a network of community law centres across the country. The Legal Aid and Advice Act 1949 was based on the principle that no-one should be prevented from obtaining the services of a lawyer through lack of means. State

funds were made available through a means test. In 1950 an estimated 80 per cent of the population was covered by legal aid.

- The abolition of the monopoly of advocacy. This was a very interesting proposal. Gifford argued that non-lawyers should have the right to represent people in court and that all qualified lawyers should have rights of audience before all courts. This would move towards the democratisation of the legal system. If implemented, it would strike a serious blow at the power of the legal profession.

Gifford also made the following points:

- Comprehensive legal services should be provided in a similar way to health services.
- Socially and culturally, the Bar is a privileged profession which is structured to exclude those who do not fit in.
- The role of judges should be to uphold the law equally and impartially. But when they have no conception of what it is to be, for example, a worker facing redundancy, they are incapable of discharging that role.

This programme of reforms was adopted as part of the election manifesto of the Labour party and then forgotten.
In reality, we have moved backwards since 1986.

It is significant that Gifford's proposals are similar, in some respects, to those put forward by the Levellers in the Seventeenth Century.

The Levellers' proposed reforms included:

- Codification and simplification of the law
- Prison reform
- Decentralisation of the legal system
- The abolition of the lawyers' monopoly on representation and advocacy.

These proposals are fully examined in Chapter 3 (Dissent).

Miscarriages of justice

Without going into detail, which is outside the scope of this book, readers might wish to be reminded of the following:

- **Guildford Four.** In summary, a group of three men and one woman who were convicted for the Guildford pub bombings in 1975. All four confessed. They were sentenced to life imprisonment. The trial judge is reported to have commented that he regretted that they had not been charged with treason, which carried the death penalty. Their convictions were quashed in 1989. They stated that their confessions had been obtained by intimidation and torture. Alibi evidence was not shown to the police. There was evidence of police collusion in fabricating evidence.
- **Maguire Seven.** Seven persons who were convicted of handling explosives and were sentenced to terms ranging from 4 to 14 years. The convictions were quashed in 1991. The court stated that police officers

had beaten some of them into confessing and had withheld information. Forensic evidence was discredited.

- **Judith Ward.** A woman who confessed to a number of bombings. She was convicted despite retracting the confessions and spent 18 years in prison before her conviction was quashed. Her confession had resulted from a mental illness. Forensic evidence was unreliable.
- **Birmingham Six.** Six men were sentenced to life imprisonment in 1975 for the Birmingham pub bombings. Their convictions were overturned in 1991. They had been forced to sign statements and there was evidence that the police had fabricated evidence.
- **Bridgwater Four.** Four men were convicted of murder in 1978. In 1997 they were released on the basis that their trial had been unfair and following allegations of serious, substantial and widespread police malpractice.
- **Tottenham Three.** Three men were convicted of murder following the Broadwater Farm riots in 1985. Their convictions were quashed four years later when it was shown that police notes of interrogations had been tampered with.
- **Stefan Kiszko.** Kiszko spent 17 years in prison for a murder to which he confessed. Forensic evidence had been suppressed by the police. He was released in 1992. The Kiszko case has been described as the worst miscarriage of justice of all time.

- **Cardiff Three.** Three men who were sentenced to life imprisonment for murder. Their convictions were quashed by the Court of Appeal. Police evidence was described as almost entirely a fabrication and largely the product of the imagination. The court stated that it was hard to conceive of a more hostile and intimidatory approach by police officers.
- **Sally Clark.** A solicitor, wrongly convicted of the murder of her two sons. She was released after serving three years of her sentence. Statistical evidence was deeply flawed. Clark was unable to recover from the effects of her conviction and imprisonment.

These are some of the most extreme and well-publicised examples of the wrongful conviction and imprisonment of the innocent. The list goes on and on but never seems to affect the constant myth that English justice is the finest in the world, that all foreign systems are in some way inferior.

In *McIlkenny v Chief Constable of West Midlands Police Force (1980)*, where the Birmingham Six, later to be released on appeal, brought civil proceedings against the police. Lord Denning struck out the action and commented:

If the six men win, it will mean that the police were guilty of perjury, that they were guilty of violence and threats, and that the confessions were involuntary and were improperly admitted in evidence and that the convictions were erroneous. That would mean that the Home Secretary would either have to recommend that they be pardoned or he would have to remit the case to the Court of Appeal. This is such an appalling vista that every sensible person in the land would say: it cannot be right that these actions should go further.

CHAPTER 1

MONEY

A lawyer with his briefcase can steal more than a thousand men with guns
(Mario Puzo, The Godfather)

Each wanton judge new penal statutes draw
Laws grind the poor, and rich men rule the law
(Goldsmith, The Traveller)

When all the buffalo have been slaughtered,
All the trees have been felled,
All the fish have been caught,
All the rivers are poisoned,
When even the air is not fit to breathe,
Only then will men discover that they cannot eat money.
(Cree First Nation)

Lord Bingham has commented that equality before the law is an aspect of the rule of law. He stated his view that the laws of the land should apply equally to all and that it is the duty of the state to make the machinery of law work alike, for rich and poor.

My own forty years of legal practice have led me to the generalised conclusion that lawyers, as a group, have a vastly inflated sense of their own importance. They see themselves as wealthy, powerful and influential. They have expressly described themselves in the legal press as "fine fellows". They are not aware that the existence of the legal profession depends on the continued existence of law – indeed, they would be shocked by any suggestion that they might be replaceable. For example, the most wealthy group of lawyers are generally those who deal with tax. They work behind the scenes, weaving webs and arranging the movement of money, dressed up in the highly technical vehicles of trusts and companies. If tax were to be abolished – which it could, because any statute can be repealed – then these lawyers would be out of a job. What needs to be realised is that it is politicians who exercise real power and that lawyers hang onto their coat tails, using their skills, contacts and knowledge of the rules to make fortunes for themselves. They are important only because they exist. If they did not exist, who would care?

This Chapter deals with money. It puts forward the argument that money is the key which unlocks the meaning of English law. It discusses the relationship between poverty and the enforcement of legal rights. No win no fee arrangements and legal aid are critically analysed. The Chapter considers lawyers' earnings, law as business and the scandal of miners' compensation. It also examines the cost of becoming a lawyer and discusses the shocking history of Claims Direct.

Poverty and the law

If people are not able to exercise their legal rights because of their poverty, then those rights have no real existence outside legal textbooks. No matter how sophisticated the legal system or how detailed the rules and procedures surrounding such rights, then in reality they do not exist for those who are too poor to exercise them. Without money, many rights under English law are illusory.

For example, English law has a highly-developed and complex set of rules aimed at protecting workers against unfair dismissal. There is a clear general right not to be unfairly dismissed. If a worker is dismissed and he or she reasonably believes that they have been unfairly treated, then in theory they have the right, in some circumstances, to complain to an employment tribunal. If they are a member of a trade union, then the union may pick up the costs of legal advice and representation and bear the risk of paying the other side's costs.

The rules and procedures surrounding unfair dismissal have become so complex (essentially because of the involvement of lawyers and the adversarial nature of English justice, resulting in a mass of decided cases which interpret complex statutes) that it is very difficult for non-lawyers to exercise these rights themselves.

For the non-unionised worker without money, it is almost impossible to exercise the right not to be unfairly dismissed. The procedural complexity of tribunal proceedings is daunting, and lawyers have made it worse.

The key to understanding the English legal system is the central role of money. I have lost count of the number of my clients who have not been able to start or continue their cases because of lack of money. My conclusion can only be that where legal rights cannot in reality be exercised because of poverty, then those rights have no

existence. Their existence, for the poor, is abstract and theoretical. Outside plush solicitors' offices, barristers' chambers, legal textbooks and university lecture rooms, legal rights have little relevance for poor people.
Almost every aspect of English law has to do with money or claims for money.

The American context is different, but the general principles are the same. The central role of money in the American legal system has been described as follows:

- Most of the law is of, by and for the wealthy, who, at every stage of its proceedings, have significant advantages over the poor. The law costs a great deal of money and, because of the poverty of many, its substantial provisions are irrelevant to their lives. Court fees, lawyers' costs and fees, transcripts, appeals, the preparation of witness statements, all these procedural deterrents are too costly when a poor person seeks to enforce legal rights.
- Poor people are not just like rich people without money.
- Poor people do not have legal problems like those of the private plaintiffs and defendants in law school case books. People who are not poor are like case book people: in so far as the law is concerned, they lead harmonious and settled private lives; except for their business involvements, their lives usually do not demand the skills of a lawyer. Occasionally, someone gets hit by a car, or decides to buy a house, or lets his dog bite someone. The settled and harmonious pattern of life is either broken or there is a threat that it may be broken. This is the law school

model of a personal legal problem. Law schools train lawyers to take care of such problems and to understand the role of a lawyer in terms of such problems.

- Poor people get hit by cars too: they get evicted: they have their furniture repossessed: they can't pay their utility bills. But they do not have personal legal problems in the law school way. Life for poor people is not a settled and harmonious affair in which the law never intrudes. It is a constant involvement with the law in its most intrusive forms. For instance, poor people must go to government officials for many of the things which not-poor people get privately. Poverty creates an abrasive interface with society: poor people are always bumping into sharp legal things. The law school model of personal legal problems, of solving them, and returning the client to the smooth and orderly world in the TV advertisements, does not apply to poor people.

In England, as in the US, for many clients, the fear of cost can be greater than the fear of the legal problems which they face. The lawyer who seeks to advise poor clients in their best interests can find himself acting as a financial adviser before he gets down to work on the legal aspects of the case. If he had worked for Claims Direct (discussed in detail below), he could also have acted as a moneylender.

The classic, ancient cry that there is one law for the rich and one for the poor rings as true as ever. Everyone knows that it is true, but it needs to be repeated.

An example of an academic/historical view of the power of money is that of Glanville Williams who commented that the lawyer must feel a sense of shame about the part played by the legal mechanism in repressing the poor in the eighteenth and nineteenth centuries.
Bankowski and Mungham stated their view that lawyers, in the long term, could have no material interest in conceding very much to the poor. The more the client knows, the less the lawyer is likely to be able to earn. And a significant erosion of the monopoly of legal knowledge is not in the lawyer's interest either, for if this base begins to wither away then so does the claim of the lawyer to power and privileges in society. The lawyer has need of the poor, but what we have yet to establish is whether the poor need lawyers.

Justice in England is often a purchasable commodity. Except that it ceases to be justice when it is bought. It then becomes class justice operating in favour of the haves against the have-nots. This is examined in more detail in Chapter 2.

The way to understand many of the apparent absurdities which emerge from the English legal system is to realise that it is, essentially, as far as most members of the profession are concerned, a business obsessed with profit and loss.
The general rule seems to be that to understand any puzzling point of law or seemingly perverse court decision, first understand the influence of money and the pursuit of profit.
A civil case is best fought, not with reference to the

rights and wrongs of the case, the relevant law, the strength of the evidence or the right to justice. The key issue is money. What, in financial terms, does the claimant seek to achieve? If this approach is adopted, the case will run smoothly and the chances of success are increased. This is the crude reality of English civil law at the start of the twenty-first century.

Any law lecturer can confirm that many students choose to study law because they hope to be able to make plenty of money from it. Many of those whose main motivation is the pursuit of justice, or helping people with legal problems, can soon find that their ideals fade away in the hard world of legal commercial reality.

Poverty

How many practising lawyers know the real meaning of poverty?

The income of lawyers, discussed below, should be seen, for example, in the context of the most recent poverty statistics compiled by the Joseph Rowntree Foundation. These statistics include:

- The low-income threshold for a couple with two children under 14 is £357 per week.
- In 2013, 13 million people in the UK were living in households below this threshold.
- 3.5 million children were living in low-income households.
- 4.4 million adults were paid less than £7 per hour.

In May 2014, the Office of National Statistics published data which showed that the richest 1 per cent of Britain's population now own as much wealth as the poorest 55 per cent put together.

In 2013/2014, the Tressell Trust reported that 913,138 people were now using its food banks, an increase of 51 per cent from the previous year.

In December 2009 Shelter, the housing charity, reported that it would take between 10 and 33 years for local authorities to clear their housing waiting lists. Approximately 1.8 million households were currently on waiting lists for social housing.

The Royal Courts of Justice Citizen's Advice Bureau (RCJCAB) deals with nearly 20,000 clients a year. It has reported the following:

- In family cases, 69 per cent of divorce matters involved at least one unrepresented party.
- In civil cases, 85 per cent of individual defendants in county court cases were unrepresented.
- There is a definite trend of solicitors being unwilling to take on cases on a publicly-funded basis in areas such as housing and family.
- 38 per cent of cases handled by the RCJCAB involve debt, mostly possession proceedings brought by banks.
- There may be a theoretical entitlement to get legal aid but the reality is somewhat different. Solicitors say that they are too busy, or the case does not look like a sure-fire winner, or there is not going to be much money in it for them.
- In relation to costs, many people do not have any concept of just how expensive litigation is.

The law industry

If all law were to be abolished, which is not necessarily to argue that it should be, then thousands of workers in the law industry would be thrown out of work. Police, prison officers, probation officers, court ushers, civil servants, judges, lawyers, paralegals, ancillary workers, workers in legal publishing and wigmakers – all have career structures built on the legal system.

It is a fundamental mistake to see this system as some sort of social service, or even as part of the state apparatus. Look at most firms of solicitors or sets of barristers' chambers. The bottom line is not academic expertise, justice or state control. It is profit. This explains why so many small, socially conscious operations fail. Groups of lawyers whose commitment is to something other than money find it very difficult to survive without taking highly-paid work to boost their bank balances.

The reality is that many solicitors, barristers, legal executives and the whole panoply of the "justice" system see law as a way of making a good living.

This general criticism of lawyers as willing participants in the money-fetish society does not include the undoubted selfless dedication of many of those involved in law centre and advice work or on the radical fringes, who do not see themselves as acting in the commercial interests of the profession.

Money is a God not only in the legal system. Materialism throughout society is reflected in the practice of law. Money control of the legal system reflects increasing money-worship in British society.

The fetishisation of money reflects its role as the supreme representation of social power, and the functioning of the legal profession is an exemplar of this representation.

Examples of poor clients who have been denied justice

Redundancy

Practice as an employment lawyer currently involves an increasing number of redundancy cases. Typical matters involve workers who have been made redundant, or threatened with redundancy. They have families to support and mortgages to pay. They have no wish to spend their limited savings on lawyers' fees. The law relating to redundancy is complex, and it is very difficult for redundant workers to be able to pay to discover the extent of their rights or the possibility of enforcing those rights.

Homelessness

Money is the key factor leading to the repossession of homes and the eviction of families. The non-payment of rent or mortgage instalments, purely a financial issue, is the basis for legally-enforced homelessness, for putting families in the street.

Personal injury

- A litigant in person, seriously injured in a workplace accident, not a member of a trade union, living on borrowed money, was told by a judge that he had plunged alone into the icy waters of the English civil procedure system and that he was unlikely to float. He persevered, with some "pro bono" help, and struggled through the preliminary stages of his claim. A week before the trial, having coped with the bullying tactics of his opponents' solicitor and barrister, he was told that the trial could not go ahead because no judges were available. He had organised all his documentation. His witnesses included a consultant surgeon whose fee was £1000 to give evidence. This fee was payable whether or not the trial went ahead. The claimant collapsed with anxiety and depression and was declared bankrupt. The case died.

- A seriously disabled young man who was badly injured when a shop display fell on him. He had very little money and tried unsuccessfully to find solicitors who would take his case on a no win no fee basis. The local Law Centre was too busy to look at the case. He was forced to rely on a charitable lawyer who helped him through the preliminary stages. The owner of the shop admitted liability. Shortly before the case was due to be settled, the shop owner went out of business. He was not insured. The young man developed serious psychological problems.

- A young man, disabled from birth with talipes (club feet), slipped on a patch of ice outside a shop. The ice was caused by water dripping from plants outside the shop onto the pavement. The young man suffered a leg fracture with complications because of his disability. He was unemployed and had no savings. He had no legal expenses insurance. He was not a member of a trade union. Legal aid was not available for a personal injury claim. After spending several weeks in hospital he was advised that he might never fully recover and might never be fit for work. He approached a firm of solicitors which refused to take his case on a no win no fee basis because the chances of success were too low. Two other firms refused to take the case. They asked for £1000 on account to look at the documentation. The local Law Centre could not take the case because it did not have the resources. Self-representation was impossible because of the nature of his disability and his injuries. All the textbook information on the common law of negligence, and procedure in personal injury cases, was simply of no relevance whatsoever.

Employment disputes

- A waitress, a Russian woman living in London, who endured years of bullying in the restaurant where she worked, hoping to reach the age of 60 when she could retire with a pension. A year before her retirement age, she was sacked for being rude to a customer. Her local Law Centre would only act on a limited basis and would provide advice but not representation. She represented herself in an employment tribunal claim for unfair dismissal. Her claim failed. She had good grounds for an appeal to the Employment Appeal Tribunal but no money for lawyers. The appeal never went ahead.
- A woman involved in an employment dispute who was told, on approaching a firm of solicitors, that she

would have to pay £500 in advance for two hours' work looking at the documentation in her case before the firm would decide whether or not to take on the case. For her, the figure of £500 might just as well have been £5 million.

- A client who was dismissed from his job as a skilled worker, whose union refused to back him and who spent most of his money on an unsuccessful employment tribunal claim. His appeal to the Employment Appeal Tribunal resulted in lawyers taking his pension fund to pay their fees in a hopeless case. He lost his job, his claim and all his money. He now works as a shelf stacker in a supermarket.

Unpaid wages

- Many contacts through my former free employment advice website related to unpaid wages. Typically, the enquirers were single mothers with unskilled or semi-skilled jobs who had been underpaid, or not paid at all, for weeks or months. They were in desperate financial circumstances. They had complained formally to their employers, without success. They were not members of trade unions. They had only a vague idea of their legal rights. Some might have contacted the Citizens' Advice Bureau or other advice agencies.

- The legal position – that there is a right to complain to an employment tribunal for unlawful deduction from wages – or a claim though the county court – has very little practical relevance for these workers.

Consulting a solicitor is out of the question because of cost. Often, a formal letter from a lawyer on headed paper will result in payment. But the cost of such letters through the mainstream profession means that this remedy is largely illusory.

- With the introduction of fees for employment tribunal applications and hearings, employees are now faced with the need to find a fee before claiming unpaid wages. This deters many unpaid workers from enforcing their rights. Figures published in June 2014 show an 85 per cent reduction in the number of employment tribunal applications.
- To some extent, the English legal profession can be seen as colluding with what can be described as a form of modern-day slavery in its failure to provide such workers with the means of redress. In recessionary times, these problems can only get worse, and lawyers will not help unless they are paid sums which are so far removed from unpaid workers' resources that the remedy does not, in reality, exist.
- The solution is a national network of community Law Centres, properly funded and staffed, offering free advice on an open-door basis. The cost of such a network is minimal compared with, for example, the amount of tax avoided by large corporations and the financing of illegal and/or unwinnable wars.

Law as a potentially corrupting profession

The rule of law by money can corrupt many young lawyers. They may start as idealists, believing that

English law can be equated with justice and that they can help to right wrongs. They have seen television programmes where glamorous young crusaders win legal battles against the forces of evil. They are ambitious, energetic and altruistic. They have invested large sums of money in the qualification process. As their careers progress, they may be changed in the following ways:

- A widespread ethos of pomposity and arrogance starts to influence them. The dependence of less informed people upon them for advice and information, and the acknowledgment by non-lawyers of their superior skills, can mean that they become patronising without even being aware of it.
- The injustices which they see every day of their working lives can harden and coarsen their attitude to clients. They become increasingly cynical and indifferent to human suffering. Gradually, they are influenced by money-worship, by materialism and by the aims of the profession seen almost exclusively in terms of financial success and failure. Their youthful idealism is replaced by an unfeeling preoccupation with profit. It is very difficult for any young lawyer entering the profession to remain untainted by hourly charging rates, success fees and bottom-line cash flow.

If a response to this is that the profession cannot function on fresh air, that if lawyers did not make a profit the profession would wilt and fade away, then a reply could be that any supposedly socially useful profession which is largely obsessed with money making could, in the interests of a healthy society, usefully fade away.

It is not as though the controlling figures in the legal establishment cannot make a reasonable living. In reality, they are paid sums of money which are unimaginable to those who have to work with their hands and their bodies.

Legal aid

Legal aid was conceived as a cornerstone of the welfare state. The current system was created by the Legal Aid etc Act 1949 as part of the welfare state at a time when free access to justice was regarded as a fundamental right in the same way as education and healthcare. At its inception, the scheme covered 80 per cent of the population. The principle was that legal aid should be available in those types of case where lawyers normally represented private individual clients. Public funding should not be limited to people normally classified as poor, but should include those of small or moderate means. Legal aid was introduced against a background of a Britain which was exhausted and bankrupt after World War II and deeply indebted to the United States.

The gradual dismantling of the welfare state and its replacement with profit-making institutions has not been limited to medicine, education and social services. It has had dramatic effects on the availability of legal remedies for the poor.

It is well known, if not often acknowledged, within the profession, that one reason why legal aid was reformed and restricted – a reason against which it was difficult to argue - was that the greed of lawyers in exploiting the legal aid system had led to runaway costs. This greed gave significant ammunition to those whose aim was the removal of welfare state principles from the legal system. Lawyers' devotion to money resulted in a drying up of money from the state. It must be recognised and accepted that the reality was that the legal aid system was abused by lawyers. This is known to those of us who practised under the old legal aid system. High fees were demanded and paid. The cost of the system ran out of control. The result of this has been its Americanisation by the introduction of conditional fee agreements.

In April 2013 the Legal Aid, Sentencing and Punishment of Offenders Act 2012 (LASPO) made sweeping changes to the legal aid system. Virtually all family law advice is now excluded from legal aid. Victims of domestic violence must obtain medical evidence of abuse. This involves a fee of £50 for a doctor's letter, £60 for a memorandum of conviction and £75 for a police disclosure report. Housing cases, immigration and personal injury claims are now generally outside the legal aid system.

The government is reported to have pledged to make further savings of £220 million each year until 2018.

This has been described as the justice gap, which is the legal aid vacuum, occupied by an increasing section of society which is neither sufficiently impoverished to qualify for legal aid nor able to afford a lawyer.

An example of the practical effects of the withering away of legal aid is given by the Legal Action Group (LAG) in its study of Dover magistrates' court on a repossessions day. There were 35 listed repossession cases. The debt adviser from the local CAB was reported to have commented that many of the defendants were traumatised, unsure of what was going on, totally ill-

informed and prepared to lose their homes because they thought that there was no alternative.
A LAG spokesperson made the point that in Britain today people can lose their homes through a legal process, often unnecessarily, in ignorance of the law and after being misled about their rights, without access to legal advice.
The English legal system now has disturbing similarities with the unreformed American healthcare system. It is mainly available only to the very rich or the adequately insured, and it bankrupts victims.

Property law

For many people, their main contact with lawyers is dealing with the solicitor who handles the procedure of buying and selling houses. "Conveyancing" law is highly structured, sophisticated and sufficiently complex to deter all but the most determined house buyer or seller who aims to avoid giving large sums of money to lawyers.
Conveyancing is essentially about the exchange of money for property. It involves layer upon layer of professionals: solicitors, legal executives, paralegals, estate agents, surveyors, mortgage brokers and bankers. Networking between lawyers and their auxiliaries controls the conveyancing system.
This massively complex and sophisticated edifice of property and tax law, aimed at the preservation of property and the transfer of property rights, is simply irrelevant to those who have no property. Those of us whose family members have died, leaving literally nothing but the clothes they stood up in, are well aware

of the reality of the irrelevance of property law in such circumstances.

Conditional fee agreements (CFAs)

In April 2000 legal aid for routine personal injury cases was abolished and replaced by "no win no fee" agreements, involving the recovery of insurance premiums and success fees from the losing party. These schemes are borrowed from the United States.

It has been commented that there are growing concerns that these arrangements may not always be operating in the interests of justice. This appears to be a mastery of understatement.

It is generally recognised that solicitors will not take on a case under a CFA unless they estimate that there is a 70 per cent chance of success.

In 2005 the Citizens' Advice Bureau made the following comments about CFAs:

- Consumers were being misled by the term "no win no fee".
- They often found that the system cost them more than they gained.
- They were subjected to high-pressure and aggressive sales tactics from non-lawyers employed by claims management companies.
- Those companies were paid a fee by solicitors to whom they referred cases.
- Consumers were not clearly informed of the financial risks involved in legal proceedings.
- They were misled into believing that the system was genuinely "no win no fee".

- The reality was that consumers had to take out insurance policies to offset legal expenses incurred if they lost the case and had to pay the winning side's costs. They were encouraged to take out loans to pay for these policies.
- Private insurance companies charged according to risk. Clients with uncertain cases could face very high insurance premiums.
- Legal expenses could be artificially inflated by claims management companies.
- It frequently happened that injured persons did not benefit from the compensation they were awarded.
- For example, the CAB dealt with a case where a woman was left with £15 from a £2150 compensation award, and another where a man received £1250 compensation but owed £2400 for insurance policies.

No win no fee can be described as "another gimmick to avoid state responsibility and to secure justice on the cheap".

The following arguments against the conditional fee system were put forward before its introduction:

- It was an open invitation to unprofessional conduct.
- Lawyers would refuse to take on weaker cases.
- There would be increased pressure to accept an early settlement.
- Lord Denning, writing in 1982, stated that English law had never sanctioned an agreement by which a lawyer was remunerated on the basis of a 'contingency fee', that is, he gets paid the fee if he wins but not if he loses. Such an agreement was

illegal on the ground that it was the offence of champerty. Never, never, said Denning, allow lawyers to work on the basis of a contingency fee.

"No win no fee"

"No win no fee", in reality, is a grotesque over-simplification which reflects the naïve innocence of clients. It has developed into an impenetrable jungle of regulations and procedures, mostly concerned with insurance premiums and payments. There is also a significant body of case law dealing with CFAs and their insurance implications.

In outline, a solicitor assesses the chance of success in a case and decides on a success fee to be paid on top of normal fees if the claim succeeds.

This includes the cost of an insurance policy to cover costs if the claim fails.

The introduction of CFAs is another example of the commercialisation of legal practice. CFAs make it less likely that poor claimants with cases which are not overwhelmingly likely to succeed will be able to find professional representation. Claims with a significant risk of failure are not taken on.

In 2009 a study by Oxford University concluded that the use of CFAs in defamation cases (essentially, libel) made such cases 140 times more expensive in England and Wales than in other European countries. Defendants who lost defamation cases faced a doubling of reasonable costs against them. Media outlets were being forced to settle claims because of the financial risks of fighting such cases. CFAs in defamation cases enabled lawyers to charge up to twice their normal fees of up to £800 an hour. The study made the point that media companies were being forced to self-censor because they had no economic incentive to defend defamation claims. Where the claimant had the benefit of a CFA, there was no longer any incentive to control the amount of work being done. This distorted the normal costs control mechanism and potentially breached Article 6 of the European Convention on Human Rights (the right of access to justice) and Article 10 (freedom of speech).

Compensation in libel cases assesses a person's reputation as if this was a commodity. The valuation of a person's reputation in money risks undermining the very thing which the law seeks to restore, namely the intangible good name of the injured person. The law of defamation is fundamentally geared towards financial compensation.

English law imposes a monetary value on injuries. Although there are a number of non-money remedies available in the employment tribunal, they are rarely ordered. Employment tribunal claims, like the vast majority of civil claims, are mainly about money.

What is the client's ultimate aim? If it is financial compensation, then the system functions. If it is otherwise, for example to "obtain justice" or to "have a day in court", the procedural aspects of the case become highly problematic.

The Bar Council's guidance on public access work for barristers makes the following points about CFAs:

- While in principle there is nothing to prevent barristers undertaking work on a conditional fee basis, there are likely to be considerable problems with their doing so in public access work.

- Barristers should consider the question of payment. Payment in advance or on completion of a particular piece of work would not be possible since, by definition, no fee is payable until success has been achieved.
- Any money paid in advance would be the client's money and barristers are not permitted to hold this.

Claims management services

Since the introduction of conditional fee agreements ("no win no fee") in England, many claims management companies, formed to profit from such agreements, have been heavily criticised for high-pressure sales techniques and the high cost of their services, which can significantly reduce the amount of compensation received by claimants.

In 1995 English lawyers were allowed to take on cases on the basis that, if they lost, they would not charge. If they won, they would charge a success fee calculated as a percentage of costs to recompense them for the risk of not being paid.

In April 2000 personal injury cases were taken out of the legal aid scheme and replaced with conditional fee agreements.

Between 2000 and 2004 there were, reportedly, 130,000 references to the Citizens' Advice Bureau related to rogue claims management companies and poor legal advice.

Part 2 of the Compensation Act 2006 responded to these criticisms by introducing strict regulation of the claims management industry.

The Act states that all claims management companies must be registered. They are obliged to comply with detailed rules which are designed to protect consumers. For example, the Act makes it unlawful for representatives of such companies to visit accident victims in hospital to encourage them to make claims.
In August 2009 the Ministry of Justice reported that 100 claims management companies had lost their authorisation to provide services since the Act of 2006 came into force. The reasons for the disqualifications included:

- Criminal convictions for fraud.
- Misleading marketing.
- Some companies targeted consumers who were in debt.
- There was a trend towards high pressure cold calling from call centres, including making unsubstantiated claims and encouraging people to hand over fees on the spot.

Claims management companies are now prohibited from advertising in hospitals and doctors' surgeries.

These companies can be seen as an example of the parasitism encouraged by the rich financial rewards of the law. They are a clear example of commercial enterprises calculating and making profit from the misfortunes of others.

Claims Direct

Claims Direct has been labelled as a leading exemplar of the cynical use of specialised professional knowledge to exploit the vulnerable. Claims Direct used lawyers as moneylenders and percentage takers. This was a fundamental and widespread debasement of the professional standards so often publicised by the Law Society and the Bar Council.

Features of Claims Direct operations

- The company required claimants to take out insurance policies costing £1500. This cost was covered by a bank loan.
- It employed high pressure sales tactics by unqualified and unregulated intermediaries.
- It engaged in unauthorised marketing in hospitals.
- It used the expression "no win no fee" in a misleading way.
- Clients could be left with 2 per cent of their compensation after the cost of the insurance was deducted.

In July 2001 the Department of Trade and Industry investigated Claims Direct, following shareholder complaints and reported allegations of false and misleading statements. The company was reported to have 5000 clients a month. It had been renamed "Shames Direct" by the mass media.

In January 2009 Anthony Sullman, the former chairman of Claims Direct, was disqualified from acting as a company director. In disqualifying him, Mr Justice Norris is reported to have made the following points:

- Sullman's whole approach to business was what he could get away with.
- His conduct could be regarded as culpable in the following ways:
- Misleading customers as to the likelihood of recovering premiums.
- Misrepresenting to underwriters and customers the failure rate of Claims Direct Protect insurance policies.
- Failing to disclose to investors the inherent risks in the business.
- Failing to properly disclose fundamental insurance arrangements.
- The protection of the public and the need to deter other directors inclined to embark on similar conduct required a period of disqualification.

Lawyers' income

Lawyers are renowned for their reluctance to discuss the level of their earnings. Memoirs, biographies and autobiographies of eminent persons of the law normally avoid the topic of money altogether or refer to it in passing in apologetic terms.

Perhaps this coyness is a survival of the reputed origins of the hood at the back of the barrister's gown. This was supposedly used by grateful clients to place coins without embarrassing the barrister or labelling him as a common tradesman selling his services.

In recent years the gap between wealthier and poorer members of the legal profession has widened. The current Guideline Hourly Rates (2010) suggest the following:

- Bristol: £195 per hour.
- City of London: solicitors with over 8 years post-qualification experience: £380 per hour.
- Barristers: up to 5 years call: £250 per hour.
- A one-hour hearing in the High Court is costed at £582 for a junior barrister with more than ten years' call.
- A one-hour hearing in the Chancery Division is costed at £757 for a junior barrister with more than ten years' call.
- A half-day hearing in the Administrative Court is costed at £1746 for a junior barrister with more than ten years' call.
- Junior Counsel with more than 10 years call: Administrative Court: £989 per hour.

There are no figures for Queen's Counsel.

These figures can be compared with the current national minimum wage (June 2014) of £6.31 per hour for workers aged over 21 and £5.03 for workers aged between 18 and 20.

In 2005 a government report was published, revealing the earnings of the top 12 barristers from criminal legal aid. The highest income from public funds during 2004/5 was £1.18 million. The twelfth was £639,000.

In August 2006, the Daily Mail, under the headline "Britain's top lawyers charge staggering £5000 per hour", reported the following:

- Two London tax barristers had each earned £3 million in the last twelve months.

- Some barristers can now charge £5000 an hour for their advice.
- Clients hoping to save millions on their tax bills are now ready to pay £50,000 for a day in conference with an expert barrister.
- A barrister's clerk was reported to have stated that if a tax specialist could save his clients millions in one hour, then he was providing them with a big financial gain in the long term.
- Senior QCs working in commercial law could earn up to £2500 an hour.
- Even the most junior commercial barristers could expect to be paid at up to £125 an hour.

In April 2008 the Financial Times, in an article on lawyers' costs, made the following points:

- Allen & Overy, a firm of solicitors, had charged £5.2 million for work on a case involving Blackberry patents. The trial lasted five days. The judge described the amount as "astonishing".
- Partners at firms like Freshfields and Clifford Chance charge £700 per hour. Senior associates in the firms charge £500 per hour.
- The high cost of litigation in London could drive foreign litigants abroad.
- The proceedings brought by the liquidators of the BCCI bank against the Bank of England lasted 12 years and cost £100 million.

In 2014, a standard high street firm of solicitors charges at least £165 per hour. This is a frightening sum for all but the very rich and those few who don't have to pay

their own legal costs. For more specialised work, the fees are much higher.
In 2001 it was reported that four former law lords and a retired High Court judge had charged £10,000 for an expert opinion on litigants' chances of success when a case reached court.

The ostentatious wealth of some members of the legal profession is illustrated by a recent issue of Counsel magazine which carried the following advertisements:

- Sir Edward Marshall Hall KC's mahogany tallboy/secretaire for sale, offers in the region of £5000.
- An 18th/19th Century Petit Chateau, Maine et Loire, midway Tours and Angers, £800,000.

Why should skilled lawyers, expert at manipulating and manoeuvring rules and strategies, earn ten times more than, for example, artists, poets, musicians, nurses, farmers and skilled workers? Lawyers seem to have a sense of superiority, in financial as well as other terms, to those who produce food or care for disabled children. They can perhaps be compared with dentists: both lawyers and dentists are highly paid, avoided as far as possible and called upon only when absolutely necessary.
Whether or not these figures are precisely accurate or justifiable is not the issue. The press reports of these costs are other examples of money-fetishism and confirm the public perception of lawyers as "fat cats". This is further supported by the reaction of the Ministry of Justice. In response to the walkout by solicitors and

barristers in January 2014, the Ministry releases figures showing that the median income of a criminal barrister is £56,000 a year. While some senior barristers earn large sums of money and reflect the fat cat image, many junior criminal barristers reportedly earn £10,000 a year. They are self-employed and responsible for their own expenses, for example travel costs and tenancy fees. Many London barristers can earn as little as £50 for a ten-hour day.

In January 2014 the Bar Standards Board extensively amended and updated its Code of Conduct. It states that a self-employed barrister is not obliged to accept instructions where a "proper fee" has not been agreed. A "proper fee" is not mentioned any further. In contrast, additional guidance on the term "integrity" is provided 19 times.

The length of time which barristers have to wait to get paid by solicitors can be a sort of badge of honour. At meetings to discuss the problem of late payment by solicitors, the following boasts might be heard:

- I am owed £100,000 by a firm of city solicitors and I can't chase them for it because they might stop sending me work.
- I am owed £10,000 by solicitors who trousered my fees.
- I am owed two and sixpence for a dock brief which I picked up in 1946.

And, inevitably, barristers who want to do public access work have to pass over a money hurdle in having to pay a preferred provider for the qualifying course.

In 2013 the Bar Standards Board announced that public access barristers would be obliged to undertake top-up training under threat of disciplinary proceedings. The new training course would cost £230 and would be carried out by trainers, two of whom were not lawyers.

Barristers who hold seminars which are free of charge and open to the public now have to pay for their accreditation by the Bar Council.

The introduction of requirements for lawyers to carry out continuing professional development (CPD) had the desirable aim of ensuring that legal professionals kept up to date with developments in their specialist fields. But, once again, money fetishism has intruded. The reality is that commercial organisations offer electronic CPD materials (for a fee) with absurdly simple test questions which mean that the professional CPD requirements have been complied with.

In the early nineteen-seventies, it was a rule of professional practice, but not of law, that where a QC was instructed, a junior barrister also had to be hired, normally for two-thirds of the QC's fee. The client therefore had to pay three times for legal advice and representation: once for the solicitor, once for the QC and again for the junior.

The role of the junior was vague. He or she often just sat next to the QC, known as a leader, perhaps taking notes, asking the occasional question or looking up points of law.

In one case, the client was involved in a messy divorce. The custody of his children had been contested and was granted to his ex-wife as mother of the children. The client was determined to take the case to the Court of Appeal despite being advised that he had little chance of success. A QC was hired for £1000 a day, financed by the client's father. The father also paid the costs of the solicitor and the junior. The case lasted two days in the Court of Appeal. The custody decision was confirmed on appeal, as seemed to be inevitable. The client was emotionally devastated. His father had to sell his house to pay the legal costs. He also had to pay the costs of the other side.

Before the Divorce Reform Act 1968 came into force, the undefended divorce case was an easy source of income for barristers. Where the divorce was not contested, and the facts were agreed, the contents of the divorce petition still had to be read out in court. The barrister simply had to take the client through the petition point by point, often bringing out the most harrowing details of cruelty or sexual perversion. For this technical exercise in public humiliation, the barrister normally picked up 25 guineas.

Recent examples of the effect of money on justice

In May 2008 a confiscation hearing was abandoned because a drug offender could not find a barrister to represent him for a legal aid fee. The offender had been sentenced to imprisonment for conspiring to supply cannabis. His assets of £4.5 million were frozen pending proceedings to confiscate one-third of the total on the basis that they were the product of a criminal lifestyle.

The offender could not use his assets to pay for representation: this is prohibited under the Proceeds of Crime Act.

His solicitor is reported to have commented that he contacted 30 sets of barristers' chambers but could find no-one to take the case for the set legal aid fee of £175 per day.
The court ruled that the proceedings should be terminated because a fair hearing could not take place without representation.
There are few clearer examples than this of the relationship between justice and money.
In May 2014 a £5 million fraud trial was halted following submissions by David Cameron's brother that legal aid cuts had resulted in a lack of competent defence barristers. The case involved 46,000 pages of evidence. Solicitors for the defence had contacted a total of 69 sets of Chambers, none of whom were prepared to take on the case.

Trial without jury

In January 2010 the first Crown Court criminal trial to be held without a jury in England and Wales for more than 350 years took place. This was justified by fears of jury tampering, and specifically that the cost of measures such as the services of police officers needed to protect jurors from interference was too high. The sentences imposed ranged from 15 to 20 years. Evidence of jury tampering was not disclosed to the defence.

Intellectual property

This area of law is a notable exception to the general rule that money is normally a footnote in law books. The absence of any discussion, in student and practitioner textbooks, of the cost implications of legal rules, is a vacuum which effectively hides the reality that the poor cannot generally enforce their rights.

The economic effects of intellectual property regimes flow from the enormous expense of intellectual property litigation.

The expense of patent litigation, for example, is such that it has given rise to patent "trolls". These are companies which collect patents, often of uncertain value, for the purpose of extracting royalties through threats of legal proceedings that it is cheaper to settle than to fight. Such companies often have no intention of manufacturing or marketing the patented invention. Patent trolls may, for example, buy a large number of patents from bankrupt companies and then complain of infringement. The cost of defending infringement actions in the United States is estimated at $1 million before trial. Defendant companies may settle such claims for hundreds of thousands of dollars even where they are frivolous. The expense of intellectual property litigation is a real burden on the ability of regimes to achieve their purposes.

This shows the effect of money on the practical application of a highly specialised area of law. This effect is, unusually, expressly recognised in intellectual property textbooks.

Employment protection

Given the far from unusual practice of employers in sacking workers shortly before the completion of the two years continuous employment requirement before they are entitled to statutory employment protection, the two-year rule should be scrapped.

Why should workers who have been employed for twenty-three months be defenceless against unfair dismissal, while those with twenty-five months' continuous employment be protected? The answer, as usual, is money. To give all workers, however short their period of employment, the right to complain to an employment tribunal if they are unfairly dismissed, would be expensive. It would mean a significant increase in the number of judges and support staff. So, once again, justice suffers at the hands of money.

Miners' compensation

It was reported in 2009 that a firm of solicitors had agreed to repay money which was deducted from miners' compensation claims and paid to a claims management company. The following points emerged:

- The firm admitted breaches of professional rules.
- It had acted for a number of claimants who had registered claims with the DTI under a scheme to compensate coal miners and their families for respiratory diseases and vibration white finger.
- The firm had bought the claims from Freeclaim IDC, a claims management company.
- The chairperson of the Solicitors Regulatory Authority is reported to have commented that complaints about the miners' compensation had seriously damaged the reputation of the profession.
- In May 2006 an MP stated in Parliament that solicitors, claims handlers and some trade unions had

raided victims' compensation. There had been a feeding frenzy.

- Of 427,969 claims for compensation which had been settled, approximately 60,000 were settled for less than £100.
- In 65 per cent of the cases, average fixed costs paid to solicitors had exceeded the amount of compensation paid to the miners.

One solicitor reportedly made £13 million in 2006, mainly from industrial disease cases.

The scam was reported as deluding people and taking payments from their compensation. This could not have gone on without collusion between solicitors, claims handlers and some trade unions.

The company reportedly handled 5000 cases a week. The defendants' insurers refused to pay out on £1250 insurance policies which claimants were obliged to take out. Tactics involved high-pressure sales tactics by unqualified intermediaries.

The national press described this affair as a series of money scandals which had seriously, perhaps irrevocably, tainted the reputation of English lawyers.

In January 2009 James Beresford and Douglas Smith, solicitors, were ordered to be struck off. The Solicitors Disciplinary Tribunal found that they had breached Solicitors Practice Rules as follows:

- A conflict of interest between their own interests and those of their clients.
- Failing to act in the best interests of their clients.
- Entering into a sham agreement with the Union of Democratic Mineworkers (UDM).

- Sharing professional fees with a non-solicitor.
- Improperly releasing confidential information.
- Failing to give their clients sufficient information about costs.

Beresford and Smith were reported to continue to deny all the allegations and to intend to appeal.

The following points were made to the tribunal:

- Beresford and Smith's firm had expanded remarkably after the government set up a compensation scheme for former miners whose health had been permanently damaged by underground work.
- In 1998 British Coal (as it then was) was found liable for vibration white finger and for chronic lung disease caused by coal dust. Beresford and Smith's firm then had 10 employees and its annual income was reported to be £684,000. In 2006 the firm made a profit of £36.2 million. £23.2 million was paid to Beresford and Smith.
- 80 per cent of the firm's income was from the coal health scheme. The firm registered 97,500 claims. There was no evidence that clients were informed, as they should have been, that the government would pay solicitors' fees and that other firms were not charging success fees.
- Thousands of UDM claims came to the firm through a company known as Vendside. This was a claims handling company wholly owned by the UDM. Beresford deducted £300 from each client who received compensation. This was paid to Vendside.
- The widow of a miner was offered £281.77 compensation by the government. Beresford's firm

had been paid £2,431.08 by the government to handle the claim. The firm charged the widow a £64.04 success fee, reducing her compensation to £217.73.

In December 2009 it was reported that Beresford and Smith's appeal to the High Court had been unsuccessful. The court commented that the Solicitors Disciplinary Tribunal made a cumulative series of findings of very serious misconduct on a huge scale and in relation to thousands of vulnerable clients in proceedings which were expensively contested in nearly every particular.

Money needed to practice as a barrister (2014)

Entrance fees:

- Non-refundable application fee: £40
- Bar Professional Training Course (varies between course providers, but course does not: £12,000 to £18,000)
- Inn fee: £100.

Basic costs:

- Gown £150
- Tunic shirts: £50
- Bands £10
- Dark Suit £250
- Wig £560
- Minimum cost of dressing up: over £1000.

Optional extras:

- Wig tin with name in gold letters: £235
- Bridle leather collar box: £65
- Blue bag with initials: £75
- Barrister's striped trousers: £71

- Wig stand: £105
- Gavel and Block: £95 (The usefulness of this item is unclear: gavels are not used in English courts).
- Sleeved bar waistcoat: £167.

These figures do not seem to sit easily with the professed aim of the bar to broaden access to the profession and to recruit the more disadvantaged.

These costs are another example of law as commodity. The system generates work for tailors and wigmakers. If barristers and judges did not wear wigs, many wigmakers would become unemployed. Perhaps this is one justification for the retention of fancy court dress – to preserve jobs in the English wig making industry.

Benefit fraud

From time to time, civil servants enforcing welfare benefit rules proudly announce that they have uncovered widespread fraud and that "welfare cheats" are to be prosecuted. These purges are welcomed and praised by sections of the mass media. The boast is that taxpayers have been saved huge amounts of money by the successful undercover surveillance and exposure of benefit cheats. Advertising campaigns urge the public to inform on welfare cheats.

The reality is that the sums of money saved and recovered are derisory in comparison, for example, with the following:

- Widely-known and accepted, legal or semi-legal, tax avoidance and evasion schemes.
- Money wasted by the state in many ways. For example ,in 2008 Joseph Stiglitz, former Chief

Economist at the World Bank, and Linda Bilmes, a leading American economist, published *The Three Trillion Dollar War: the true cost of the Iraq conflict.* Their conclusion was that the total cost of the Iraq war to the US would be $3 trillion and the total cost to Britain would be £20 billion.

It has been commented that the bloodhounds who track down the benefit cheats should be let loose on the tax avoiders, the arms traders and those who have wasted unimaginable amounts of money on illegal wars.

The Americanisation/money fetishism of the English legal profession: examples

- Conditional fee agreements based on the American model
- A vast increase in the number of lawyers
- The withering away of the welfare state
- The virtual abolition of legal aid
- The increasing supremacy of the free market
- The commercialisation of legal services
- Conferences originating in the US.

Parasitism

Wherever large amounts of money are to be made from the law, increasing levels of parasitism can be seen to develop around the law-commodity. Layer upon layer of non-lawyers skim percentages from the system.

For example, personal injury compensation claims are surrounded by claims farmers, insurance companies, television and press advertising companies. Other examples include:

- Companies operating on the Internet which offer to help students to obtain pupillage. A customised application form is offered for £650 and customised interview answers for £800. The company states that its services are organised to maximise the chances of successfully navigating the application process. The top-end "Magic Service" costs £4500.
- A QC selection consultancy which, for a considerable fee, offers coaching in the QC appointment process.
- Employment and health and safety law also attracts layers of commercial activities aimed at extracting profits from employment tribunal claims. Consultancy companies, as well as providing unqualified representation, may offer insurance schemes for employers to "protect" them from the cost of employment tribunal proceedings. Such companies may offer free seminars as a means of pitching their insurance sales. Thus the organisations providing seminar facilities also profit from employment disputes.
- Mediation services, offered as a cheaper alternative to litigation (again, money is the key).
- Bar Select. This is an agency for clients wanting to instruct barristers online. It is described by its promoters as "an exciting new marketing channel". Barristers are asked to sign up for £99 per month for a minimum of 12 months. This electronic introduction agency is, we are told, "supporting the process of change and modernisation designed to serve the interests of both clients and the legal profession".

- Expresso sack trucks. The company which produces these devices states that it is aware that travelling between Chambers and Courts with a large amount of documentation can cause a great deal of problems. These can be solved by using an Expresso sack truck, price £279.95.

Costs

The concept of "costs" – by definition, exclusively concerned with money – is a highly sophisticated and complex area of law in its own right. It has spawned detailed procedures and weighty textbooks. It has developed layer upon layer of money-related rules, for example the costs of applications for costs. In practice, costs often take priority over justice.

In relation to the employment tribunal, one of its guiding principles was that costs, as a general principle, would not be awarded. This principle has been diluted and costs threats are not unusual in employment tribunal proceedings, often made by large defendant corporations.

The cost of costs textbooks includes the following:

Greenslade on Costs: £654.00

Butterworths Costs Service: £695.00

The very word "costs" sums up the central feature of the legal system. How many cases have been abandoned, and justice violated, because of fear of costs?

Begging

Begging is a criminal offence, set out in section 3 of the Vagrancy Act 1824. It is punishable with a maximum fine of £1000. Since December 2003, begging has been a recordable offence. Details including fingerprints and DNA are now stored on the Police National Computer when a person is convicted of begging.

The offence of begging, by its definition, can only be committed by poor people. It is utter fantasy to imagine any wealthy person sitting on the pavement and asking for change.

In this connection, it is interesting to note that social parasitism is not a criminal offence, nor is tax avoidance.

Law publishing

Those of us with an interest in law publishing have experienced the following developments in recent years:

- Globalisation, involving the concentration of the production of law books by fewer multinational companies of greater size.
- Steadily increasing prices.
- An increasing emphasis on electronic publishing.
- Attempts, largely unsuccessful, to outsource aspects of the publishing process to developing countries, purely in search of financial advantage.

One effect of these developments has been to make an understanding of English law more difficult for non-lawyers.

The profitability of law publishing

Law books are almost always prohibitively expensive. Some titles, costing hundreds of pounds, are marketed as "essential" texts. They have a guaranteed sale of perhaps tens of thousands. Selling books is notoriously difficult.

These books sell themselves. They are updated annually and thus the sales and profits are guaranteed every year. Small, independent legal publishers have virtually disappeared in England. The production of law books is increasingly under the control of American multinational companies. These companies are purely profit-driven.

The legal publishing industry is very profitable. A core number of legal textbooks have a guaranteed minimum sale. For example, Stone's Justices Manual, Archbold on Criminal Procedure and the White Book (the leading Civil Procedure textbook) are as essential to sections of the legal profession as pliers are to an electrician.

These books cost several hundred pounds. They are not generally available to non-lawyers because of their price, which makes guaranteed profits for the American-controlled multinational companies which largely run English legal publishing. The detail of most legal rules is contained in these publications which the vast majority of the population cannot access. The mysteries of the law, once again, are surrounded by a money fence.

The difficulty of access to law publishing by non-professionals further removes knowledge of the law from professional specialists.

The money imperative of the English law business and its attendants is well-illustrated by the price of law books.

Some areas of law are crucially important for non-lawyers in their everyday lives. For example, employment law deserves to be intelligible to the averagely literate person, and employment law rules should be easily available to anyone with problems in the workplace.

The key source for employment law is Harvey on Industrial Relations and Employment Law, a five-volume looseleaf work, priced at £1,179, or almost 200 hours of work at the national minimum wage.

Another key sourcebook is Sweet and Maxwell's Encyclopedia of Employment Law, price £1,397.

Recently, a book entitled "Employment Court Practice" has been published, price £275. This closely follows the style of the White Book and is a new court reference book for employment practitioners. The strange thing about this book is that there appears to be no employment court in the United Kingdom. This publication marks a further step in the move away from public accessibility to the employment tribunal and its domination by lawyers.

More specifically, in the area of disability discrimination, Doyle's Disability Discrimination: Law and Practice, costs a mere £49, or nine hours at the national minimum wage.

Books on health and safety law are also out of the range for most workers, for example:

- Sweet and Maxwell's Encyclopedia of Environmental Health law and Practice at £1,165.
- Redgrave's Health and Safety is cheaper, at £242.

Turning to family law, it may be idle to expect that literate people with family problems should have access to the legal rules. If they want to buy books to educate themselves through the family law labyrinth, they should be advised of the following:

- Rayden and Jackson on Divorce and Family Matters: £935.

- Duckworth's Matrimonial Property and Finance: £478.

Perhaps the right to a fair trial, guaranteed by the European Convention and the Human Rights, is of such basic importance that all citizens should be able to know its implications. They may be dismayed to know that the leading book on Human Rights Practice costs £540, and a text on Human Rights and Criminal Justice is priced at £153.

Criminal law is also of real interest to those whose liberty or reputation might be at risk from a criminal prosecution. If they want to own a copy of Archbold, Criminal Pleading, Evidence and Practice, they will need to find £475. Stone's Justices Manual, the magistrates' bible, costs £645.

Tax law is best left to specialists and the rich, given the price of Simon's Direct Tax Service at £2,900.

Civil procedure is also best avoided by the averagely well-off. The White Book Service is advertised as being the biggest source of reference on civil procedure in the country. Its authority is considered to be second to none by judges, barristers and solicitors alike as well as amongst in-house counsel and many other users of civil court texts. The price? A mere £510.

Other examples include:

Luxton, Law of Charities, Oxford University Press, £225

Principles of Mental Health Law and Policy, Oxford University Press, £230

Law of Freedom of Information, Oxford University Press, £275

Health and Safety Enforcement, Oxford University

Press, £130
Monaghan on Equality Law, Oxford University Press, £145
Police Misconduct, Complaints and Public Regulation, Oxford University Press, £99.95.

Law books do not have to be ruinously expensive, incomprehensible or produced in electronic form. The Legal Action Group (LAG) has a fine record of publishing books which are detailed, accurate, practical and extremely good value. They manage to demystify whereas many legal textbooks obfuscate the law beyond impenetrability. At a time when legal publishing is moving towards expensive electronic products for specialists, LAG books mark a significant contribution to accessibility and demystification at prices which non-lawyers can afford.
LAG, among its other activities, publishes textbooks which are models of what law books should be. For example

- Employment Tribunals: tactics and precedents: £38
- Legal Adviser's Handbook: £42
- Prisoners: Law and Practice: £40
- Disabled Children: a legal handbook: £40
- Repairs: tenants' rights: £45.

These books are clearly written, contain masses of practical information for lawyers and, above all, are priced within the reach of most non-lawyers.

Taxonomy

This is defined as "classification".

In the context of law publishing, taxonomy refers to a system, imposed by a publisher, for simplifying English legal terms. In reality, it reduces legal terminology to a number of standardised words and phrases which can easily fit into a classification suitable for all the electronic publications of a multinational company.

The system eliminates the subtleties of the English language and distorts the precise meaning of authors' words. For example, many taxonomical indexes bear little relation to the terms used by the author in the text.

Not surprisingly, this technique for blurring the meaning of words has run into significant opposition from authors concerned with the precision of the language in which their thoughts are expressed.

The legal taxonomy means that the English language is simplified and classified in interests of an American legal electronics company and reduces the number of words in the English language. These developments should be resisted by anyone who believes in the integrity of the English language. Legal taxonomy has echoes of Orwell's description of Newspeak in *1984* – the reduction of the English language to a minimum of words and phrases with meanings imposed from above, without any opportunity to preserve the intricacies and subtleties of language developed over centuries.

The true reason for the imposition of a taxonomy is certainly not demystification. Rather, the suspicion must be that the standardisation of legal terms to fit the plans of a multinational publishing company to produce electronic materials covering the whole of the law are based on the profit motivation.

The Legal Taxonomy contains the keywords assigned by Sweet and Maxwell editors to products such as the Legal Journals Index. It is available to subscribers as a desktop tool (the Taxonomy Viewer) that can be downloaded to view and use the taxonomy. The taxonomy is regularly updated and complete subject and alphabetical term lists are also provided.

For example, we are told that the index to Criminal Law Review involves the allocation of keywords from the Legal Taxonomy utilised by Sweet & Maxwell to provide a standardised way of describing legal concepts. These keywords are identical to those used in Westlaw UK.

This can be seen as an example of the move to electronic publishing, supposedly for benefit of user, but in reality for increased profits for American parent companies.

Topics covered by leading law journals

An analysis of a recent issue of Lawyer magazine shows the following topics:

- Of the 84 pages of the journal, 56 are advertisements for jobs
- Merger of transnational law firms
- "Realignment" of firms of solicitors
- Market opportunities
- Insolvency
- Disputes between partners of large law firms
- Corporate reorganisations
- Corporate governance
- Asset management company's legal team

- Banking supervision disputes
- Management of large law firms
- Construction deals
- Horseracing funding
- Offshore financial services
- London Stock Exchange
- Global telecoms sector
- City lawyers
- Supervision of law firms
- International firms
- Chinese employment law
- Quarter page on pro bono.

This is really what legal practice and publishing in England in 2014 is all about.

An experienced lawyer from an ethnic minority background has commented recently that he has concluded that money, rather than race, gender, disability, sexual orientation or age, is the main discriminating factor in the English legal profession. The main issue in interviews for places is sets of chambers was, in his experience, how much work and money would be brought in.

Charity

No society can legitimately call itself civilised if a sick person is denied medical aid because of lack of means.
(Aneurin Bevan, 1947)

The Labour government which came to power in 1945 was committed to replace charitable good works in

essential public services with state-provided welfare. Aneurin Bevan, who created the National Health Service, was passionately opposed to the patronising reliance upon private charity for the treatment of the sick. Bevan was involved in the formation of the Tredegar Medical Aid Society. This is fully discussed in Michael Foot's biography of Bevan. The Society has been described as the forerunner of the National Health Service. It involved workers clubbing together and paying small regular sums into a fund for the payment of doctors and hospital services. Foot points out that the Society partly achieved the aim of making the cost of sickness a communal burden, thus lifting the worst shadow which fell across working-class homes.
The creation of the legal aid and advice scheme was part of the same reforms. The scheme is now in tatters. The huge gaps left by the withdrawal of the state from legal help for the poor are, it appears, to be filled by the adoption of conditional fee agreements, private charity, the whim of the rich, benevolent lawyers and detailed regulations issued by insurance companies.

It is clear that many lawyers involved in institutionalised legal charities are highly motivated, with strongly developed social consciences. They could earn many times more than their modest salaries by working as commercial lawyers. This does not exempt them from criticism or from a need to subject their activities to rigorous theoretical analysis.

The following criticisms of altruistic pro bono lawyers are not aimed at their humanity. It is clear that lawyers who work for free, and the dedicated staff and volunteers who run the professions' charitable schemes, are mainly motivated by simple humanity. Charitable schemes operated by lawyers can provide free advice and assistance to those who need it most and who cannot afford normal lawyers' fees. These criticisms, rather, reflect their lack of theoretical analysis of the reality of their charitable work, their failure to give priority to campaigning for a properly funded network of Law Centres, and their acceptance of public plaudits.

Charity law

This is an industry in itself. Charity law is a massive subject in its own right, overlapping significantly with company law, trusts law and tax law. The basic motivator of the charity law industry is tax avoidance.

The role of charity law as an element of the traditional legal system, and as a commodity, is illustrated by the cost of charity law textbooks, for example:

Picarda, Law and Practice Relating to Charities: £395

Luxton, Law of Charities £225

Charity Market Monitor £370

Leadership in Nonprofit Organizations A Reference Handbook £230

Top 3000 Charities £304

Charity law reflects the institutionalisation of philanthropy as part of the edifice of English property law. The complexity of charity law, and its close relationship with tax and company law, reflects an increasing reliance on "charity" as the gains made by the welfare state are rolled back.

English charities are granted fiscal privileges by the law. These privileges are not universal but are granted to selected charities, for example Eton College, the British Goat Society and the British Society of Dowsers. Charitable status may be withheld from organisations aimed at changing the law.

The key to understanding the true role of charity law is that it provides for tax exemptions. As with most other issues surrounding the English legal system, the answer is money.

Charity, it has been commented, involves the expectation of gratitude and admiration for the giver and the stigmatising status for the receiver of being a beggar. These concepts have no place in relationships based on social and economic rights rather than vague moral obligations on the part of the haves towards the have-nots.

Theoretical approaches to charitable work by lawyers are ambivalent, to say the least. For example, in October 2006 the President of the International Bar Association, writing in *The Lawyer*, made the following points:

- Many countries do not have the benefit of the rule of law.
- The effects of this can be measured in a lack of certainty for investment.
- This commercial reality conspires to prevent the economic fillip which these countries so badly need.
- Internationally focused pro bono work can advance the rule of law.
- There is a need to emphasise more strongly the nexus between respect for the rule of law and the benign

investment climate which it necessarily presents to the international community.

- Social and economic stability is a prerequisite for the attraction of investment.
- The legal profession can do much to help countries construct the framework of the rule of law and help to bring about an environment in which international investors can bring a much-needed injection of capital.

These statements can be seen as an overtly expressed link between pro bono, profit-making and successful capitalism.

Use of Latin

The dictionary definition of "pro bono", an abbreviation of *pro bono publico*, is "free, used to denote the giving of free legal advice and services". "Free" is a simple word of Old English origin, easily understood by anyone of normal intelligence, which can easily replace three Latin words.

Why do lawyers who provide their services without charge continue to use the term "pro bono"? References to Latin maxims and phrases in Law Reports are now so rare that they attract considerable attention. The use of Latin is discredited and is often criticised by the judiciary. "Pro bono" continues to be used by those who assume that it's a "good thing" without any rigorous theoretical analysis. But there are a number of question marks and a need for self-examination and criticism on the part of those who unquestioningly accept the benefits of legal charity and who fail to reject Latin terminology.

How do non-charging lawyers who label themselves "pro bono" react, for example, to the statement of Lord Justice May in *Fryer v Pearson and Another (2000),* that people should stop using maxims or doctrines dressed up in Latin which are not readily comprehensible to those for whose benefit they are supposed to exist?

Or, a judicial statement of 1940 which made the following points:

Counsel has strenuously contended that the master's action was novus actus interveniens, which broke the nexus or chain of causation, and reduced the unseaworthiness from causa causans to causa sine qua non. I cannot help deprecating the use of Latin or so-called Latin phrases in this way. They only distract the mind from the true problem, which is to apply the principles of English law to the realities of the case.

There is a suspicion that the continued, unquestioning use of the phrase "pro bono" reflects the increasing Americanisation of the English legal system. For many American lawyers, pro bono work is an essential element of their career progression and a crucial factor in the corporate identity of large law firms.

Former Attorney-General Lord Goldsmith is reported to have made the following comments:

We are fortunate to live in a country with a mature and effective legal system. People in many other countries are less fortunate. A lack of functioning and effective courts, corruption and shortages of competent lawyers are affronts to justice and to basic human rights. They also hold back a country's development. They lead to people taking the law into their own hands. And refugees will stream from countries where legal systems offer no protection.

This can be seen as an argument that unless we give charitable legal help to the unfortunates of this world who are not blessed with the English legal system, we will face a flood of lawless refugees.

Objections to Charity

Just as the worst slave-owners were those who were kind to their slaves, and so prevented the horror of the system being realised by those who suffered from it, and understood by those who contemplated it, so in the present state of things in England, the people who do most harm are the people who try to do the most good; and at last we have the spectacle of men who have really studied the problem and know the life, coming forward and imploring the community to restrain its altruistic impulses of charity, benevolence and the like. They do so on the ground that such charity degrades and demoralises. They are perfectly right. Charity creates a multitude of sins. It is immoral to use private property in order to alleviate the horrible evils that result from the institution of private property. It is both immoral and unfair ... we are often told that the poor are grateful for charity. Some of them are, no doubt, but the best amongst the poor are never grateful. They are ungrateful, discontented, disobedient and rebellious. They are quite right to be so. Charity they feel to be a ridiculously inadequate mode of partial restitution, or a sentimental dole, usually accompanied by some impertinent attempt on the part of the sentimentalist to tyrannise over their private lives. Why should they be

grateful for the crumbs that fall from the rich man's table? They should be seated at the board.
(Oscar Wilde, The Soul of Man under Socialism)

Camus, The Fall

This is the story of a successful barrister who appears to be the epitome of good citizenship and decent behaviour. Circumstances explode his sleek self-esteem. He sees through the deep-seated hypocrisy of his existence to the condescension which motivates his every action.
The feeling of the law, the satisfaction of being right, the joy of self-esteem... I loved to help blind people cross streets. From as far away as I could see a cane hesitating on the edge of a pavement, I would rush forward, sometimes only a second ahead of another charitable hand outstretched, snatch the blind person from any solicitude but mine, and lead him gently but firmly over the pedestrian crossing amidst the hazards of the traffic towards the quiet haven of the other pavement, where we would separate with a mutual emotion... I always enjoyed telling people the way in the street, giving a light, lending a hand with heavy barrows, pushing a stranded car, buying a paper from the Salvation Army girl.
Being stopped in the corridor of the law courts by the wife of a defendant you represented for the sake of justice or pity alone – without charging a fee – hearing that woman whisper that nothing could ever repay what you had done for them, replying that it was quite natural, that anyone would have done as much, even offering some financial help to tide over the bad days ahead, then – in order to cut the effusions short and preserve their

proper resonance – kissing the hand of a poor woman and breaking away...

In 1957, Camus was awarded the Nobel Prize for literature, with a prize of $42,000. He deposited the cheque in a bank in Stockholm and forgot about it until some months later, when he was asked by the bank what he wanted them to do with the funds.

Camus' attitude to prizes and honours forms an interesting contrast with the ethos of lawyers' charitable work. For example, in November 2009 it was reported that more than 50 "pro bono heroes" attended a Parliamentary reception hosted by the Attorney-General. She is reported to have commented that it was not in the nature of lawyers who acted pro bono to seek recognition or praise for their efforts. The reception was a way of celebrating the work of pro bono heroes. The glaring contradictions of this statement were not recognised.

Richard Abel, in *English Lawyers between Market and State,* makes the following comments on pro bono services:

- They allow elite lawyers conspicuously to enact independence on behalf of vulnerable clients confronting powerful adversaries (frequently the state) thereby mystifying those lawyers' profound dependence on a few large clients (many of which oppress and exploit the very same clients).
- Pro bono services contain their own contradictions.
- The recession was not in general a climate in which an extension of pro bono work was sought.

- There is a fundamental contradiction between the Law Society's exhortation that solicitors must run their practices on strict business lines and its message that they have surplus time, resources and cash to work for nothing to prop up under-funded organisations.

Claire Dyer wrote in the Guardian, June 3, 2003, that the reasons for pro bono work were "a complex interaction between professional idealism, political pressure and commercialism".

Only lawyers?

- Is the legal profession apparently the only group of professionals which feels it necessary, when it gives fellow human beings a helping hand without demanding money in return, to organise such actions into an institution, to give such actions a Latin tag, to bask in the assumption of public admiration, to accept plaudits at glittering social events and to reap commercial benefits from an improved public image?
- Do any other professions have pro bono schemes? Are there pro bono plumbers or motor mechanics? Bookmakers? Doctors don't do pro bono work because their work is funded by the state and runs parallel to a private system.
- Do lawyers work for free because they are the only group of professionals with a social conscience?
- If other groups of professionals do free work on a large scale, which is questionable, why is this so little

publicised in comparison with lawyers' pro bono schemes?

- How do lawyers react to the argument that they make so much money that they can easily afford to do some work for free?

- Another profession which is well-known for its readiness to do unpaid work is teaching. Many primary and secondary school teachers regularly take on unpaid professional activities beyond the scope of their contracts of employment. For example, a typical conscientious inner-city comprehensive schoolteacher may habitually spend about ten hours a week on unpaid out of school activities, including drama, adventure trips, fundraising activities, pastoral and advisory work. This work is not given a Latin label, receives little public recognition, will not lead to an award, and is not organised by a central body. There are no ceremonies for schoolteacher "pro bono heroes".

Legal charitable institutions

The Bar Pro Bono Unit

This is a national charity which aims to assist those with deserving cases who cannot obtain public funding or pay privately for legal assistance.

This immediately raises the questions of, first, what is "deserving", with its echoes of the concept of the "deserving poor", and, second, who decides what is deserving.

All applications to the Unit must be referred from advice agencies or solicitors.

The Bar Pro Bono Unit publishes an annual review. The 2005 edition, for example, states, on its front cover, that access to the legal system, irrespective of means, is essential to ensure that the rule of law prevails. It goes on to comment that the Unit, with its committed staff and volunteer team, allows barristers to put something back into society of real importance. Not only do they help individual clients – just as importantly, they demonstrate to the wider public the value of lawyers to society.

On the back cover, the following advertisement by Coutts Bank appears: "Expert Wealth Management for Private Clients".

Criteria for charitable assistance

Lawyers' "pro bono" schemes generally operate criteria for eligibility in a similar way to that used by the legal aid authorities. It is not easy to get charitable help.

The schemes operate as a sort of charitable Legal Aid Board.

For example, the Bar Pro Bono scheme states the following:

- It is for people who cannot obtain legal aid.
- Who cannot afford to pay or get help elsewhere.
- The case must usually have legal merit.
- A single piece of work must not involve more than 3 days work.
- Applications must be made through a solicitor or an advice agency.

- Applications are reviewed by one of a number of senior barristers who consider the legal merit of the case.

The Bar defines "pro bono" work as legal advice or representation provided by lawyers to individuals and to community groups who cannot afford to pay for that advice or representation and where public funding is not available.

The Bar Pro Bono scheme was founded in 1996. On the tenth anniversary of its creation, the founders made the following points:

- The unit had helped to ensure that access to justice was never just for the rich.
- The foundation of our society is the rule of law.
- Access to justice is the gateway to the rule of law.
- Pro bono can only ever be an adjunct to, and never a substitute for, a proper system of publicly funded legal aid.
- The unit co-ordinates the Bar Pro Bono Award, an annual award which celebrates an outstanding contribution in the pro bono field by an individual barrister or set of chambers.

There was no mention of any campaign for increased legal aid and/or more Law Centres.

In the Annual Review for 2007, a barrister doing voluntary work for the Bar Pro Bono unit commented that nearly all barristers, no matter how superb their reputations might be, would do well to seriously consider providing their expertise to the Unit. Not only were people in dire need assisted but there was no doubt that barristers would bolster their chances of success as they enjoyed their journey through the legal marketplace.

The Bar Pro Bono Unit believes that pro bono work is not a substitute for a proper system of publicly funded legal services. There is, however, no evidence of campaigning to achieve a proper publicly funded system. The Unit's refusal of complex cases is understandable from its own viewpoint but this policy only reinforces the patronising nature of charity: law is not as important as medicine but the same principles apply: legal assistance should be a right and not a charitable act. The policy of refusing to take on complex cases can be compared with a doctor refusing to treat the seriously ill.

Law Works

The solicitors' pro bono scheme, now known as "LawWorks", excludes crime, family and immigration matters. Applications must be made through advice agencies. They are reviewed by a senior solicitor who decides whether they are suitable for pro bono work. Clients with no money can be turned down by pro bono organisations for a number of reasons and it can be seen that the very act of choosing which clients to assist is, in itself, patronising and amounts to the exercise of power to decide the future of claims.

Free Representation Unit

The Free Representation Unit provides legal advice, case preparation and advocacy in tribunal cases for those who could not otherwise obtain legal support for want of personal means or public funding. It is staffed by student caseworkers, predominantly enrolled on the BPTC (Bar training course) who view it as an important training ground to gain experience so as to enhance their pupillage prospects. This assistance is available only if the case has already started and is referred by a referral agency.

Law Centres

In the Southeast of England, outside London, there is one Law Centre in Surrey and one in the Isle of Wight. There is one in Wales. Since LASPO came into force, Birmingham Law Centre has closed, as have Wythenshawe and Trafford Law Centres (both in Manchester). Harehills and Chapeltown (Leeds), Barnet, Greenwich and Streetwise Community Law Centres (all in London) have also ceased to operate. The Law Centres Federation predicted in 2011 that 1 in 3 Centres would close because of funding cuts.

Pro bono is presented to the public as professional altruism but is sold to members of the profession as self-interest. Pro bono practitioners are advised that the advantages of well-publicised free work include creating a high profile, attracting top quality new recruits, supplying useful advocacy and trial preparation experience and refreshing established fee earners. For those starting their careers in the profession, experience of pro bono work can be a useful addition to their CV.
The former President of the International Bar Association, Francis Neate, commented that:
... we need to emphasise more strongly the nexus between respect for the rule of law and the benign investment climate that it necessarily presents to the

international community. Social and economic stability is a prerequisite to the attraction of investment.

Pro bono schemes admit that formalised free work should not usurp the proper role of the state, but there is no campaigning for proper state-funded legal advice and representation, and in particular for a properly funded national network of Law Centres. Those whose consciences dictate that poor people should not be left without legal assistance might consider the option of employment at a low salary in a Law Centre or another advice organisation, if only for a short period.

Criticisms of the pro bono movement

- Reliance on private charity for the enforcement of social and economic rights is unacceptable in an advanced society. We have witnessed, over the last couple of decades, the formalisation and acceptance of the charitable ethos to deal with social and economic problems. In this context, although law is less important than, for example, medicine and education, these are all social and economic rights and should not depend on the consciences of the wealthy and powerful.
- There has been a significant expansion of the charitable sector since the 1980s, linked to the notorious assertion by the powerful that there is no such thing as society. Street collections for medical problems, especially in relation to children, should not be necessary in the eighth richest country in the world and are an affront to those who suffer from

such problems. My own discussions with charitable street collectors have revealed that very few have ever considered the theoretical implications of charity and are astonished to find someone who regards charity as a "bad thing" and is prepared to argue the issue.

- It can be argued that all charitable work is necessarily patronising. To have to explain to clients the meaning of "pro bono" simply reinforces the "us and them" syndrome and is supposed to make clients grateful for being able to enjoy their rights and give the charitable lawyer the warm glow felt by Ebenezer Scrooge when he gave Bob Cratchit a day's holiday. Simply to say "no charge" or "pay what you can when you can" is enough.

- Pro bono awards are self-congratulatory. These awards and ceremonies reflect not only doing work for nothing but being seen to do so. These awards and ceremonies are regarded with amazement outside the profession but with not a trace of embarrassment within. There appears to be no realisation of the irony of being feted for doing work for nothing. Perhaps lawyers are so well-paid that when one works for nothing, a well-earned glass of champagne is in order. The system of pro bono awards and ceremonies is another example of the legal profession's astonishing lack of awareness of the public perception of lawyers.

- Justice does not come cheap and is too important to be left to charitable initiatives.

- Those of us who regularly come into contact with people who cannot afford justice have drawn the conclusion that the solution to the problems of poverty do not lie in organised charitable institutions.
- Charity is always double-edged. Surveys suggest that the poor give far more than the rich. One of the most pernicious ways in which governments use people's generous instincts is by transferring responsibility for the most desperate people onto charities.
- It is known that there is a massive unmet need for legal advice and representation, particularly in the areas of, for example, welfare law, housing and employment. It seems likely that the number of redundancies and repossession of family homes will increase sharply. These problems are not essentially legal, but lawyers can help to reduce the hardships caused. This legal assistance should be provided by properly funded and resourced community law centres: it must not be left to charitable initiatives.
- Public funding of legal advice is in permanent retreat and there is an increasing "legal aid desertification", leaving tracts of the country without cover. The concept and culture of pro bono are expanding.
- The increasing Americanisation of the English legal system can be seen in, for example, the institutionalisation of pro bono, the introduction of conditional fees, ambulance chasing, claims farmers, and more lawyers than any healthy society needs.
- For most people, employment law, for example, is almost prohibitively complicated and they can't get

hold of the advice they need, even though it has been designed to protect them. Neither do they know where to go for help because it's either expensive or difficult to access.

Pro bono initiatives

Old books for the third world

The organised distribution of secondhand law books to sub-Saharan Africa, the poorer parts of Asia and the Caribbean has been hailed as a contribution to the underpinning of individual liberty and democratic government. The organisers do not seem to have realised the contradictions inherent in this scheme.

First, an old law book is more like out-of-date food than like an old overcoat. Old overcoats can keep you warm, but old law books, like food which is past its sell-by date, are worse than useless – they are dangerous. If it were to be suggested to a successful British lawyer that he or she might rely on old editions of legal textbooks donated by inhabitants of former colonies, this would rightly be regarded as an insult. Developing countries deserve more than our castoffs, just as poor people deserve more than our old clothes.

No decent British lawyer would use an out of date textbook. If she did, she would risk liability for negligence. Old law books are simply wrong, and valueless, because they contain out of date material. If you are involved in litigation and your opponent has a new book, while you have an old one, you are suffering a tremendous disadvantage.

Second, the distribution of such useless material to the

deserving poor is one of the clearest examples of the pro bono movement not thinking its actions through. If law books are essential for democracy in "the poorer parts of Asia", then why should those who thirst for democracy not have access to up to date material? Are we seriously expected to believe that a poverty-stricken Asian lawyer will give heartfelt thanks when he receives an old edition of Archbold? The attitude seems to be that old law books are no use to us, but the colonies will be grateful for them.

Third, it has been reported that the major law publishers are involved in this patronising exercise. But it seems clear that their largesse stops short of giving new law books away, even though they are essential for democracy. Law publishing is known to be a highly profitable business, and the cost of new editions of law books makes them unavailable to anyone other than the very rich or those with access to a law library. The distribution of new editions of law books to the deserving colonies would carry more weight if useful texts, rather than useless castoffs, were given away. Lawyers in developing countries will have a long wait if they expect deliveries of new law books from multinational publishers.

One of the organisers of the distribution of unwanted old law books is reported to have said that all of those who work on the project feel that what they are doing is in tune with the times.

CHAPTER 2

CLASS

The law doth punish man or woman
That steals the goose from off the common.
But lets the greater felon loose
That steals the common from the goose.

The law in its majestic impartiality forbids both rich and poor alike to sleep under bridges, to beg in the streets and steal bread.
(Anatole France, Crainqueville)

I went from having an idealistic view of the law as a sword of justice to a perception of the law as a tool used by the ruling class to shape society in a way favourable to itself. I never expected justice in court, however much I fought for it and though I sometimes received it.
(Nelson Mandela)

This chapter concerns Class. It attempts to define, discusses and gives examples of the concept of class justice. These examples include the Crimewatch television programme as an exemplar of the spectacle of class justice, alcohol prohibition in the United States and the English system of Crown immunity. The current role of the English judiciary is considered. The Chapter also looks at class justice in the context of examples of revolutionary legal systems including the Paris Commune and Cuba.

Summaries of recent health and safety prosecutions are spread throughout this Chapter as examples of what might be described as reverse class justice, operating in favour of workers against employers.

Class justice

Class justice means, essentially, that the principles of justice operate inequitably in favour of one class of people in relation to other classes. A basic definition of "class" is a division of society according to status, or a number of individuals possessing common attributes and grouped together under a general or class name.
Class justice functions when justice is done in favour of one class against another. In England in the early twentieth century, this means that justice can often be seen to operate in favour of the rich and powerful against the poor and the weak.
Class justice is exemplified by the prosecution of petty offenders against property while major criminals can appear to be immune.
This is not purely a theoretical concept. It has serious implications for people in their everyday lives.

Crown Immunity

The case of John Wynne and the Royal Mint

The case of John Wynne, employed by the Royal Mint at Llantrisant, South Wales, has highlighted the legal rules and procedures surrounding Crown immunity as a clear example of class justice. The facts, in summary, were that in 2001 Mr Wynne (W), suffered fatal crushing injuries when a six-tonne furnace fell from a crane. W, aged 50, had worked in the metal rolling department of the Mint for 21 years.

The Health and Safety Executive (HSE) found itself unable to prosecute the Mint for breaches of health and safety legislation. Instead, it brought Crown Censure proceedings. At the hearing of these proceedings it was stated that the Mint had failed to follow safety procedures. The hearing was not open to the public. A report of the hearing was sent to the government, the Royal Mint and the HSE. W's widow was not entitled to a copy of the report.

W's widow is reported to have commented that she was shown pictures at the hearing which showed the furnace hanging from a crane, but not sitting on the hook properly. The furnace was balancing on the top and it fell. It had fallen once before, and no-one was hurt. The Mint's management had not carried out safety checks. If they had done so, they would have realised that it was faulty and the accident could never have happened.

An HSE inspector is reported to have made the following points to the hearing:

- W's death was an accident waiting to happen.
- There was sufficient evidence to bring a criminal prosecution against the Mint.
- Although Crown property, including the Mint, has to comply with health and safety regulations, it cannot be prosecuted because the Crown cannot prosecute itself.

The shadowy issue of Crown immunity arises in the context of both criminal and civil proceedings. Crown immunity is an ancient, obscure and complex area of law with significant practical implications. The concept is inextricably bound up with the development of the unwritten British Constitution and the relationship between the monarch, central government, legislation and the enforcement of criminal law.

Criminal proceedings

The following points may help with an understanding of Crown immunity:

- The literal meaning of "Crown" is "an ornamental badge of regal power worn on the head of sovereign princes". In general terms, it means the monarch. This involves a consideration of the constitutional position of the monarchy as the head of state.
- In strict legal and constitutional theory, legislation cannot come into force until it has received the Royal Assent, that is, consent by the monarch.
- The "Crown" now applies to the collective structure of central government in the United Kingdom.
- The monarch is personally immune from prosecution or criminal proceedings. This is one reason why the execution of Charles I was deemed to be illegal after the restoration of the monarchy.
- In constitutional law, the King (or Queen) can do no wrong. He/she is never a minor and never dies.
- Crown immunity also applies, by implication, to the ruling sovereigns of other states. This does not extend to deposed or exiled sovereigns who happen to be within the jurisdiction. The authority for this is

cited by Archbold (the barristers' bible) as *R v Mary, Queen of Scots (1586).*

- Criminal prosecutions are conducted on behalf of the Crown and generally brought in the name of the Queen. Criminal cases are cited as "R v …" which is an abbreviation of "Regina v…".
- The general principle is that the Crown is not bound by any statute. This principle may be displaced where there is an intention stated in the statute that the Crown should be bound.
- The principle extends to Crown servants acting in the course of their official duties, Crown property and property occupied by the Crown for public purposes. It covers, for example, the Ministry of Defence, the Prison Service and the Royal Mint.
- Section 48 of the Health and Safety at Work, etc., Act 1974 states, in summary, that sections 1 to 54 of the Act, except for sections 21 to 25 and 33 to 42, shall bind the Crown. But this does not mean that criminal proceedings may be brought against the Crown. It should also be noted that liability under the 1974 Act cannot, in itself, give rise to civil liability.
- It is also significant that the Working Time Regulations 1998, regulation 37, states in summary that the regulations have effect in relation to Crown employment. No act or omission by the Crown shall make the Crown criminally liable, but the High Court or the Court of Session in Scotland may make a declaration that such act or omission is unlawful.

There appear to be no reported examples of such declarations.

Crown Censure proceedings are brought by the Health and Safety Executive as an alternative to criminal prosecutions. These proceedings have no formal legal basis and it is difficult to find information about them through standard sources. It is thought that the HSE has reached agreement with the government that the proceedings will be used in appropriate circumstances. The proceedings have been used in a number of reported cases, mostly involving the prison service and the Ministry of Defence.
The proceedings are not open to the public. Trade union representatives may be invited to attend. The procedure is not a trial and it is chaired by a senior HSE inspector. The procedure has no statutory basis but is set out in a Cabinet Office Personnel Information Note. The aim of a Crown Censure hearing is to seek acknowledgment of the problem and to improve standards of health and safety. The absence of an agreed and documented procedure led to "some difficulties". This resulted to the issue of the Cabinet Office note.

Crown Censures taken by the Health and Safety Executive since April 1999

The following summaries illustrate the scope of deaths and injuries for which no-one could be prosecuted because of Crown immunity.

- March 2007: breach of section 2(1), Health and Safety at Work, etc., Act 1974: Ministry of Defence (Army): Albemarle Barracks, Newcastle upon Tyne:

failure of MOD in May 2004 to ensure the safety of a soldier who was crushed between a moving armoured fighting vehicle and another stationary vehicle. The soldier suffered fatal injuries.

- May 2006: breach of section 2 (1), 1974 Act:Ministry of Defence (Royal Air Force): Resources Initiative Training Centre, Fairbourne: failure to ensure, so far as was reasonably practicable, the safety of employees, in that the risks of climbing Lockwood's Chimney, Snowdonia, during the conduct of adventurous training, was not adequately controlled.
- June 2005: breaches of sections 2 and 3, 1974 Act and regulations 3 and 5, Management of Health and Safety at Work, etc., Act: Ministry of Defence (Royal Navy): Hamworthy Barracks, Poole: in relation to a specific Royal Navy equipment procurement project, failure to ensure the health and safety of employees and others, failure to carry out suitable and sufficient risk assessment and failure to make and give effect to such arrangements as were appropriate, having regard to the nature of the activities and the size of the undertaking, for the effective planning, organisation, control, monitoring and review of the preventive and protective measures.
- January 2005: breach of section 2(1), 1974 Act: Ministry of Defence (Army): Porth–yr-Ogof caves, Powys: failure to ensure, so far as was reasonably practicable, the safety of employees, including Apprentice Tradesman Kevin Alan Sharman, in that the risks of them drowning whilst caving, during the

conduct of adventurous training, were not adequately controlled.

- January 2005: breach of section 2(1), 1974 Act; Ministry of Defence (Royal Navy); failure to ensure the safety of employees, including a recruit marine, at Woodbury Common, Devon.
- December 2004: breaches of section 3(1), 1974 Act; Ministry of Defence Main Building, Whitehall, London: MOD employees were required to make 11,000 volt switchgear safe for contractors to maintain, but failed to recognise live terminals and failed to lock the shutter in the closed (protective) position. A contract electrician gained access to the live terminals and died as a result of the electrical explosion. Another contractor was injured at the same time. Safety programmes for previous years contained similar errors but they were not detected by the auditing process.
- August 2004: breaches of section 2(1), 1974 Act and Regulation 3 (1) (a), Management of Health and Safety at Work Regulations 1999: Ministry of Defence (Royal Navy):Defence Diving School, Horsea Island, Portsmouth: failure to ensure the health and safety of employees during the conduct of military diver training courses.
- April 2003: breach of section 3 (1), 1974 Act: Ministry of Defence: James Callaghan Drive, Portsmouth: MOD resurfaced the road with an unsuitable limestone macadam which became dangerously slippery over time. Two fatal accidents

occurred in 1997 and 1998. The road had by then been adopted by the Highway Authority and the MOD was no longer responsible for it.

- August 2001: breach of regulation 5(1), Management of Health and Safety at Work Regulations 1999: Ministry of Defence (Army): Sennybridge, Brecon: failure to put into place proper arrangements for the monitoring and review of preventative measures. The case arose from an investigation into the accidental shooting of a soldier with a general purpose machine gun support weapon being used in an improvised firing position.
- November 2000: breaches of regulations 5 (1) and 6(2), Provision and Use of Work Equipment Regulations 1998: Ministry of Defence (Royal Navy): HMS Raleigh, Cornwall: failure to maintain spin driers in an efficient state, in efficient working order and in good repair. Failure to ensure that spin driers exposed to conditions causing deterioration liable to result in danger were inspected at suitable intervals.
- July 2000: breaches of section 3 (1), 1974 Act and regulation 3, Management of Health and Safety at Work Regulations 1992: Ministry of Defence (Army): Longmoor Training Camp, Hampshire: cadet fatally injured when she was run over by a vehicle during a night exercise. Poor planning and risks not properly identified and controlled.
- October 1999: breach of section 2 (1), 1974 Act: Ministry of Defence (Army): Central Ammunitions Depot, Carlisle: failure to ensure safety of employee

engaged in slinging of large containers. Risk of falling. Being a Crown employee prevented prosecution.

- May 1999: breaches of regulations 7 and 12, Control of Substances Hazardous to Health Regulations 1994: Defence Evaluation and Research Agency Porton Down: research worker potentially exposed to hazard group 3 pathogen following centrifuge accident. Risks not properly controlled. Failure to adequately instruct and train laboratory staff.

In 2007 it was reported that the Health and Safety Executive had issued a Crown Censure on the Ministry of Defence following the deaths of two soldiers in transport accidents.

In May 2003, Corporal Eirian Rees was killed when he was trapped between two armoured vehicles in Middlesborough. He was in charge of the transportation of the vehicles to the Persian Gulf. As he was guiding a vehicle onto a low loader, the second vehicle rolled down and caused fatal crushing injuries.

An investigation by the HSE concluded that the MOD had failed to conduct a risk assessment into the hazards of loading armoured vehicles or to ensure that there was a safe system of work.

In May 2004 Lance-Bombardier Robert Wilson was washing an artillery vehicle. The vehicle moved forward and crushed him to death.

In both cases, the MOD was censured under section 2(1) of the Health and Safety at Work, etc., Act 1974.

A spokesperson for the HSE is reported to have commented that the vehicles involved in these incidents were heavy and powerful. Army personnel had to work closely alongside them. The risk of personal injury was potentially high.
In bringing these censures, the HSE wished to emphasise to the MOD, and to other employers, the importance of assessing, managing and controlling the operational risks arising from the use of workplace transport.

In 2006 the Ministry of Defence was issued with a Crown Censure following the death of an RAF officer during a mountaineering course.
Flight Lieutenant Elizabeth Bond died when she fell 200 feet while mountaineering in Snowdonia during a course at the RAF's Resource and Initiative Centre. She was a novice climber and should have been attached to a rope at all times. She was not.
The risk of her falling had been significantly increased by inadequate levels of supervision and poor weather conditions. The RAF had not adequately assessed the risks of falling and had failed to identify and implement effective control measures or to carry out adequate monitoring.
At a private hearing in Cardiff, it was ruled that the RAF had been in breach of section 2(1) of the 1974 Act for failing to ensure the health and safety of employees.
A spokesperson for the RAF is reported to have commented that remedial action has now been taken in response to the censure. It now carries out site-specific risk assessments for all activities and has introduced

random inspections to ensure that safety standards are being met.

In 2006 employees at the HMRC call centre in Bathgate, West Lothian, complained to the Health and Safety Executive about thermal comfort. An HSE investigation revealed a number of problems with the installation and design of the centre's ventilation system. There was a lack of means of monitoring relative humidity or of maintaining humidity at between 40 and 70 per cent. There were also draughts from the system which meant that staff felt very uncomfortable.

In January 2007 the HSE served an improvement notice on HMRC. The deadline for compliance with the notice was extended from March until April 2007, but it was not complied with.

The investigation also concluded that HMRC had failed to obtain or to act upon relevant competent advice to resolve concerns over thermal comfort and that it had failed to manage the matter in a timely manner. The problems had continued from 2004 until 2007.

HMRC was formally censured.

The director of HSE Scotland is reported to have commented that the problem arose from the conversion of what were industrial premises, with ventilation designed for the factory process, into office premises. HMRC had taken too long to take the matter seriously but were now determined to establish improved working conditions.

More recently, in 2011, Greenwich Hospital, a Royal Navy Crown charity, received a Crown Censure from the

HSE after the investigation of an incident at the Royal Hospital School in Holbrook, Suffolk. The school is run by Greenwich Hospital.

In March 2009 12 pupils at the school were taking part in a PE class which involved the use of a climbing wall. One of the pupils was a 15 year old girl. She fell six metres in an uncontrolled descent from the top of the wall onto a wooden gymnasium floor below. She suffered a fractured spine and spent two weeks in hospital. She had to wear a body cast for two weeks and continues to receive medical treatment.

The school admitted failing to have a suitable and sufficient risk assessment, written operating procedure and inspection and maintenance regime related to climbing activities and the use of climbing wall equipment in the gymnasium.

The school also admitted that climbing wall supervisors had not been given refresher training and that there was no system in place to provide access to technical advice dealing with the use of climbing wall equipment.

Greenwich Hospital is a Crown body and is immune from criminal prosecution.

In January 2013 the Ministry of Defence was censured in relation to the death of a 14- year old Army Cadet who died in August 2007 when she was trapped under a boat when in capsized on Loch Carnan. The MOD could not be prosecuted. The HSE took the view that evidence of primary failings during the activity would have been sufficient to provide a realistic prospect of conviction in the civilian courts.

One of the meanings which Dicey gave to the rule of law is that no-one is above the law, as follows:

We mean, when we speak of the rule of law as a characteristic of our country, not only that with us no man is above the law, but that here, every man, whatever be his rank or condition, is subject to the ordinary law of the realm and amenable to the jurisdiction of the ordinary tribunals.

Crown immunity and the Crown Censure system directly contradict this assertion.

Civil proceedings

Until 1948 the Crown could not be made a party to a civil action. This was an offshoot of the principle of sovereign immunity. The Crown Proceedings Act 1947 changed this rule. The Crown may now be sued in contract or tort, with minor exceptions. A reigning monarch may not be sued.

The application of Crown immunity in relation to civil proceedings in the health and safety field was recently considered by the Court of Appeal in the case of *Matthews v Ministry of Defence (2002)*. The facts were that M was an electrical engineer in the Royal Navy from 1955 until 1968. He worked on board a number of ships and he claimed that he developed an asbestos-related illness during the course of his work. It was not until 1999 that he became aware that his illness was attributable to his service in the Navy.

M sought compensation from the Ministry of Defence. The MOD claimed immunity under section 10 of the Crown Proceedings Act 1947. This section, which was repealed in 1987, continues to apply to acts or omissions carried out before 1987. It provides for the Crown's immunity from actions for compensation by members of the armed forces who died or suffered injury in the course of their duties.

As a preliminary issue, it was argued on behalf of M that section 10 of the 1947 Act was incompatible with the right to a fair trial, as guaranteed by Article 6 of the European Convention on Human Rights and incorporated into English law by the Human Rights Act 1998.

At first instance, the High Court made the following points:

- The aim of section 10 was to achieve efficiency and discipline in the armed forces. This aim could be undermined if personnel thought that they might be liable in negligence. The section imposed a blanket ban on negligence claims. The fact that it had been repealed in 1987 showed that that objective no longer needed to be met.
- Section 10 was incompatible with Article 6 because its all-embracing nature meant that it was not rationally connected to the limited objective which it was intended to achieve.

On appeal to the Court of Appeal, this decision was reversed. The Court ruled that a statutory provision which exempted the Crown from liability for injuries to members of the Armed Forces as a result of events occurring before 1987, and which thus deprived service personnel of their civil right to claim compensation and substituting a right to a pension, was a provision of substantive law to which Article 6 and the Human Rights

Act did not apply.

Technical immunity of employers

The Rosepark case (HM Advocate v Balmer and Others (2007))

Thomas Balmer, Anne Balmer, Alan Balmer and Balmer Care Homes Ltd were charged with a number of offences following a fire at the Rosepark Nursing Home, Uddington in 2004. Fourteen people were killed in the fire. The three Balmers were partners in the firm which ran the nursing home. In summary, the court ruled that the alleged offences could only be committed by employers. The Balmers were not, as a matter of law, employers.

The charges were prefaced by the accused "being partners in the firm of Rosepark Nursing Home, also known as Rosepark Care Home, and carrying on the business or undertaking of a residential care and nursing home registered to provide care and nursing for up to 43 residents in the categories of frail elderly, elderly with mild mental illness, terminally ill and young physically disabled at Rosepark and being employers in terms of the Health and Safety at Work Act 1974".

- At the date of the alleged offences (January 31, 2004), the Balmers were the only partners of Rosepark carrying on the business specified in the charges.
- The legislation specified in the charges imposed legal duties upon employers.

- The partnership had been the employer for the purposes of the Health and Safety at Work, etc., Act 1974.
- The partnership was dissolved on February 28, 2005.
- The partners transferred the business to Rosepark Care Home Limited. The Balmers were directors of the company.
- Criminal proceedings against the Balmers were started in November 2005.
- The prosecution could have charged the partnership if it had not been dissolved.
- The now dissolved partnership could not be charged.

Lord Hardie made the following points:

- The charges alleged that each of the Balmers were employers in terms of the Health and Safety at Work, etc., Act 1974.
- The status of employer was necessary for the commission of the offences specified in the indictment.
- If the prosecution considered that thc commission of an offence by an employer was "due to the act or default of some other person", that other person could be charged and convicted of the offence under section 36 of the 1974 Act.
- The prosecution did not rely on this section and was unable to do so as long as it maintained that the accused were employers.
- If that special capacity as employers did not exist, the prosecution could consider whether any or all of them should be charged under section 36.

- In view of the admission by the prosecution that the partnership was the employer, it could not be maintained that any of the Balmers were employers. The contract of employment was with the firm.
- The basis for the prosecution's assertion that the individual Balmers were employers was based in the law of partnership. Employees could have had recourse to the assets of individual partners if the firm failed to pay debts due to them, but it was quite a different matter to attribute personal criminal responsibility to partners for the criminal acts of the firm.
- One consequence of such a course of action might be to expose individuals to sentences of imprisonment, whereas the limit of their liability for offences committed by the firm would be a financial penalty.
- The dissolution of the firm was fatal to any charge against it. This did not necessarily end the prospect of proceedings against individual partners. If the prosecution sought to attach criminal responsibility to the accused as partners of the now dissolved firm, any future indictment should make that clear.
- It might seem inappropriate to permit people to escape criminal liability, and at least the prospect of substantial financial penalty, by taking steps to dissolve the firm after a criminal investigation is underway. However, it is essential that any allegation of criminal liability against partners of a dissolved firm is well founded.
- If prosecution has been made impossible by the actions of others in the course of a criminal investigation, such actions may give rise to a charge

of perverting or attempting to pervert the course of justice, assuming that the essential ingredients of that charge exist.

- The charges against the Balmers would be dismissed because the accused were not party to the contracts of employment of the employees at Rosebank and were therefore not employers.
- Lord Hardie wished to emphasise, for the benefit of the relatives of those residents who perished in the fire, and the injured residents and their relatives, that this decision did not signal an end of proceedings against the accused.

The Rosepark case can be seen as a clear example of the application of class justice, with the details of the law governing commercial legal interests overriding individual justice in the interests of employers.

Hunger and homelessness: *London Borough of Southwark v Williams (1971)*

Homeless families in London squatted in empty houses in Southwark. The local authority applied for immediate possession of the houses. The families pleaded necessity. The court (Lord Denning) made the following points:

- Homelessness did not amount to necessity.
- The doctrine of necessity was confined within very narrow limits, for example urgent and transient situations of great and imminent danger to life in which the law permitted some encroachment on private property.
- If hunger were to be allowed as an excuse for stealing, it would open a way through which all kinds

> of disorder and lawlessness would pass. If homelessness were admitted as a defence to trespass, no-one's home could be safe. The courts must, for the sake of law and order, take a firm stand. They must refuse to admit the pleas of necessity to the hungry and the homeless and trust that their distress will be relieved by the charitable and the good.

Thus the rights of the homeless depend, as a matter of law, on charity.

Saudi Arms Inquiry

The story of the Saudi Arms Inquiry throws mainstream criminal law and criminology theories into chaos and illustrates the application of English criminal law in favour of one class.

The inquiry involved allegations of massive corruption. No prosecutions were brought in the "interests of the state". This can be compared with thefts of small amounts of property resulting in prison sentences.

In December 2006 the Serious Fraud Office abandoned its investigation into a multimillion pound arms deal between BAE and Saudi Arabia. This followed a private threat from Saudi Arabia that intelligence cooperation with Britain would be cut unless the inquiry was abandoned. The Attorney-General stated that the decision to end the inquiry had been taken in the public interest. The investigation would cause serious damage to UK/Saudi security, intelligence and diplomatic co-operation. It would be likely to have seriously negative consequences for the UK public interest in terms of national security and foreign policy objectives.

The inquiry concerned allegations that a multimillion pound slush fund was linked to the deal. The Saudi government had threatened to cancel a £10 billion order for 72 Eurofighter Typhoon jets.

In April 2008 the High Court ruled that the decision by the government and by the Serious Fraud Office to stop an investigation into allegations of corrupt dealings between BAE Systems and Saudi Arabia was a threat to the reputation of British justice, unlawful and an abject surrender.

Lord Justice Moses and Lord Justice Sullivan are reported to have made the following comments:

- They feared for the reputation of the administration of justice if it could be perverted by a threat.
- Any similar future unlawful threats to the rule of law must be resisted by the government, or the courts would intervene.
- No-one is entitled to interfere with the course of our justice. The rule of law is nothing if it fails to constrain overweening power.
- The Director of the Serious Fraud Office had ceased to exercise the power to make the independent judgment conferred on him by Parliament.
- The Director (in reality the government) contended that he was entitled to surrender to the threat and that such threats were a part of life. So bleak a picture of the impotence of law invited at least dismay, if not outrage.
- The government had failed to recognise that the threat uttered was not simply directed at this country's commercial, diplomatic and security interests but was aimed at its legal system.

- If such a threat had been made by one who was subject to the criminal law of this country, he would risk being charged with an attempt to pervert the course of justice.
- There was no evidence that any consideration had been given as to how to persuade the Saudis to withdraw the threat, let alone any attempt made to resist the threat.

On appeal to the House of Lords (2008) by the Director of the Serious Fraud Office, the appeal was allowed. The Lords stated that where he took the view that protecting the lives of British citizens outweighed the public interest in pursuing an investigation into allegations of corruption, the Director was entitled to exercise his discretion to discontinue the investigation, following threats by a foreign state as to consequences affecting national security if he did not do so.

The issue was not whether he had been right or wrong but whether the decision was one which he was lawfully entitled to take. In the opinion of the Lords, it had been.

Law as a weapon of class conflict

E. P. Thompson made the following points about English law in the historical context of class:

The common law tradition has so frequently been associated with concepts of fundamental right and justice that it is at first startling to find that it was used as the main doctrinal justification for preventing the advancement of working people of both sexes, notably in conspiracy cases, and of women of the upper and middle classes, primarily in the male monopoly cases. What maintained continuity between the ideas of the common law over the centuries was that it continued to be the instrument of the judges and to express in a vigorous if indirect form the interest of the social group with whom the judges were associated. The fundamental rights of the English people thus amounted to little more than the fundamental rights of the judges, and chief amongst these was the right to determine how social claims could be legally classified and what procedures should be followed for their enforcement.

The opinion has been expressed that law is one aspect of the control of social behaviour by the ruling class as major wielders of the instruments of force and coercion. The primary purposes of law are the orderly processing of claims of competing capitalists for more money through rules drawn for and by capitalists in accordance with their own custom, and the quelling of violence and civil strife arising out of their "rule of law".

Almost every aspect of law has to do with money or claims for money. Most of the law is of, by and for the wealthy, who, at every stage of its proceedings, are accorded more than the poor. The law costs a great deal of money and, because of the poverty of many, its substantial provisions are irrelevant to their lives. Filing fees, lawyers' costs and fees, transcripts, appeals, all these procedural deterrents are too costly when the poor person has been wronged. This is examined in more detail in Chapter 1 (Money).

From a class justice point of view, disadvantaged groups include the poor, homeless, illiterate, young, old, low waged, disabled, casual workers, ethnic minorities, migrant workers and those who have no choice but to work in dangerous conditions.

They may be employed by American multinational companies which refuse to recognise trade unions and have a record of their employees suffering serious injury and death.

Most lawyers would not analyse these imbalances but would act for the party offering the most money.

Criminal law and class justice

The argument that the concept and reality of crime is created through political actions by those groups and institutions which possess the power to enforce their will, and that the state decides from time to time, in the best interests of the ruling class, what activities should be treated as crimes, is not new.

Frederick Engels' overview of the condition of the English working class, written in 1844 at a time of acute class conflict and against a background of European revolution, includes the following:

... the law is sacred to the bourgeois, for it is his own composition, enacted with his consent and for his own benefit and protection. He knows that, even if an individual law should injure him, the whole fabric protects his interests; and more than all, the sanctity of the law, the sacredness of order as established by the active will of one part of society, and the passive acceptance of the other, is the strongest support of his social position. Because the English bourgeois finds himself reproduced in his law, the policeman's truncheon has for him a wonderfully soothing power.

But for the working man quite otherwise! The working man knows too well, has learned from too-oft experience, that the law is a rod which the bourgeois has prepared for him....
The state does not care whether starvation is bitter or sweet; it locks people up in prison or sends them to penal settlements, and when it releases them it has the satisfaction of having converted people without work into people without morals.
What inducement has the proletarian not to steal? It is all very pretty and very agreeable to the ear of the bourgeois to have the sacredness of property asserted; but for him who has none, the sacredness of property dies out of itself. Money is the god of this world: the bourgeois takes the proletarian's money from him and so makes a practical atheist of him.
If a rich man is brought up, or rather summoned, to appear before the court, the judge regrets that he is obliged to impose so much trouble, treats the matter as favourably as possible, and, if he is forced to condemn the accused, does so with extreme regret.

Another twentieth-century writer who developed the theory of class justice is Victor Serge. Serge, whose real name was Victor Kibalchich, was a Russian anarchist who later converted to communism. He was expelled from Soviet Russia because of his opposition to Stalinism. He wrote a number of novels exposing the evils of Stalinism.
In an appeal for the rejection of "bourgeois legality", Serge pointed out that in every country the workers' movement has had to fight against the criminal law for

the right to associate. In conflicts between capital and labour, the armed forces have often intervened against labour, but never against capital, and the overwhelming majority of crimes come into the category of attacks on property. Serge concluded that

... the state is a mesh of institutions designed to defend the interests of the property owners against non-owners, that is, to maintain the exploitation of labour; the law, always decreed by the rich against the poor, is enforced by judges almost invariably belonging to the ruling class, along rigorous class lines.

Hillsborough

In April 1989, 96 football supporters were killed, and 766 injured, during a crush at the FA cup semi-final at the Hillsborough stadium. The survivors and the families of the deceased have campaigned since 1989 to discover the facts of the disaster. The victims were labelled as lawless hooligans by the media and the police. The Hillsborough disaster can be seen as yet a further example of class (in)justice in that it exemplifies the difficulty of less-powerful victims to obtain justice against powerful institutions.

Causes of crime

Private legal practice is not permitted in Cuba. Under Cuban law, the private practice of law is a criminal offence. This means that English barristers and solicitors would be criminals under the Cuban system if they were transported, en masse, to Cuba. (This is not to suggest that they should be).What would be the causes of this mass crime? Genetic factors? Social deprivation? Innate evil? The shape of their heads? The true cause of this criminalisation is the declaration by the state that certain types of behaviour are criminal.

It is sometimes argued that, although many types of crime are specific to state prohibitions, certain "core" crimes are common to the whole of humanity. These are said to include:

- Murder, basically intentional killing. But it can be seen (and the Iraq War, fully examined in Chapter 5, is a clear example of this) that the crime of murder applies only in the circumstances laid down by the state, and mass murder on behalf of the state may not be considered criminal and may not result in prosecution.
- Theft, essentially a dishonest taking. Again, the reality is that stealing is regarded as a crime in very limited circumstances. This is illustrated by the prosperity of the tax avoidance/evasion industry and is underlined by the ongoing MPs expenses scandal. When is dishonest taking a crime? When it is committed by individuals whom the state considers should be prosecuted and punished.

Emma Goldman (1869-1940)

Born in Russia, Emma Goldman was described as one of the most dangerous women in America. She has also been described as the heroine of modern feminists. She was imprisoned for urging the unemployed to steal the food which they needed.

Emma Goldman's prison sentence for incitement to riot

led to the following:

The revolutionary contention that crime is the result of poverty is based on fact. Most of the defendants who were awaiting trial came from the lowest strata of society, men and women without friends, often even without a home. Unfortunate, ignorant creatures they were, but still with hope in their hearts, because they had not yet been convicted.

In the penitentiary, despair possessed almost all of the prisoners. It served to unveil the mental darkness, fear and superstition which held them in bondage. Among the seventy inmates, there were no more than half a dozen who showed any intelligence whatsoever. The rest were outcasts without the least social consciousness. Their personal misfortunes filled their thoughts; they could not understand that they were victims, links in an endless chain of injustice and inequality. From early childhood they had known nothing but poverty, squalor, and want, and the same conditions were awaiting them on their release.

Working classes

The phrase "working class" has significant legal connotations and has been the subject of judicial definition in a number of cases. The courts have had some difficulty dealing with the concept. For example, in *Re Sanders' Will Trusts (1954)* Mr Justice Harman ruled in a case where a will stated that money should be left for providing dwellings for the working classes and their families in Pembroke Dock. The judge stated that a gift for the working classes was not a gift for the relief of poverty and did not have charitable status. He made the following points:

- The expression "working classes" means persons who have to work for their living.
- The "working classes" in Pembroke Dock were merely men working in the docks. An element of poverty could not be inferred.

Another example is *Green & Sons v Minister of Health (1947)* where the court commented:

- "Working classes" fifty years ago denoted a class which included men working in the fields or the factories, in the docks or the mines, on the railways or on the roads, at a weekly wage. The wages of people of that class were lower than those of the other members of the community, and they were looked on as a lower class. That has all now disappeared. The social revolution in the last fifty years has made the words "working class" quite inappropriate today. There is no such separate class as the working classes.

Again, in *Re Niyazi's Will Trusts (1978)*:

- … the adjectival expression "working men" plainly has some flavour of "lower income" about it, just as "upper class" has some flavour of affluence, and "middle class" some flavour of comfortable means. Of course there are impoverished members of the upper and middle classes, just as there are some "working men" who are at least of comfortable means, if not affluence: one cannot ignore the impact of such things as football pools.

We see the spectacle of judges whose experience of manual labour is limited to a few weeks during their university vacations, pontificating on the detail of the working life of those who know the real meaning of work, who have had their health ruined by shift work or who have faced redundancy. Finding against manual workers who have been seriously injured during their employment, delivering judgments in a world so remote from that of ordinary working people's daily lives that one might as well be in fairyland, except that their arcane rulings can ruin lives.

Political trials

Peter Hain, writing in 1985, stated his view that an understanding of the operation of the law was impossible without acknowledging that British society remains rigidly stratified, with pronounced class divisions, most wealth in the hands of a tiny minority and effective political power exercised by a few. Parliament, in Hain's view, was forced merely to go through the motions of exercising power. Real decisions were taken by the City, in the boardrooms of the giant multinationals, the pension and insurance companies, the Common Market and NATO.

Further, stated Hain, over 90 per cent of serious crime involves property and the whole law enforcement apparatus is directed at tackling it. This could be contrasted with the tiny team of factory inspectors trying to enforce health and safety regulations, and the fact that although several thousands of people are killed at work each year, prosecutions of companies are most unlikely and if they occur at all, fines are puny.

Hain's analysis of political trials in Britain included the following observations:

- There was no evidence that the Prevention of Terrorism (Temporary Provisions) Act 1974 had in any way curbed terrorism. The ability to detain suspects for up to seven days without being charged was one of the biggest attacks that there had been during peacetime on the rights and freedoms of the people of Britain.
- We were experiencing an insidious growth of state power, as expressed in the strengthening of the security forces, computerized collection of intelligence, sophisticated techniques made possible by new technology, and above all a tightening of the law, with judges showing an enthusiasm for political trials and for exercising their own political preferences.

Crimewatch: an exemplar of the spectacle of class justice

The crimes presented in the Crimewatch television programme by glamorous personalities placed in lavish sets are portrayed, essentially, as entertainment. The programme is reported to have viewing figures of around 6 million.

"Crime", in the context of the Crimewatch spectacle of dramatic reconstructions, is almost always presented as being committed by individuals or small groups of individuals against other individuals or groups.

The most serious crimes against humanity, in terms of numbers of people affected or numbers of deaths or serious injuries, are never put across as part of the Crimewatch spectacle. For example, although we are shown details of a particularly vicious rape of a UK citizen, and treated to theatrical self-congratulation by celebrities and the police when an arrest is made, we must wait in vain for the following:

- Pictures of dead and horrifically injured children in wars involving the UK military, with requests for information about the immediate perpetrators and their superiors. There is no hotline number to call with information about war criminals.
- Dramatic reconstructions of incidents on construction sites and in factories which have resulted in multiple injuries and deaths, with pictures of the employers allegedly responsible for such crimes.
- Information about the activities of arms manufacturers, the construction of weapons of war and the consequences of their use.
- Requests for the identification and tracing of those responsible for research, development and production of instruments of torture.

Who are the real criminals? Individuals whose background and upbringing has resulted in actions labelled as crimes by the state? Or those in power whose cynical manipulations and amoral choices have caused mass murder? Or both? The Crimewatch spectacle never addresses and least of all attempts to answer these questions.

The following remote possibility should be considered: Crimewatch publishes photographs of war criminals, arms manufacturers, tax avoiders, landlords and employers whose crimes may make those actually featured on Crimewatch sink into insignificance.

Health and safety law and class justice

The common law gave no health and safety protection for employees. The first Act intended to protect the welfare of people at work was passed in 1802. This followed revelations of the abuse of children in textile mills. The Act was widely evaded and rarely enforced. Further legislation in 1819, 1825 and 1841 was also largely ineffective. By the end of the nineteenth century, an ad hoc patchwork of statutes and regulations was in place.

These Factories Acts have been described as having been wrung step by step from masters after a civil war of half a century.

Engels, who toured England during the 1840s, gives a detailed description of working class life, including employment in mines and factories with non-existent safety measures. In general terms, Engels made the following comment:

If one individual inflicts a bodily injury upon another which leads to the death of the person attacked we call it manslaughter. On the other hand, if the attacker knows beforehand that the blow will be fatal we call it murder. Murder has also been committed if society places hundreds of workers in such a position that they inevitably come to premature and unnatural ends. Their death is as violent as if they had been stabbed or shot... murder is committed if thousands of workers have been deprived of the necessities of life or if they have been forced into a situation in which it is impossible for them to survive... murder has been committed if society knows perfectly well that thousands of workers cannot avoid being sacrificed so long as these conditions are allowed to continue. Murder of this sort is just as culpable as the murder committed by an individual. At first sight it does not appear to be murder at all because responsibility for the death of the victim cannot be pinned on any individual assailant. Everyone is responsible and yet no-one is responsible, because it appears as if the victim has died from natural causes. If a worker dies no-one places the responsibility for his death on society, though some would realise that society has failed to take steps to prevent the victim from dying. But it is murder all the same.

Engels' description of working-class life in England in the 1840s includes the following:

Condemned to mass starvation during periods of recession, employed in mines and factories with non-existent measures, housed in disease-ridden slums. What is true of London, is true of Manchester, Birmingham, Leeds, is true of all great towns. Everywhere barbarous indifference, hard egotism on one hand, and nameless misery on the other, everywhere social warfare, every man's house in a state of siege, everywhere reciprocal plundering under the protection of the law, and all so shameless, so openly avowed that one shrinks before the consequences of our social state as they manifest themselves here undisguised, and can only wonder that the whole crazy fabric still hangs together.

The origins and significance of health and safety law

Health and safety law is of crucial significance to any analysis of English law. It is different from most other aspects of law in that it expressly protects the interests of the working class.

Health and safety in its widest sense, includes statutory rules and regulations, common law negligence and aspects of employment law. Health and safety suffers from not being taken seriously and from its enforcement being seriously underfunded in comparison with other areas of criminal law.

The historical context of health and safety law

The industrial revolution of the early nineteenth century resulted in a massive, rapid and uncontrolled increase in the number of workers employed in factories. Workplace conditions were observed and described by a number of contemporary reformers.

In 1815 Robert Owen toured the main factories of Britain. He observed that "in some large factories from one-fourth to one-fifth of the children were either cripples or otherwise deformed, or permanently injured by excessive toil, sometimes by brutal abuse".

EP Thompson has described working conditions in Manchester in 1832 as including eight-year old children being forced to work a fourteen-hour day. Thompson concluded that the exploitation of little children, on this scale and with this intensity, was one of the most shameful events in our history.

History of factories legislation

The first factory legislation was passed in 1802. It aimed to regulate the hours of work of apprentices in cotton mills and to set standards for lighting, heating and ventilation. These rules were only sporadically enforced. In 1833 new legislation appointed inspectors to enforce the law. During the nineteenth century, a series of ad hoc Acts were passed which consolidated the law, and its administration, in relation to factories and workshops.

Health and safety law outwardly appears to be for the benefit of the working class. It has been argued that it was never properly enforced and was never intended to be. The argument goes that health and safety laws were introduced to give employees the false impression that their interests were promoted and to deflect their militancy.

In reality:

- The promoters of the early factory legislation were genuinely concerned to improve workplace conditions.
- Within the employing class, competing industrialists supported the new laws because they would increase their competitors' costs.
- The Health and Safety at Work Act 1974 was introduced against a background of pressures from the civil service to simplify the legislation, from the TUC, from public concern and from individuals such as Foot and Lord Robens.

Health and safety legislation is starved of resources for its enforcement. In 2012-2013, 706 cases were prosecuted for health and safety offences.

The Health and Safety Executive (HSE) receives income from a number of sources, including the proceeds of fines, sales of publications, EU and investment income, and funding from the Department of Work and Pensions

(DWP). Its budget from the DWP however has been cut by 35 per cent. A further 9.5 per cent reduction is scheduled for the year 2014/2015. The number of HSE employees has been reduced by 6 per cent. It has been reported that deaths in the construction industry increased by 8 per cent in the year 2013-2014. A trade union spokesperson is reported to have commented that dangers in the construction industry were exacerbated by the massive cuts that the government had made to the HSE's budget and its continued attack on safety laws and regulations.

Health and safety law and practice, however imperfect and underfunded, clearly operates to protect workers and to improve safety standards. If there were no health and safety law, could it seriously be argued that employers would voluntarily cut profits to improve safety standards?

During the Franco regime, advertisements for investments in Spain regularly appeared in the British press. These stated that one of the main advantages of investing in companies in a country with a fascist government was that there were minimal health and safety regulations and little legal employment protection.

Health and safety law is the Cinderella of the English legal system. It rarely features in law school syllabuses, is under constant attack for populist journalists and is subjected to government cuts. In reality, it is one of the few elements of English law which operates in favour of workers in relation to employers.

For example, in May 2011 East Sussex County Council was fined following an incident in which a man died and five others were seriously injured when they drank dishwasher fluid.

A group of persons from the St Nicholas Centre in Lewes, a day care facility for adults with learning difficulties run by the council, were taken to Plumpton Agricultural College to use the sports facilities.

They were given a drink which had been prepared at the day centre and brought to the sports hall. This should have been orange squash but actually contained sodium hydroxide, a cleaning chemical.

The six who drank the fluid started vomiting blood and fitting. Colin Woods, who had Down's Syndrome, died 17 months after drinking the chemical. Five others suffered burns to their mouths, throats and stomachs. Most had to undergo repeated surgery.

Three will never be able to swallow normally again.

East Sussex County Council had failed to ensure that the fluid was safely stored away. It was left on the side in an unlocked kitchen. The chemical was marked as corrosive but it was similar in appearance to that of orange squash.

Surviving service users at the day centre were too traumatised by the incident to be interviewed about who had mixed the drink.

East Sussex County Council was fined £50,000, plus £27,000 costs, for a breach of section 3 of the Health and Safety at Work,etc., Act 1974, for failing to ensure the health and safety of non-employees.

A spokesperson for the HSE is reported to have made the following comments:

- This was one of the worst incidents which he had investigated in all his time as a health and safety inspector.
- It was impossible to adequately imagine the suffering and terror that the victims must have felt as the tragedy unfolded.
- The terrible thing was that the incident and its horrific consequences could so easily have been prevented by simply locking away the container of sodium hydroxide.
- Mr Woods had died a slow, painful and unnecessary death and others had suffered terrible and preventable injuries, some painful and permanent, because the council had failed in its responsibility to take proper care of them. It was imperative that authorities properly protected vulnerable people in their care.

Another recent example is that of a worker who was dragged through a CD-sized gap in a machine.
Compass Engineering Ltd and Kaltenbach Ltd, a machine supply company, were fined at Sheffield Crown Court in July 2011 after a worker was seriously injured when he was dragged through a gap in a machine. The gap was no wider than a CD case.

- In December 2008 Matthew Lowe, an employee of Compass, was working at the company's site in Barnsley. He looked into the machine's outlet point to check a line of work.
- Lowe was caught on a conveyor used to move heavy steel beams. He was dragged through a 125mm

opening between a moving measuring head and a wall.

- Lowe suffered serious injuries including a ruptured stomach and bowel, a fractured spine, both hips, his right arm, several ribs and a fractured pelvis. He has lasting physical and psychological damage.
- There was no guarding in place to protect Lowe from dangerous moving parts. This was a serious safety failing for both Compass and for Kaltenbach, which had supplied the machine.
- Both companies were responsible for ensuring that adequate guarding was in place. Although the machine belonged to Compass, Kaltenbach had installed the equipment and signed it off as being fit and ready for use.
- Lowe was inexperienced in operating the machinery after he had been moved from a different line at the premises because of a lull in his regular workload.
- The lack of guarding was the decisive factor.

Compass Engineering Ltd was fined £45,000 plus £24,000 costs under section 2 of the Health and Safety at Work, etc., Act 1974, for failing to ensure the health and safety of employees.

Kaltenbach Ltd was fined £30,000 plus £16,000 costs for a breach of section 6 of the Act.

An HSE inspector commented that it was remarkable that Lowe had survived. If appropriate guarding had been in place, the incident would never have happened. The prosecution would live long in the memory because of the shocking details. He hoped that it served as a reminder to those involved in the manufacturing, processing and supply of machinery of the need to prevent access to dangerous parts.

Lowe is reported to have made the following comments after the case:

- What mattered most was that the industry learned from his experience. His life had changed forever and no matter how well he recovered from his physical injuries, he would still have the psychological impact of the accident hanging over him.
- He hoped that his case highlighted the dangers posed by not following health and safety regulations. It would not put his life back to how it was before the incident, but at least it might prevent others suffering in the future.
- Too many people are needlessly killed and injured in accidents at work. If hearing his story made them think twice about safety, and about the daily risks which they faced in the workplace, then he would be happy.

Section 6 of the 1974 Act states, in outline, that it shall be the duty of any person who designs, manufactures, imports or supplies any article for use at work to ensure, so far as is reasonably practicable, that the article is so designed and constructed that it will be safe and without risks to health at all times when it is being set, used, cleaned or maintained by a person at work.

Health and safety in prisons

Pullen v Prison Commissioners (1957)

From 1951 until 1953 George Pullen served a sentence of imprisonment in Pentonville prison. During most of his sentence, he worked in the prison workshop making coir mats. Dust was given off during this process. In 1954 Pullen was diagnosed as suffering from tuberculosis. He claimed compensation from the Prison Commissioners, who at that time were responsible for prisons. The basis for his claim was that the Commissioners had been in breach of their statutory duty under section 47 of the Factories Act 1937 in failing to take measures to protect him from dust and fumes, and that the Commissioners had been negligent.

On behalf of the Commissioners, it was argued that a prison workshop was not a factory within the meaning of the Factories Act.

The High Court ruled that Pullen's claim failed and made the following points:

- A prison workshop was not a factory.
- The Act of 1937 was designed for the protection of persons working in factories.
- The Act placed obligations on employers of labour in factories to take various precautions for the protection of their workpeople. It applied to people working under contract and not to prisoners employed on labour as part of penal discipline.
- If Parliament had intended to include prisons for the purposes of the Factories Act, a reference to prisons would have been inserted.
- If the definition of "factory" is to apply, there must be a relationship of master and servant and employment for wages. There is no employment for wages in the case of prisoners.

- The work which is carried on in prisons is work which is penal in the sense that prisoners are obliged to work as a consequence of their sentence.
- Pullen had not been employed in unhygienic conditions. His health had not been undermined by the conditions in which he was working. There was a certain amount of dust in the place where he was working. An extractor was provided.
- This had not been a dangerous occupation nor had the conditions under which he worked such as to cause Pullen ill-health.

This decision, that prisoners are not employees of the prison in the course of their work, remains good law. It means that the Health and Safety at Work, etc., Act 1974 cannot normally be invoked by prisoners.

Negligence

Prisoners who are injured at work may be able to claim compensation in common law negligence. For example, in the case of *Ferguson v Home Office (1977)*, F was serving a sentence for armed robbery in Maidstone prison. He was working in the prison carpenter's workshop. As he was cutting gate posts with a circular saw, his hand came into contact with the saw. His hand was severely mutilated.

F claimed compensation from the Home Office on the basis of common law negligence. On his behalf, it was argued that he was authorised to use the machine and was doing an authorised job. He had not been properly trained in the use of the machine, which was defective.

The High Court ruled that the claim succeeded and awarded F £15,500 compensation. The cause of the accident was that F was wholly unskilled in the use of the machine. His training in its use was so inadequate that he should not have been permitted to use it. The Home Office owed F a duty of care because he was a "neighbour" for the purposes of common law negligence. There was a duty on the prison authorities to instruct prisoners in the use of machinery.

Another recent case is *Cox v Ministry of Justice [2014] EWCA Civ 132*. The facts were that C was the catering department manager at Swansea prison. A prisoner dropped two 25kg sacks of rice onto her, causing injuries. It was not disputed that the prisoner had been negligent. C claimed compensation from the MOJ, arguing the following:

- The MOJ was more likely to have the means to compensate her than the working prisoners
- The tort had been committed as a result of activity being undertaken by prisoners on behalf of the MOJ
- The activity was part of the catering business and benefitted the MOJ by allowing catering for the whole prison without employing significant numbers of staff or paying outside agencies
- By causing the prisoners to carry on the activity, the MOJ had created the risk of the tort being committed
- The prisoners were under the control of the MOJ and were treated as though they were employees and were paid for their work.

At first instance the claim was dismissed. The court stated that the engagement of prisoners to perform work for pay was a statutory requirement for the purposes of prison discipline and the efficacy of the penal system. It was not a voluntary mutual arrangement entered into by the MOJ for its own advantage or for commercial reasons to further a business or enterprise of running prisons.

C appealed to the Court of Appeal. The appeal was allowed. The Court made the following points:

- The relationship was akin to employment. The features of ability to compensate, creation of risk and control clearly applied.
- The relevant work was clearly done on behalf of the MOJ and for its benefit.
- The activity was different from the activity of a prisoner engaged in education, training or sport.

Crown immunity in the prison context

Rule 31(1) of the Prison Rules states that convicted prisoners are required to do a maximum of ten hours work a day. Forced labour is prohibited by Article 4 of the European Convention on Human Rights, but work done in the ordinary course of detention is excluded from this prohibition.

The health and safety of prisoners at work is also closely connected with the issue of Crown immunity. The general principle is that most of the Health and Safety at Work Act 1974 applies to the Crown (generally, the government) but no prosecutions can be brought, except against individuals. The Crown Censure procedure may apply.

The only recently reported Crown Censure involving prisoners was issued on May14, 2004. It concerned the prisons at The Verne and Erlestoke. The offences listed in the Censure were as follows:

- Failing to ensure that effective measures were taken to prevent a person falling more than 2 metres or being struck by a falling object during work on flat roofs resulting in serious harm to an employee who was hit on the head by a falling concrete block.
- Failing to make and give effect to appropriate health and safety management arrangements including those for risk assessment, management training and for monitoring and review of performance.
- Failing to make a suitable and sufficient assessment of the risks to employees and prisoners from exposure to hazardous substances in connection with work including the use of cleaning chemicals in the wings, use of acids in the boiler house, and exposure to wood dusts and paints in woodworking, resulting in two prisoners being exposed to chlorine gas.

The Health and Safety at Work, etc., Act 1974

The Robens Report (1972) formed the basis for the Health and Safety at Work, etc., Act 1974. The Report included the comment that it was a melancholy fact that much of our preventive legislation was introduced following events which were both unforeseen and disastrous. The existing law was one of "bewildering complexity".

There were seven separate inspectorates (factories, mines, agriculture, explosives, nuclear installations, radiochemical and alkali). These were amalgamated into the Health and Safety Executive by the Act of 1974.

The Act of 1974 was passed when Michael Foot was Secretary of State for Employment. He regarded the Act as one of his greatest achievements. In the House of Commons he referred to the Gresford mining disaster in North Wales in 1934 when 266 miners were killed. Foot regarded the Act as an affirmation of three socialist principles:

- It mobilised the power of the state for a great cause.
- It meant the active participation of working people.
- It empowered ministers to give leadership.

Most health and safety law is relatively easy for non-lawyers to understand. It is administered and enforced by professionals who are mostly non-lawyers and who do not have a vested interest in "legalising" health and safety. In sharp contrast with other pieces of employment legislation, the Act of 1974 is clearly drafted. It operates mainly to protect vulnerable employees and it may deter some employers from the worst excesses of dangerous workplaces. Much of the case law which has interpreted and developed the Act of 1974 is also relatively clear. Examples of this clarity are examined in detail in Chapter 6 (Mystery).

It has been commented that health and safety offences are not seen to be as serious as other crimes. The Simon Jones case is quoted as an example of this.

In 1998 Simon Jones was sent by an employment agency to work at Shoreham docks. He was employed by Euromin. Jones' work involved the unloading of bags of cobblestones from the hold of a ship. The system for this involved workers standing near an open grab bucket attached to a crane. The lever in the driver's cab for closing the bucket was very sensitive. When it was operated, the bucket closed in one second. Jones was decapitated when the grab bucket closed on him.

The Health and Safety Executive (HSE) and the police investigated the killing. The HSE issued improvement and prohibition notices and decided to prosecute Euromin for statutory offences. The Director of Public Prosecutions decided not to prosecute the company for negligent manslaughter. This decision was challenged in the High Court on behalf of Jones' family.

The decision of the High Court was as follows:

- The DPP's decision not to prosecute would be quashed.
- The DPP had been wrong in applying a test of subjective culpability rather than objective liability for the dangerous system of work.
- The test for negligent manslaughter was objective. Negligence would be criminal if, on an objective basis, the defendant showed a failure to advert to a serious risk going beyond mere inadvertence in respect of an obvious and important matter which the defendant's duty demanded he should address.

This case is significant in a number of respects:

- It illustrates the devastating consequences of failing to provide a safe system of work.
- It is also an example of the problems which may arise in prosecuting companies for manslaughter.

Significant recent developments in health and safety

The most significant recent developments fall into the following areas:

- European law
- Common law: work-related stress
- Corporate manslaughter
- Funding of civil claims
- Migrant workers

European law

European Directives have had an increasing influence on British health and safety law. Directives resulted in the introduction of the "six-pack" of Regulations. The 'six-pack' is the name given to the half-dozen most widely quoted health and safety Regulations. They came into effect in Britain after six European Directives were issued by the European Commission.

- The main Regulations are the Management of Health and Safety at Work Regulations 1999. These first came into force in 1993, and were updated in 1999. Regulation 3, placing a legal duty on employers to carry out a risk assessment as a first step in ensuring a safe workplace, lies at the centre of a modern approach to health and safety at work.

- Other 'six-pack' Regulations cover: heating, lighting and ventilation at work; the safe use of computer screens and keyboards; handling heavy or awkward loads; rest breaks; and personal protective equipment.

Following the introduction of the Enterprise and Regulatory Reform Act 2013, the aims of the European legislation have been significantly undermined. The purpose of the 2013 Act was "to remove the right of civil action against employers for breach of statutory duty in relation to certain health and safety legislation, other than where such a right is specifically provided for". The Act amended section 47 of the Health and Safety at Work, etc., Act 1974 by removing civil liability for most health and safety breaches. This greatly reduces the protection of workers under the previous legislation.

Common law: work-related stress

As well as legal duties under statutes and regulations, employers have obligations under duties imposed by the common law. These duties are essentially judge-made and consist of a mass of decided cases.

With reference to work-related stress, one positive point about the English common law is that it is prepared to protect people who have been driven mad, to use a colloquial term, by workplace conditions. English judges have created a rule that mental illness caused by the conduct of employers can be treated in a similar way to physical injury.

Cases of bullying, harassment and exploitation at work, where a recognised psychiatric illness has resulted, can lead to the victims obtaining compensation.

The leading case on work-related stress is *Hatton v Sutherland and Others (2002).* Baroness Hale's judgment in this case extends to almost 30 pages of the report. There are no Latin words or phrases in the judgment. Baroness Hale deals with a case with complex facts in a difficult area of law. The judgment examines and analyses psychiatric illness in general, defines and describes workplace stress, and goes on to explain the relevant law. Anyone with an interest in work-related stress should be advised to read this judgment for its clarity. It can safely be recommended to non-lawyers: a rarity. This judgment is further discussed in Chapter 6 (Mystery).

Corporate manslaughter

The Corporate Manslaughter and Corporate Homicide Act 2007 came into force on April 6, 2008. The Act represents the culmination of more than ten years of lobbying, consultation and discussion. The prosecution of companies for manslaughter was a matter of such complexity and technicality that very few prosecutions were successful. Following pressure from trade unions and health and safety organisations, we saw White Papers, consultation exercises, conferences, numerous articles in the specialist and national press, Bills, interviews and speculation.

The death of a worker because of the negligence of an employer, rather than being treated as an unfortunate accident, should be one of the most serious crimes known to English law. The Act of 2007 goes some way towards addressing this. It creates the new statutory offence of corporate manslaughter. In summary, a company will be guilty of the new offence if the way in which its activities are managed or organised, by its senior management, amounts to a gross breach of the duty of care which it owes to its employees, the public or other individuals and those failings have caused a person's death.

On February 15, 2011, Cotswold Geotechnical Holdings became the first company to be convicted of the new offence of corporate manslaughter under the Act of 2007.The case concerned the death of Alex Wright, a geologist employed by the company. In September 2008 he was investigating soil conditions in a 3.5 metre deep trench on a development site in Stroud, Gloucestershire, when it collapsed and killed him.

Wright was left working alone in the trench to finish up when the director of the company left work for the day. Two people who owned the site, who were present, heard a muffled noise and a shout for help. One of the owners called the emergency services. The other went to the trench where he saw that Wright had been buried up to his head. He removed some soil so that Wright could breathe. More earth fell into the trench, completely covering the victim. He died from traumatic asphyxiation.

The prosecution made the following points:

- Wright was working in a dangerous trench because the company's systems had failed to take all reasonably practicable steps to protect him from working in that way.
- The company had ignored well-recognised industry guidance which prohibited entry into excavations more than 1.2 metres deep.
- The company required junior employees to enter into and work in unsupported trial pits, typically from 2 to 3.5 metres deep.

Cotswold Geotechnical Holdings was a small company which employed eight people. Its director, Peter Eaton, was in overall control of the way in which the company managed its affairs. Eaton was charged with gross negligence manslaughter and a health and safety offence. In 2010 a judge ruled that he was too ill to stand trial.

The jury at Winchester Crown Court found the company guilty of corporate manslaughter after a trial before judge and jury which lasted three weeks. The dock was empty because the sole defendant was a company – an entity with a virtual legal personality based on general principles of company law.

Mr Justice Field is reported to have commented that the gross breach of duty to Wright was a grave offence. He fined the company £385,000. The company, which was stated to be in a parlous financial state, could pay the fine over ten years at £38,500 per annum.

The fine aimed to mark the gravity of the offence and the deterrent effect which it would have on companies, to strongly adhere to health and safety guidance.

The company was on a small scale and a larger fine would cause it to be liquidated. This would result in four people losing their jobs.

It might well be that the fine would put the company into liquidation. If that was the result, it was unfortunate but unavoidable. It was a consequence of the serious breach.

Reaction to the result of this, the first corporate manslaughter trial, has included the following:

- Criticisms of the length of time from the date of death to the guilty verdict – two and a half years.

- This case had not been a real test of the effect of the Act. Cotswold Geotechnical Holdings was a small company run by a sole director. The first real test would come when a large, perhaps multinational company, with a complex management chain, was charged with an offence under the Act of 2007.
- Solicitors were reported to have commented that the case would herald an "avalanche" of similar cases. The accuracy of this view remains to be seen.

In relation to the level of the fine, this may be gauged against the definitive guidelines laid down by the Sentencing Guidelines Council (SGC) for the sentencing of organisations on or after February 15, 2010, where such organisations have been convicted of corporate manslaughter and health and safety offences causing death.

The SGC guidelines include the following:

Factors likely to increase seriousness:

- How foreseeable was serious injury?
- How far short of the applicable standard did the organisation fall?
- How common was this kind of breach in the organisation?
- How far up the organisation did the breach go?

Mitigating factors:

- Prompt acceptance of responsibility
- High level of co-operation with the investigation
- Genuine efforts to remedy defects
- A good health and safety record
- A responsible attitude to health and safety.

In relation to financial information:

- The law must expect the same standard of behaviour from large and small organisations.
- Size is relevant: the means of any defendant are relevant to the level of a fine.
- The court should require information about the financial circumstances of the organisation.
- The best practice will usually be to call for the relevant information for a three-year period including the year of the offence.
- The court should look at turnover and profit and also assets to gauge the resources of the organisation.

The court should consider the following factors relevant to the financial consequences of a fine:

- The effect on the employment of the innocent
- The effect of shareholders will not normally be relevant
- The effect on directors will also not normally be relevant
- Whether the fine will put the organisation out of business will be a relevant consideration but this may be an acceptable consequence.

Fines should normally be paid within 28 days by larger organisations. For smaller organisations, this may be extended.

The offence of corporate manslaughter normally involves a level of seriousness significantly greater than a health and safety offence. The appropriate fine will seldom be less than £500,000 and may be measured in millions.

The fine in the Cotswold Geotechnical Holdings case - £385,000 – is therefore less than the starting point recommended by the SCG.

Following the trial, a spokesperson for the CPS stated that the death of the deceased had been a tragedy and would never have happened if Cotswold Geotechnical Holdings had properly protected him. It was hoped that the conviction had offered his family some sense of justice.

More recently a company was fined £100,000, plus £10,450 in court costs, at Belfast's Laganside Crown Court for health and safety failings under the Act of 2007 in connection with the death of 47-year-old employee, Norman Porter.

The conviction followed a joint Police Service of Northern Ireland (PSNI) and Health and Safety Executive for Northern Ireland (HSENI) investigation into the fatal incident, which took place on an animal feed mixing plant owned by J Murray & Son Ltd at Ballygowan, Co. Down on 28 February 2012.

Mr Porter, who had only been working at the company for eight weeks, died after he became entangled in moving parts of a meal blending machine.

The investigation revealed that the company had removed safety panels from the top of the mixer to allow raw ingredients to be added more easily.

This had the undesired effect of exposing the dangerous moving parts of the machine, which the company failed to identify and correct.

The investigation also revealed that the blender was operated without the safety guards for approximately three years.

Following the hearing, Kevin Campbell, an inspector with HSENI's Major Investigation Team said: "This case highlights the importance of proper management of health and safety in the workplace... The removal of safety guards from the machine and the continued use of the machine ultimately led to the death of Norman Porter".

Funding of civil claims

The virtual abolition of legal aid in civil cases has radically changed the funding of civil claims for compensation for health and safety-related injuries and deaths. It is now very difficult for victims of breaches of health and safety law to afford legal advice and representation. Legal costs may occasionally be covered by the following:

- Trade union membership.
- Legal expenses insurance: victims often do not know that they have such cover and should always be advised to check house and contents insurance, motor insurance, credit cards and other possible "hidden" legal insurance. A significant drawback of these insurance policies is that the insured is denied a choice of lawyer: claims must almost always be referred to the insurance company's lawyers. This cosy arrangement has been successfully challenged in *Brown Quinn & Another v Equity Syndicate Management Limited & Another [2012] EWCA Civ 1633.*
- "No win no fee" schemes. This deceptively simple phrase hides the reality of complex, insurance-driven

arrangements. These are fully analysed in Chapter 1 (Money)

- Law centres. In theory, these should provide legal assistance to victims who cannot afford any other means of obtaining guidance. In reality, they are overworked and underfunded. Large areas of the United Kingdom have no access to law centres.
- Pro bono (charitable) schemes. These are discussed in detail in Chapter 1 (Money)
- Private funding. It is by no means unusual for victims of health and safety breaches to be asked for £5000 in advance before lawyers will look at their case.

The shortcomings of the current funding arrangements are well illustrated by the scandal of miners' compensation claims, which is fully discussed in Chapter 1.

Migrant workers

Since the enlargement of the European Union, with the general principle that citizens of EU states have the right of free movement to work, increasing numbers of migrant workers have found employment in the United Kingdom. Migrant workers are generally regarded as being highly motivated, reliable and committed. Many of these workers do not have a fluent grasp of English and may be particularly vulnerable to failings in health and safety practices. The large number of migrant workers from Central and Eastern Europe currently employed in the United Kingdom has started to make an impact on health and safety and employment law.

These workers may be prepared to accept lower wages than their British counterparts, because wages in their home countries are far lower than those in the United Kingdom for comparable work. Those migrant workers who are highly educated find themselves in a position where they are not familiar with their employment rights. They may feel that they are in a vulnerable position in a foreign country with whose laws and customs they are unfamiliar. English employment tribunals and courts are increasingly demonstrating an awareness of this position.

The Health and Safety Executive has shown itself to be well aware of these problems. It has issued detailed advice and guidance on the proper management of migrant workers' health and safety. The HSE recognises that factors such as poor language skills and unfamiliarity with the workplace can magnify the effects of existing health and safety problems. It advises that migrant workers with better English should be asked to interpret for their less fluent colleagues. Internationally recognised signs, videos or audio materials can be used to communicate health and safety messages.

In general, tribunals and courts have expressly recognised the problems arising in relation to large numbers of workers with a limited grasp of English language, law and culture. Spokespersons for the HSE have repeatedly commented on the vulnerability of such employees in relation to health and safety.

Examples of health and safety prosecutions involving migrant workers

In July 2009 Thomas Thomson, the director of Thomas Thomson (Blairgowrie) Ltd, a fruit farming company, was fined following the death of a migrant worker by electrocution.

In July 2006 Gerard Faltynowski, a Polish migrant worker, was helping to build a polytunnel in a field near Blairgowrie in Scotland. The polytunnel was placed below three overhead power lines carrying 11,000 volts.

Faltynowski had slotted thirteen poles, each one half a metre in length, and was carrying them vertically. The pole touched the cables. He was killed instantly.

Thomson was fined £1800 under Regulation 3 of the Management of Health and Safety at Work Regulations 1999 for failing to make a suitable risk assessment of working below power lines.

In August 2006 a gangmaster in charge of Chinese migrant cockle pickers was sentenced to 14 years' imprisonment on 21 counts of manslaughter. The facts, in summary, were that 23 Chinese migrant workers died after a group of 35 cockle pickers were cut off by the tide after dark in February 2004. Twenty-one bodies were later recovered.

The gangmaster – Lin Liang Ren – was also convicted of perverting the course of justice and facilitating illegal immigrants to work in the United Kingdom. His girlfriend, Zhao Xiao Qing, was sentenced to two years and nine months imprisonment for perverting the course of justice and facilitating. His cousin, Lin Mu Yong, received a sentence of four years and nine months imprisonment for helping cocklers to break immigration laws.

In August 2007 Shah Nawaz Pola was fined and imprisoned following an incident in which a worker suffered life-threatening injuries on a construction site.

Pola employed a number of migrant Slovakian workers to build an extension to a house in Bradford. He paid them each £30 a day in cash.

In November 2005 Dusan Dudi, one of the workers, fell from inadequately constructed scaffolding when the wall which he was demolishing collapsed on him. A concrete lintel struck him on the head. He suffered injuries which it was thought would be fatal.

Although Dudi's life support machine was switched off in hospital, he survived. He was left with severe disabilities and needs constant care. It is thought that he will never work again. He is ineligible for benefits in the United Kingdom and in Slovakia.

Pola had no experience of running a construction site. When he was told by an HSE inspector what needed to be done to protect the safety of workers, he replied that he did not care.

Pola had made no concessions at all to health and safety. He had not written a risk assessment nor method statements. He had failed to provide welfare facilities, proper scaffolding, adequate fall guards or personal protective equipment for his workforce. A number of contractors had left the site because safety standards were so poor.

Pola denied being in charge of the site and refused to accept responsibility for the incident.

Health and safety law and practice, however imperfect and underfunded, clearly operates to protect workers and to improve safety standards. If there were no health and safety law, could it seriously be argued that employers would voluntarily cut profits to improve safety standards?

Anyone who doubts the importance of health and safety law should attend a coroner's inquest into a workplace death. The tragic reality of these proceedings, and the devastating effect of such incidents on the family of the deceased, illustrate the crucial significance of health and safety.

Some employers appear more than once in recently reported health and safety prosecutions. For example:

Corus (UK) Ltd, the steelmaking company, was fined £170,000 in April 2007 after a worker was killed by a falling crane.

In July 2003 Shane Eastwood, an employee of Corus, was working at the company's site in Rotherham. He was working on machinery in an engineering workshop under an overhead crane. The crane's hoist block, which weighed 260 kg, fell seven metres onto Eastwood, causing fatal injuries.

A limit switch, which was designed to cut power to the crane if its block was hoisted too far, and which was safety-critical, had failed. As a result, the hoist rope snapped and the block fell.

The accident had been entirely avoidable. Corus had failed to properly maintain the limit switch. The switch was defective and had progressively failed.

This was reported to have been the ninth time in five years that Corus has been fined for health and safety offences.

Corus was also fined £1.3million at Swansea Crown Court on December 15, 2006, for health and safety offences relating to fatalities at its Port Talbot plant.

In November 2001 a blast furnace exploded at the plant. The explosion lifted the top half of the furnace two feet into the air and resulted in molten metal falling on workers. Three were killed, twelve suffered serious burn injuries and five others were injured. The explosion was caused by water leaking into the white hot centre of the furnace, which had been in operation for 47 years. Some of the injured, and those who witnessed the incident, were still receiving psychological treatment five years after the explosion.

The Crown Court Judge criticised the company's casual attitude to safety. During a two-day hearing, evidence was given of a catalogue of errors which resulted in the explosion. These included years of recommendations by senior employees at the plant, relating to the furnace, which were ignored.

In 1993 a decision was taken to prolong the life of the blast furnace. A committee was set up to discuss and report on the furnace four times a year. The committee made a series of recommendations, none of which were acted upon.

One example was a recommendation to carry out a comparative study into the benefits of electrical and diesel pumps. The failure of a succession of electrical pumps, which circulated cooling water to the furnace,

resulted in the explosion. The furnace had suffered many pump failures before the explosion.
The power plant log for the period before the incident showed that an electrical transformer had been damaged by rain and needed repair. A plan to repair it was the start of events which eventually caused the incident. The transformer had to be partially isolated before repairs were carried out. This meant that the current to a furnace pump was transferred to another transformer. This operation needed monitoring to ensure that voltage remained constant.
The team of employees working on the furnace on the day before the explosion was not told about the repair work. When the current was transferred, the voltage in the transformer dropped. This caused a pump to trip and an auxiliary pump, which then came into operation, also tripped. The result of this was that water to cool the system ceased to circulate and approximately 50 tons leaked into the furnace. Employees who were sent to deal with the leak thought that it had been repaired. In fact, the water remained in the furnace. It reacted with the molten metal in the furnace and caused the explosion when the metal core was reheated on the next day.
Corus pleaded guilty to breaches of health and safety law. Defending counsel stated that this did not mean that the company acknowledged that it had foreseen that lives would be at risk. Modern blast furnaces went back to the Victorian era. There were no records of similar explosions having happened. The inquest into the deaths had recorded verdicts of accidental death. An internal report issued by Corus at the time of the inquest had

concluded that the explosion was neither foreseen nor foreseeable.

Senior management responsible for the furnace had met to discuss problems with it one hour before the explosion. The risk of a discharge, but not an explosion, had been discussed at the meeting.

The families of the victims of the explosion were reported to have made the following comments:

- They were disgusted and shocked at the outcome.
- It was quite unbelievable that the company should have been fined such a meagre sum.
- Corus should have been fined up to the maximum allowable. A large fine would have ensured that other companies sat up and listened and understood the consequences of not doing enough for health and safety.
- The judge had stated that Corus had made £143 million this year after tax, so what they had been ordered to pay was a pinprick.

A spokesperson for Community, the trade union representing steelworkers, is reported to have made the following comments:

- The fine was substantial but the union would have expected it to be higher. It did not begin to reflect the scale of suffering of the workers and their families and of the traumatised community of Port Talbot.
- The union had put all its resources at the disposal of the community and had spent more than £500,000.
- The disaster had been horrific, with hot molten metal flying everywhere.

- The sentence was a warning to industrial companies everywhere and their duty of care towards their employees must be paramount.

Class justice and British magistrates' courts

The realities of class justice can be seen in the magistrates' court on any day when it is in session.

A visit to a magistrates' court in any city will show class justice at its clearest. At the top of the class, the haves: magistrates, lawyers, probation officers, social workers, well-educated, well-dressed, well-fed, articulate, self-confident, secure and in control. The courts are their realm. They have the knowledge and the power.

At the bottom of the class, the have-nots, defendants and witnesses, poorly-educated, confused, inarticulate, out of control. The weak, vulnerable, inarticulate, inadequate, excluded. They wait to be processed by a system which excludes them except as victims.

There is never the slightest doubt as to which class they belong. It is impossible to confuse a twenty-year old charged with burglary with a twenty-year old trainee solicitor, or a fifty-year old woman accused of petty theft with a magistrate of the same age.

You may see the odd radical lawyer or the unusual white-collar accused.

You are unlikely to spot a tax evader, a weapons salesman, a loan shark, a polluter or an employer who negligently kills or injures workers. You will never see a war criminal. You are more likely to see an obese young single mother in handcuffs, waiting to be sent to prison for shoplifting. The prisons fill up with the have-nots, while the war criminals excuse themselves from responsibility. But the machine of the criminal courts grinds on, processing the alienated and excluded.

Tabling

The class stratification of British society extends to the law publishing industry. An exemplar of this is the work of the tablers.

Most law books have detailed lists of the cases and statutory materials which are mentioned in the text. The compilation of these lists, known as "Tables", is a task of almost inconceivable monotony and drudgery. It is carried out manually by teams of casual workers whose working hours are devoted to the alphabetisation of case names, the checking of references and the identification of the details of statutes and statutory instruments.

A large legal textbook, running to perhaps 2000 pages, will involve immeasurable work on the tabling of cases and statutes. The tabling of law books can make oakum picking and mailbag sewing seem like work of infinite interest and variety. Senior lawyers earning £300 an hour and more depend for much of their information on teams of low-paid drudges.

Prohibition

At midnight on January 16, 1920, alcohol was criminalised in the United States of America. The Volstead Act, the Eighteenth Amendment to the US Constitution, made it unlawful to manufacture, sell, barter, transport, import, export, deliver, furnish or possess any intoxicating liquor. The Act set out specific exemptions, for example industrial alcohol, sacramental wine, doctors' prescriptions and "near-beer" with a maximum 0.5 alcohol content.

The Volstead Act made liquor advertising illegal and also stated that any room, house, building, boat, vehicle, structure or place where intoxicating liquor is manufactured, sold, kept or bartered was declared a common nuisance.

Prohibition lasted until 1933. It is generally accepted that its main effect was the encouragement of organised crime to evade the law and that the legacy of gangsterism developed by the Volstead Act continues to the present day.

The contemporary socialist analysis of Prohibition was that it was a deliberate attempt by the dominant bourgeoisie to avoid the real issues of poverty and exploitation. The ideals of the Prohibitionists – sobriety and hard work – meant that industrial workers would work more efficiently.

This analysis is supported by the activities of Henry Ford. He had required his employees to abstain from alcohol. He used a private police force for surveillance and anyone buying liquor a second time was dismissed. Ford's only concern was efficiency. Alcohol consumption slowed the Ford assembly lines and caused accidents.

The circumstances in which Prohibition was repealed also support the contemporary socialist analysis. Edward Behr states the view that the reasons for the end of Prohibition were essentially economic. The stock market crash of 1929 and the Depression which followed it led to an increasing awareness on the part of industrialists that one of the effects of Prohibition had been to cut off tax revenues from the sale of alcohol. The Du Pont family, owners of munitions factories, stated that if America adopted Britain's alcohol tax system, income tax could be abolished. John D Rockefeller, previously a strong advocate of Prohibition, argued strongly for its repeal in 1932.

Behr estimates that 500,000 people were convicted of offences under the Volstead Act. In some states, mandatory sentences were imposed for a fourth violation. In Michigan, two persons were sentenced to life imprisonment for possession of a pint of gin. These half a million people were generally those who lacked political or financial influence. Throughout the Prohibition era, politicians, enforcement officials and professional criminals dealt in alcohol with impunity. Bribery and corruption were endemic.

If traditional criminological questions are applied to the half million, some interesting answers emerge. Why did these people commit crime? Was it a genetic disorder? The shape of their heads? Peer pressure? Social deprivation? Inherited characteristics? Alcoholism? Psycho-sexual disorders? Did they suddenly cease to be subject to these factors on December 5, 1933, when the Eighteenth Amendment was declared void? Or is the truth that they were victims of a system which decided, for partly altruistic but essentially political and economic reasons, to criminalise them?

Prohibition is a clear example of the proposition that criminal law is what the state declares it to be. The half million Prohibition criminals were criminals because the state made them so. The state then decriminalised them thirteen years later when economic considerations prevailed. They ceased to be involved in criminal behaviour, and traditional criminological analyses became irrelevant.

Prohibition also provides a very clear example of class justice operating in an advanced capitalist society. Millions of citizens were criminalized, without their consent, by a combination of forces including corrupt politicians, puritans and the raging xenophobia unleashed by the US's entry into World War I as it was nearing its end. The owners of the means of production were also instrumental in the enactment of the Volstead Act because they believed that sober workers meant larger profits.

Once enacted, the enforcement of Prohibition impacted most severely on the poor and disadvantaged. Those responsible for the Volstead Act took the naïve view that the law would be obeyed purely and simply because it was the law. The opposite was true. The huge profits to be made from illicit liquor sales led to massive corruption in government and an explosion of organised crime. The greatest profiteers were not prosecuted because they were the greatest profiteers and could bribe their way to immunity. The enforcement of Prohibition was at its most successful against small-time operators, the poor and the inadequate, who could not afford lawyers and who had no influence with politicians. If this is not class justice, then what is?

Alcohol prohibition in the United States is a clear example of the relativity of criminal law and makes nonsense of many theories of the causes of crime. The only sensible definition of criminal behaviour is that which the state, from time to time, declares to be a criminal offence. There are many examples of this, including the prohibition of alcohol in Muslim countries, different ages in different countries for sexual consent, and the reported illegality of Red Bull in France.

Why do people in France break the criminal law by drinking Red Bull? Why are prosecutions brought for possession of marijuana in some countries but not in others? How do we explain this criminality? Social deprivation? A genetic disposition to break the law? The shape of their heads? The reality is that the state has created this criminality in otherwise law-abiding citizens. No other explanation is meaningful or necessary.

Oral tobacco

In Sweden and parts of Finland, the use of oral tobacco as an alternative to smoking is fairly widespread. Oral tobacco is a legal product in Sweden but is banned elsewhere in Europe including Finland and the Aland Islands. These are an archipelago of 6500 islands in the Baltic Sea. They are a Swedish-speaking autonomous province of Finland.

Ferry ships operating between Sweden and Finland have oral tobacco for sale. The current state of European law appears to be that ferries registered in Sweden and operating via the Aland Islands are allowed to sell oral tobacco. Alandic registered vessels are not. Criminality, in this context, depends upon the place where a ship is registered. A passenger on a Swedish ship can lawfully buy oral tobacco. A passenger on an Alandic ship is a criminal if he does so.

It may be assumed that we will wait in vain for

Crimewatch to denounce the oral tobacco chewers of the Aland Islands or for criminologists to seek explanations for their criminal behaviour.

George Orwell

Orwell had little interest in the law, but he commented that it was not that anyone imagined the law to be just. Everyone knew that there was one law for the rich and another for the poor. But no one accepted the implications of this, everyone took it for granted that the law, such as it is, would be respected, and felt a sense of outrage when it is not. Remarks like "They can't run me in; I haven't done anything wrong" or "They can't do that; it's against the law" are part of the atmosphere of England. Everyone believes in his heart that the law can be, ought to be, and on the whole will be, impartially administered.

In his essay *The Lion and the Unicorn* (1941) on the nature of Englishness, Orwell states the following:

... the gentleness of English civilisation is mixed up with barbarities and anachronisms. Our criminal law is as out-of-date as the muskets in the Tower. Over against the Nazi Storm Trooper you have got to set that typically English figure, the hanging judge, some gouty old bully with his mind rooted in the nineteenth century, handing out savage sentences. In England people are still hanged by the neck and flogged with the cat o'nine tails. Both of these punishments are obscene as well as cruel, but there has never been any genuinely popular outcry against them. People accept them (and Dartmoor, and Borstal) almost as they accept the weather. They are part of 'the law' which is assumed to be unalterable.

Orwell also refers to the English respect for constitutionalism and legality, the belief in 'the law' as something above the State and above the individual, something which is cruel and stupid but at any rate incorruptible. He also refers to

...the hanging judge, that evil old man in scarlet robe and horse-hair wig, whom nothing short of dynamite will ever teach what century he is living in, but who will at any rate interpret the law according to the books and will in no circumstances take a money bribe, is one of the symbolic figures of England. He is a symbol of the strange mixture of reality and illusion, democracy and privilege, humbug and decency, the subtle network of compromises, by which the nation keeps itself in familiar shape.

Class justice and the judiciary

Every student of history knows that many of the most significant victories for freedom and justice have been won in the English law courts, and that the liberties of Englishmen are closely bound up with the complete independence of the judges (Lord Hewart, The New Despotism, 1929)

The myth of judicial neutrality continues to flourish in Britain, and all evidence inconsistent with it is either explained away or, more frequently, ignored.
(Albie Sachs)

You will find, I am sure, that judges will still be of the same type whether they come from major or minor public schools, grammar schools or comprehensives,

and whether they like to spend their leisure in a library or a club. They will all be the same type of men who do not seriously question the status quo, men who whose ambition it is to serve the law and not to be its master. You can see this already at the university, where students in law faculties all over the world are nearly always on the right while those in sociology are on the left. Lawyers are not naturally interested in social reform, any more than policemen are or soldiers.
(Lord Devlin)

The nineteenth-century Law Reports may be searched in vain for cases involving exploitation by employers who required their workers to labour for long hours at starvation wages, or conspiracies involving combinations which resulted in death or injury to employees because of dangerous conditions in mines and factories. There are no reported trials of masters for profiteering, speculation or the accumulation of capital. It is impossible for such activities to be offences under capitalist economic conditions.
For example, in the case of *Mogul Steamship Co v McGregor, Gow & Co (1889)*, the court ruled that concerted action by a powerful group of tea traders to suppress competition was not a conspiracy because they had acted with the lawful object of protecting and extending their trade and increasing their profits. In a capitalist society, their actions were justifiable even though they involved ruining weaker businesses.

In 1932, Harold Laski calculated that between 1832 and 1906, sixty percent of High Court judges had been

Members of Parliament, of whom three-quarters had been appointed to the Bench by the party which they supported. Well over seventy percent had received an Oxford or Cambridge education. Laski's conclusion was that the most important judicial posts are, in England, largely the appanage of the chief legal advisers of the Cabinet of the day and that it was possible that such judges would, particularly in cases where the liberty of the subject was concerned, find themselves unconsciously biased through over-appreciation of executive difficulty.

In 1999 a survey compiled by Labour Research reported that of the 85 judges appointed since 1997, seven were female and 79 per cent had been educated at public schools. 73 per cent had been to Oxbridge.

John Griffith stated the view (*The Politics of the Judiciary* 1977) that, in our society, political power is exercised by a relatively small number of people. These include Cabinet ministers, senior civil servants, the executives of local authorities, senior police officers, leading members of the armed forces, industrialists and some trade union leaders. The senior judges must also be included in this list, as must senior bankers and individuals who control the mass media.

Griffith's concluding thesis is that the judiciary in any modern society, however composed, under whatever system, is an essential part of the government of that system and its function may be described as underpinning the stability of that system and protecting it from attack.

This can now seen to be out of date or just demonstrably wrong in day-to-day developments. The judiciary now protects us from the government. In 21st century Britain, the courts may be seen to have replaced Parliament as protectors of the rights of the individual.

For example, in *A v X and Others (2004)*, nine appellants, all foreign nationals, were certified by the Home Secretary as suspected international terrorists. They were detained under Part 4 of the Anti-Terrorism, Crime and Security Act 2001. This breached Article 5(1) of the European Convention on Human Rights which guarantees the right to liberty of the person. The UK government therefore derogated from that Article under Article 14, on the basis of "war or other public emergency threatening the life of the nation".

Under the Act of 2001, the Special Immigration Appeal Tribunal (SIAT) had exclusive jurisdiction over this matter.

The detainees challenged the government's decision. They succeeded in the SIAT but this was overturned by the Court of Appeal.

The House of Lords ruled against the government. The Lords made the following points:

- There was a state of emergency which justified derogation under Article 15.
- The measures taken by the government did not comply with Article 15 because they were not "strictly required by the exigencies of the situation".
- The government's response had not been proportionate because it did not address the threat posed by UK nationals, and it permitted foreign terrorists to pursue their activities abroad. The provisions imposed the severe penalty of indefinite

detention on those foreign nationals who remained in the UK.

- The legislation was discriminatory because it applied only to non-British nationals.
- In the words of Lord Hoffmann, the life of the nation was threatened by the Spanish Armada and by Hitler but not by terrorists. The real threat to the life of the nation came not from terrorism but from laws like these.

Another recent example of the changing role of the judiciary is the reported comments (October 19, 2005) of Lord Steyn, a former law lord, and Lord Alexander of Weedon's assessment of the constantly shifting grounds for intervention in Iraq. They agreed that none of the grounds offered by the British government had any plausibility. The earlier Resolution 678, preceding the driving of Iraq from Kuwait 12 years earlier, had no relevance to the contemporary international position. The sole reason for harking back to it was that it was impossible to obtain Security Council approval for intervention in Iraq. This is expanded further in Chapter 5 (War).

Another example is the reported comments of Lord Ackner, Lord Lester and Lord Carlile (October 16).
Lord Ackner stated that there was a contradiction between the government's efforts to separate Parliament and the judiciary through the creation of a Supreme Court, and its instinct for directing judges how to behave. He thought that it was terribly important that there should not be this apparent battle between the

executive and the judiciary. The judiciary has been put there by Parliament in order to ensure that the executive acts lawfully. If we take that away from the judiciary we are really apeing what happened in Nazi Germany. The government's proposals to hold terrorist suspects for three months without charge was overblown.
Lord Lester expressed concern that the government was flouting human rights law and meddling with the courts. He warned against the whittling away of historic civil liberties. In the United States the Patriot Act included a system whereby a witness to a terrorist incident could be detained for up to a year. This was in the land of the free. Judges had now replaced MPs as the defenders of basic human rights.

It is difficult to justify views like those of Laski and Griffith in 2014. We now seem to be in a position where the judiciary regularly finds itself in conflict with the government. We find ourselves in the position, unforeseeable even ten years ago, where a senior figure in the legal establishment expresses views very similar to those of Edward Thompson, the scourge of the establishment, and in absolute legal and moral opposition to government.
In decision after decision, the courts have ruled against the government. Is this because the current government is particularly authoritarian, or were the commentators totally wrong about the nature and role of the judiciary? Are the judges really the main bastion of defence against a government which threatens fundamental rights? Was New Labour a particularly vicious organisation? There are a number of possible explanations.

1. The fundamental nature of the judiciary has changed. From being part of the establishment it has metamorphosed into a progressive, even radical body, determined to uphold the rights of the individual against the state. This seems unlikely, given that methods of choosing and appointing judges have changed only marginally. Judges, particularly senior ones, are chosen almost exclusively from the ranks of successful barristers who have managed to climb from one or two universities through pupillages and tenancies to successful practices and appointment as Queen's Counsel. It is difficult to find evidence that the social and economic background, and the political ethos of this tiny elite, has significantly changed. The conclusion must be that the fundamental nature of the judiciary has not changed.
2. The commentators were wrong. The judges do not act in favour of the state. The Labour government, despite having introduced the Human Rights Act, was so authoritarian and control-oriented that the traditional establishment view of the judiciary, as an essentially neutral body which enforces laws which protect human rights, had been proved correct.
3. The state has moved so far towards totalitarianism that even the legal establishment, with its undoubted commitment to common law principles and the rule of law, is in a state of rebellion.

Mozambique

Following the Frelimo revolution of 1976 most judges

and lawyers, who were Portuguese, left the country.

The legal priority of the revolutionary government was combating crime and re-educating criminals. Its view was that criminals are nearly always drawn from the ranks of the exploited classes who had absorbed a corrupt and exploitative mentality from their exploiters and who tried to solve their personal difficulties, which were caused by a society divided into classes, not by a struggle to destroy this type of society, but through the exploitation, oppression and humiliation of the people themselves.

Paris Commune

For ten weeks in 1871, workers, artisans, students and veterans of revolutions took control of the second largest city in Europe. It was said that for the first time since 1848 the streets of Paris were safe without any police of any kind.

The Commune's law-making activities included the following:

- The abolition of military conscription: the permanent army was replaced with the National Guard which was a democratic body of citizen soldiers.
- A moratorium on rents.
- The requisition of abandoned apartments and their distribution to the homeless.
- The prohibition of the sale of articles deposited at pawnshops.
- Teachers' salaries were raised: there was no distinction between the pay of male and female teachers.

- Equal pay for equal work.
- The transfer of requisitioned property to worker co-operatives.
- The separation of church and state.
- The suppression of public funding for religion.
- Nationalisation of church lands.

The Commune was destroyed by force of arms. Many communards were executed without trial in a frenzy of killing and thousands of others were transported to New Caledonia. This is an extreme example of a historical truth – that when the state is sufficiently threatened, it uses violence to deal with the threat. In extreme conditions, the criminal law is essentially about violence, no matter how it attempts to deny this and to dress itself up as machinery for suppressing violence. The state, in crisis, asserts its monopoly of extreme violence.

French illegalists

Following the suppression of the Paris Commune in 1871, all forms of working-class political activity were banned by the state. Trade unionists were forced to operate in illegal or marginally legal ways.

This criminalisation of working class organisation was accompanied by anarchist "propaganda by the deed" which involved insurrection, assassination and bombing.

In the words of some elements of the anarchist movement, the wish for expropriation of the expropriators was reduced to individual acts of re-appropriation of bourgeois property.

These ideas were taken to the extreme concept of "revolutionary criminality" as expressed, for example, by Ravachol and others, who justified robbery and killing on the basis that revolutionary acts must necessarily be criminal. If actions were not criminal, then they were ineffective, because effective actions must be in breach of the criminal law.

It is not, of course, surprising that Denning, in the case of *London Borough of Southwark v Williams (1971)*, stated the opposite view from that of the French illegalists, referred to above.

Nazi law: extreme class justice

The National Socialist theory of law in Hitler's Germany included the following:

- The "leadership principle". The state is a group and a group has no strength or unity without a leader. The leader is the mystical personification of national unity. Law and the state mean the same thing. Since the leader is the embodiment of the state, law is what the leader commands. Therefore, unquestioning obedience is demanded; the law serves political ends; nothing must stand in the way of implementing the will of the leader.
- The "racial principle". Law is inherited by blood. It should serve the ends of the state and its policies. It should help to preserve racial purity. The German Code of 1900 was based on Justinian's version of Roman law. It was therefore "Jewish" in origin. The only international system which could be tolerated was a Nordic one. Every state has a natural privilege and power to prevail over other states and to take

their land as room for its people. Any treaty which attempted to restrict this privilege could be ignored.

Nazi law was not central to the exercise of power by the National Socialist party, but it formed part of a system which brought unimaginable suffering to millions.

Cuba

Debra Evanson is regarded as the leading American authority on the Cuban legal system. She has published widely in this area. She describes herself as a critical supporter of the Cuban Revolution.

The following material should not be seen as an uncritical analysis of the Cuban system, nor as an acceptance of its practical effects. The Cuban system is analysed as an expressly socialist legal system which gives deep insight into the English capitalist system.

Evanson's work has been described by contemporary academics as a penetrating analysis of how law and society interact in a revolutionary setting. Her views include the following:

- Cuba is described as a democratic-centralist state organized according to a Marxist-Leninist model. The Supreme Court of Cuba is the country's highest judicial branch of government and also operates as a court of last resort for appeals from lower courts.
- Cuba is divided into 14 provinces and numerous municipalities. Provincial courts deal with serious crimes, civil matters including divorce, and appeals from municipal courts. Municipal courts are courts of first instance for less serious crimes and civil matters.

- The Cuban legal system reflects Cuba's historical status as a Spanish colony. It is a civil law country with an emphasis on written codes rather than judicial precedent as sources of law. The inquisitorial system of criminal procedure is similar to that of France and Spain.

Aspects of the Cuban system

- Husbands are legally obliged to share equally in household chores and child rearing.
- Mortgage payments are set at a maximum of 10 percent of salary.
- Personal injury lawsuits are rare.
- Lay judges, chosen from the workplace, sit alongside traditional judges at trials.
- The welfare of society is put ahead of individual rights.
- In balancing social good with individual interests, the emphasis is on collective welfare. There is a deep sense of community.
- In 1994, a severe economic crisis resulted from the collapse of the Soviet bloc. One consequence of this was that it was thought that more lawyers were needed. New areas of law have been developed, including tax, trademark registration, a new labour code, consumer rights, an updated contract, a new criminal code and bankruptcy.
- The Cuban revolution of 1959 was based on humanistic and egalitarian aims. These included gender and race equality, the redistribution of wealth, land reform and the realisation of social and

economic rights to housing, health care and education.

- The legal system was of minor relevance to these aims. During the early part of the Castro regime, law comprised a large number of decrees made by the revolutionary leadership.
- In 1976 a new Constitution came into force, together with new codes dealing with, for example, the legal profession, the judicial system, employment law and criminal justice. Legislation came to be seen as a primary instrument for social change.
- The central, general aim of the revolution has been the creation of a system of economic well-being founded on the equitable distribution of resources. Achievements in universal free education, health care and equality are now regarded in Cuba as fundamental rights. It is generally recognised that individual freedoms have been subordinated to these collective aims. It is clear that those who oppose the socialist system are subject to limitations on their freedom of expression and association.
- The question of human rights in Cuba can only be properly considered in the context of the fact that the United States has continuously attempted to undermine and destabilise Cuba's government. These attempts have included an invasion, assassination attempts, an economic embargo and travel restrictions.

The origins of Cuban law

American and Spanish colonialism have had a significant influence on Cuban law. For example, the

Spanish Penal Code was in force until 1979 and the Spanish Civil Code until 1987. Slavery was not abolished in Cuba until 1886.

Before the Revolution, Cuba was notorious as a haven for organised crime controlled from the US.

After the Revolution, law was made by the post-revolutionary Council of Ministers. Early legislation included agrarian reform and nationalisation. Revolutionary Tribunals and people's courts were created.

The Cuban concept of socialist legality

- Law must establish the basis for social stability and create the conditions for social development.
- Socialist legality includes the value system according to which laws are evaluated and amended, as well as the method by which the state governs society.
- Socialist Constitutions are dynamic agents in the evolution of communism.
- This can be contrasted with capitalist Constitutions which preserve the status quo.

Key elements of "socialist legality"

- An emphasis on substantive rather than judicial measures of justice.
- The use of law as a pro-active tool for socialist development.
- Limited use of formal legal mechanisms for the resolution of private disputes.
- The use of informal "social courts" to resolve, for example, housing and labour disputes.

- Direct citizen involvement in judicial and crime control processes.
- State-organised law collectives to provide free or low-cost legal services.

Commentators have analysed legal developments in post-revolutionary Cuba according to four phases:

- From 1959 (the year of the revolution) to the early 1970s: a period of revolutionary experimentation, for example the creation of People's Courts without the involvement of the legal profession.
- From the early 1970s: a phase of institutionalization, for example the creation of a new Constitution, the development of a hierarchical and more formal court system and the creation of *bufetes colectivos.*
- The mid 1980s: a "rectification" phase including a new penal code.
- The "special period" of severe economic crisis following the collapse of the Soviet bloc.

Cuba and human rights

The Cuban Constitution of 1976 sets out all the rights recognised by the Universal Declaration of Human Rights and includes the following:

- The obligation of the state to assure the economic and social well-being of the collective.
- Positive social and economic rights: the right to work, right to social security, free health care and free education. The right to work is balanced by a duty to work.
- Equality of rights and duties and the prohibition of discrimination.

- Individual liberties, for example freedom of speech in keeping with the objectives of a socialist society.

Capitalist democracy is seen as a democracy for a majority of exploiters and as a form of oppression of the majority.

US and UK jurisprudence puts individual autonomy and property rights above group rights and collective economic and social well-being.

Socialist legality is concerned with collective well-being based on egalitarian values. It imposes limitations of individual liberties for the collective good. Political expression is restricted where it conflicts with state policy. The Cuban Communist party is the only lawful political party.

All efforts to organise internal dissent have been linked to US efforts to destabilise the government.

Lawyers in Cuba

Evanson reports the following:

- The 1959 revolution destroyed the private practice of most Havana law firms. The practice of law was considered to be a parasitic bourgeois profession.
- In many countries, the practice of the law tends to smack of professional elitism and questionable ethics.
- The revolution resulted in a decline in the role of the courts for dispute resolution. Legal education shrank to virtual extinction.
- The Law on the Organization of the Judicial System (1973) eliminated the private practice of law.

- Legal services are provided by bufetes colectivos (collective law offices) which are the exclusive providers of legal services. Services are provided at modest rates or free for those who cannot pay. The National Organization of Collective Law Offices (ONBC) comprises 2000 lawyers supplying free or low price legal services. The bufetos colectivos reportedly provide legal services to almost one million people every year. Issues range from traditional civil, administrative, penal and labour matters to more specialized matters, for example banking and commercial cases. The ONBC has staff who obtain official documents on behalf of clients. There is a fixed tariff for each procedure. Contracts for legal services specify the price of the service and the rights and obligations of the parties.
- Cuban lawyers are expected to support socialist ideology and to work for the perfection of socialist law. Lawyers are called upon specifically to educate their clients and other citizens with respect to their legal rights.
- Legal education, room and board are free. Books are available at highly subsidised prices. In return, law graduates must work at a bufete for three years.

The Cuban population has come to expect relatively easy access to legal services in a system which has substantially diminished inequality in law and the legal process. Legal representation is no longer a privilege of class. Cuba is closer to guaranteeing access to justice than most countries.

Cuban judicial system

People's Popular Courts were established after the revolution to deal with private disputes and petty crime. Judges were elected and sat on a part-time basis.
Revolutionary Tribunals under military control dealt with war crimes and imposed death sentences.
Under the reforms of 1973, Revolutionary Tribunals and People's Popular Courts were abolished. Part-time lay judges now sit alongside professional judges in all cases. Lay judges in Cuba, who sit alongside professional judges, are elected peasants, workers and housewives. The comment has been made that, in this context, justice can be seen as reflecting the popular will.

Cuban law and equality

Under the 1976 Constitution discrimination because of race, colour, sex or national origin is forbidden and is punished by law. The institutions of the state educate everyone, from the earliest possible age, in the principle of equality among human beings.
For example:

- In 1979 all criminal penalties for abortion were eliminated.
- In 1961 all private schools were abolished.
- The private renting of housing has been abolished.
- There is freedom to practise religion except Jehovah's Witnesses because their beliefs oppose service to the state, especially military service.
- There are no religious holidays and Christmas is a work day.

- The primary aim of the family, and the aim of family law, is to contribute to the development and upbringing of children in accordance with socialist values, and to provide for the emotional needs of individuals.
- There is a legal obligation for men and women to share housework.

Cuban criminal justice

Under the 1987 Criminal Code, every socially dangerous action or omission, prohibited by law resulting in a penal sanction, is a punishable crime.

Social dangerousness is defined as habitual behaviour which shows a special proclivity to commit criminal acts, as demonstrated by observed conduct, which is manifestly against the norms of socialist morality. This has resonances with the British concept of anti-social behaviour, where no conviction is required for an ASBO.

There are few examples in Latin America where the criminal justice system is as fair and efficient as in Cuba.

Cuban criminal law includes offences against socialist organization, for example:

- The misuse of employment in a state enterprise for illegal personal gain.
- Obtaining money or property illegally channelled from a state economic entity.
- Trading in foreign currency.
- Attempting to leave Cuba without complying with formal emigration requirements.

Inmates in Cuban prisons are expected to complete their education to the equivalent of US high school degree level and are also expected to learn a trade.

Prisoners are obliged to work and are paid the same wage which they would expect to receive outside prison. Prisoners are entitled to conjugal visits every two months.

Private property in Cuba

- The revolution resulted in a fundamental change in property relations. All means of production were nationalised.
- Landlords were prevented from evicting delinquent clients.
- Cuba is a country of homeowners, based on the individual ownership of private homes. Most Cubans are homeowners.
- Housing law has the primary social objective of providing shelter to all citizens. It is based primarily on the recognition of the social function of housing as opposed to its commercial or investment value.
- In no case can the ownership of a home become a mechanism of enrichment or exploitation.
- Private rental housing is prohibited. Housing is a public service with the state as primary landlord.
- State constructed housing is transferred through sale to individuals by the Popular Savings Bank. The price is amortised over 15 to 20 years. There is no foreclosure or repossession. Arrears are collected by the attachment of the debt to the debtor's salary.

- Inheritance rules are designed mainly to protect the occupiers of homes.
- There are virtually no homeless people in Cuba.

Economic regulation

In capitalist states, private contract law can be seen as a fundamental regulatory device which enables competitive markets to function. Parties to private contracts act voluntarily and out of self-interest.

In the Cuban socialist economy, a contract is seen as an instrument in the implementation of the national economic plan which attempts to allocate resources to provide the greatest and most equitable societal benefit.

The Cuban Communist party is reported to have approved a plan to reform the Cuban economy by moving 20 per cent of the state labour force to non-state sector. A new foreign investment law will include improved guarantees and incentives to foreign investors.

Somc aspects of the Cuban system are viewed as "draconian" by human rights organizations. These are justified by Cubans as being national security measures necessitated by US aggression.

The US economic embargo, which in itself can be seen as a form of human rights abuse, is viewed as impeding Cuba's ability to adopt more permissive policies in the area of political freedoms.

The Cuban model, as reported by Evanson, can be seen not as an ideal to be achieved but as a comparative and alternative model for a legal system, which could be described as English class justice in reverse.

CHAPTER 3

DISSENT

Those to the tyrant serve, who, skilled to snare
The feet of justice in the toils of law,
Stand, ready to oppress the weaker still:
And right or wrong will vindicate for gold,
Sneering at public virtue, which beneath
Their pitiless tread lies torn and trampled, where
Honour sits smiling at the sale of truth.
(Shelley, Queen Mab)

The aim of this Chapter is to set out extracts from the work of writers and others who have dissented from the prevailing views of English law and lawyers. These dissenting voices are now rarely heard.

This Chapter sets out summaries of opinions which do not merely indulge in marginal debate about arcane aspects of particular laws, but which fundamentally challenge preconceptions and assumptions about the essential nature of law and lawyers. These opinions range from those of anarchists and socialists to anthropologists, historians and journalists.

This selection of dissenting voices shows the width of critical views of the law. Devastating criticisms of law and lawyers have a long and well-respected intellectual pedigree.

These views provide a new perspective for an analysis of English law and lawyers. They need to be considered and discussed in the context of a critical analysis of the English legal system. The author does not necessarily agree with any of these views except insofar as they generally challenge accepted assumptions about the role of law in society.

This Chapter summarises elements of the views of the following:

- The Levellers
- William Godwin
- Tolstoy
- Kropotkin
- French illegalists
- Emma Goldman
- Strong state theorists
- Jessica Mitford
- Nelson Mandela
- Albie Sachs
- E P Thompson
- Harold Barclay's Anthropology of Anarchism
- DN Pritt
- Haldane Society
- Modern American radical lawyers
- George Monbiot
- Up Against The Law
- The McLibel Case

The Levellers

Some of the earliest and most devastating criticisms of English law and lawyers were made by the Levellers in the seventeenth century in the context of revolutionary changes in English society following the Civil War and the execution of Charles I. The Leveller movement advocated popular sovereignty, extended suffrage, equality before the law and religious tolerance. The Levellers proposed radical reforms, most of which have not yet been carried out in Britain. The Levellers put forward a revolutionary programme, including the codification of the common law in a brief and intelligible handbook, the abolition of barbarous punishments and the reform of the prisons. Its keynote was decentralisation, so that the common man and his neighbours should govern themselves through their juries and elected magistrates.

HN Brailsford states that, during the 1640s, the courts were distrusted and the legal profession disliked. In Brailsford's view, the legal profession was greedy and corrupt and its technical habit of mind was even more unintelligible to the common man than it is today. Official documents and statutes were in Latin or Norman French. Indictments were not valid until they were read out in court in Latin. The fees lawyers charged were generally felt to be exorbitant and some of them were shameless in protracting litigation until their clients were ruined. In 1653 it was said that 23,000 cases had been waiting for settlement in Chancery for ten, twenty and even thirty years.

It happened constantly, Brailsford states, that peasants allowed their cases against landlords who robbed them of their common land by enclosure to go by default, because they could not afford to hire a Chancery lawyer. Workers who had grievances against their employer were in the same position. They had no trade union and could not face the cost of litigation at Westminster whereas the employers could.

Brailsford also points out that it would be easy to compile from the memoirs of this period a long list of the fabulous fortunes made by lawyers, beginning with Sir Edward Coke who is said to have made £100,000 in a single year.

Based on innumerable and sometimes conflicting precedents, the common law could be understood and applied to particular cases only by a skilled body of professional lawyers, who levied a heavy toll on the rest of the nation and made a resort to the courts so costly that only the rather rich or the very rash would venture on litigation.

In every rank of society below the upper layer to which the legal oligarchy belonged, a dread of the law courts and a detestation of lawyers were widespread.

The Levellers invoked the law of nature. Their statements, set out in a series of manifestos, included the following:

William Walwyn, Leveller, author of the Remonstrance, July 1646

Ye know the laws of this nation are unworthy a free people, and deserve from first to last to be considered and reduced to an agreement with common equity and right reason... Magna Carta itself being but a beggarly thing, containing many marks of intolerable bondage... the Norman way for ending of controversies was much more abusive than the English way, yet the Conqueror, contrary to his oath, introduced the Norman laws and his litigious and vexatious way amongst us. The like he did also for punishment of malefactors, controversies of all natures having before a quick and final despatch in every hundred. He erected a trade of judges and lawyers, to sell justice and injustice at his own unconscionable rate and in what time he pleased, the corruption whereof is yet remaining upon us to our continuing impoverishing and molestation.

He further commented:
...a society in which judges grew rich and potent and a wise man would let go his right or inheritance rather than be eaten to the bare bones by grasping judges and avaricious lawyers, where a poor man was hanged for stealing food for his necessities and a luxurious courtier could be pardoned after killing the second or third man.

John Lilburne, Regal Tyranny Discovered

Lilburne advocated a return to Anglo-Saxon days and "ridding this kingdom of those vermin and caterpillars the lawyers, the chief bane of this poor nation".
Lilburne proposed the abolition of national courts and Quarter Sessions. He advocated the *Gemot* which decided everything once a month in every hundred. All cases would be decided in the hundred (an Anglo-Saxon administrative district) by a jury of twelve men. The only appeal would be to the House of Commons. Lilburne also supported the idea that a register should be kept in every county for all leases and conveyances of landed property.

Brailsford's view is that every revolution which brings a new class to power adopts as a matter of course a new system of law which embodies its own view of property and social relations. The French Revolution substituted the clarity of the Code Napoleon for the traditions of feudalism. The Russian Revolution broke with tradition and set up its own characteristic system of civil and criminal law, with a new procedure. The English Revolution was the exception. Its lawyers defeated every attempt at an organic reform of the common law. There was no Code Cromwell.

Imprisonment for debt was common: jailers, who came from the governing class and normally paid a commission to get their jobs, ran prisons as a commercial enterprise.

The Levellers believed that prison served no useful purpose. They proposed that imprisonment should only be used for safe custody until time of trial and not as a punishment for offences.

The Case of the Army truly stated

Law should be overhauled by laymen and decentralised. All laws should be codified in a single volume intelligible to everyone.

Third Agreement of the People

- All are equal before the law.
- No man may be condemned under a law passed after the commission of the offence.
- No-one may be required to incriminate himself by answering questions in a criminal case.
- All proceedings in law must be terminated within six months.
- All laws and legal proceedings must be in English.

- Any man may plead his own cause or call in whom he will to plead for him (the lawyers' monopoly is broken).
- Imprisonment for debt to be abolished.
- Capital punishment abolished except for murder.
- All trials to be by twelve sworn men of the neighbourhood – a return to Anglo-Saxon traditions.
- All law courts in Westminster to be abolished.
- No judges appointed by central government to go on circuit.
- Codification of the civil and criminal law.

Winstanley, The Law of Freedom: True magistracy restored

- Magistrates to be elected annually.
- All citizens must work.
- Legal sanctions to include whipping, forced labour and loss of civil rights.
- Death penalty for murder, buying and selling, rape or following the trade of lawyer or priest.

William Godwin

Godwin (1756-1836), was a political writer and novelist who was one of the earliest and most trenchant critics of law. He proposed a decentralised and simplified society based on voluntary associations of free and equal individuals. He lived with Mary Wollstonecraft, an early feminist, and was an influence on Shelley. Godwin's views included the following:

- Man-made law is unnecessary because immutable reason is the true legislator. Men can do no more than declare and interpret the rules of universal justice as perceived by reason.

- The main weakness of law is its status as a general rule. No two actions are the same and yet the law absurdly tries to reduce the myriad of human actions to one common measure. As such it operates like Procrustes' bed which cuts or stretches whoever lies on it.
- Law is inevitably made in the interest of the lawmakers and as such is a venal compact by which superior tyrants have purchased the countenance and alliance of the inferior.
- Like government, law fixes the human mind in a stagnant condition and prevents that unceasing progress which is its natural tendency.
- Punishment threatened or imposed by law is not an appropriate way to reform human conduct. Men are products of their environment. They cannot strictly speaking be held responsible for what they do. An assassin is no more guilty of the crime he commits than the dagger he holds. Because men are controlled by circumstance, they do not have free will. There can be no moral justification of punishment, whether it is aimed at retribution, example or reform.
- All punishment is a tacit confession of imbecility. It is worse than the original crime because it uses force instead of rational persuasion. Coercion cannot convince or create respect. It can only sour the mind and alienate the person against whom it is used.
- Law, like government, is not only harmful but unnecessary. Godwin's answer to anti-social acts was to reduce the occasion for crime by eradicating

its causes in government and accumulated property and by encouraging people, through education, to think in terms of the general good rather than private interest. Because human vice is mainly error, enlightenment would be enough to make people virtuous.

- Even in a free society it may be necessary to restrain violent people on a temporary basis. They should be treated kindly and kept within the community as far as possible.
- Instead of resorting to courts and to professional lawyers, disputes should be resolved by popular juries who consider the specific circumstances of each case.
- Every case is a rule to itself. The aim should be to resolve conflict rather than to apportion blame. Eventually, it would be necessary to recommend rather than to enforce the decisions of juries.
- In place of law, the power of public opinion would check anti-social acts. When the rules of justice were understood by the community, laws would become unnecessary.
- Laws are inconsistent with the nature of the human mind and the progress of truth.
- All man-made laws are by their very nature arbitrary and oppressive. They represent the venal compact of superior tyrants, mainly enacted to defend economic inequality and unjust political power.
- Law tries to reduce the multiple actions of people to one universal standard.
- Once begun, laws inevitably multiply. They become increasingly confusing and ambiguous and

encourage practitioners to be perpetually dishonest and tyrannical.

- Punishment is immoral and ineffective. It is barbaric if used for retribution and useless if used for reformation or example. Wrongdoers should only be restrained as a temporary expedient and treated with as much kindness and gentleness as possible.

Tolstoy, Count Leo Nikolayevich (1828-1910)

Tolstoy has been described as a writer, aesthetic philosopher, moralist and mystic, the greatest European novelist. *War and Peace* and *Anna Karenina* are generally acknowledged to be the two greatest novels ever written. Tolstoy read law at Kazan University.

During the last twenty years of his life he wrote a number of essays expounding an innovative brand of non-violent anarchism, including the following commentary on law:

- Laws are framed, and repealed, by human beings. It is not some sociological "iron" law, but ordinary man-made law, that produces slavery. The slavery of our times is very clearly and definitely produced by human enactments: about land, about taxes and about property.
- There is one set of laws by which any quantity of land may belong to private people, and may pass from one to another by inheritance, or by will, or may be sold; there is another set of laws by which everyone must pay the taxes demanded of him unquestioningly; and there is a third set of laws to the effect that any quantity of articles, by whatever means acquired, may become the absolute property

of the people who hold them. And in consequence of these laws, slavery exists.

- We are so accustomed to all these laws that they seem to us just as necessary to human life, as the laws maintaining serfdom and slavery seemed in former times. No doubts about their necessity and justice seem possible, and we notice nothing wrong in them. But just as a time came when people, having seen the ruinous consequences of serfdom, questioned the justice and necessity of the laws which maintained it, so now, when the pernicious consequences of the present economic order have become evident, one involuntarily questions the justice and inevitability of the legislation about land, taxes and property which produces those results.
- Land ownership: history shows that property in land resulted from the seizure of the common land by conquerors and its distribution to those who served the conquerors.
- Taxes are taken by those who have the power to take them.
- People formerly established laws enabling some people to buy and sell other people, and to own them, and to make them work, and slavery existed. Now people have established laws that men may not use land that is considered to belong to someone else, must pay the taxes demanded of them, and must not use articles considered to be the property of others – and we have the slavery of our times.
- The essence of legislation is organised violence. According to science, legislation is the expression of the will of the whole people: but as those who break

the laws, or who wish to break them and only refrain from doing so through fear of being punished, are always more numerous than those who wish to carry out the code, it is evident that legislation can certainly not be considered as the expression of the will of the whole people.

- There is one characteristic common to all laws, namely, that if any one man does not fulfil them, those who have made those laws will send armed men, and the armed men will beat, deprive of freedom, or even kill, the man who does not obey the law.
- For every non-fulfilment of the established laws there is punishment: the offender is subjected, by those who make the laws, to blows, imprisonment or even loss of life.
- Everywhere and always the laws are enforced by the only means that has compelled, and still compels, some people to obey the will of others, by blows, by deprivation of liberty and by murder. There can be no other way. It cannot be otherwise. For laws are demands to obey certain rules and to compel some people to obey certain rules can only be done by blows, by deprivation of liberty and by murder. If there are laws, there must be the force that can compel people to obey them. There is only one force that can compel people to obey rules (to conform to the will of others) and that is violence; not the simple violence which people use on one another in moments of passion, but the organized violence used by people who have power in order to compel others

to obey the laws that they, the powerful, have made, in other words, to do their will.

- The essence of legislation lies in the fact that people who wield organized violence have power to compel others to obey them and do as they like.
- Laws are rules, made by people who govern by means of organized violence, for non-compliance with which the non-complier is subjected to blows, to loss of liberty, or even to being murdered.

Kropotkin, Prince Peter (1842-1921)

Kropotkin was a Russian geographer and revolutionary. His work included the following comments:

- Prisons do not moralise their inmates; they do not deter them from crime.
- Our penal institutions have been nothing but a compromise between the old ideas of revenge, of punishment of the "bad will" and "sin", and the modern ideas of "deterring from crime", both softened to a very slight extent by some notions of philanthropy.
- Most people who are kept now in jails, or put to death, are merely people in need of the most careful fraternal treatment.
- The higher instincts of human nature have been checked in their growth by the abominable conditions under which thousands and thousands of children grow up, and millions of adults are living, in what we call our centres of civilisation.
- If we analyse ourselves, we should see that all of us have had some feelings and thoughts such as

constitute the motive of all acts considered as criminal. We have repudiated them at once; but if they had had the opportunity of recurring again and again; if they were nurtured by circumstances, or by a want of exercise of the best passions – love, compassion and all those which result from living in the joys and sufferings of those who surround us; then these passing influences, so brief that we hardly noticed them, would have degenerated into some morbid element in our character.

- That is what we ought to teach our children from the earliest childhood, while now we imbue them from their tenderest years with ideas of justice identified with revenge, of judges and tribunals. And if we did this, instead of doing as we do now, we should no longer have the shame of avowing that we hire assassins to execute our sentences, and pay warders for performing a function for which no educated man would like to prepare his own children.
- Humanity has seldom ventured to treat its prisoners like human beings; but each time it has done so it has been rewarded for its boldness.
- Prisons do not cure pathological deformities, they only reinforce them; and when a psychopath leaves a prison, after having been subjected for several years to its deteriorating influence, he is without comparison less fit for life in society than he was before.
- The shameful practice of legal assassination – of hiring for a guinea an assassin to accomplish a sentence which the judge would not have the courage to carry out himself – this shameful practice has not

even the excuse of preventing murder. Nowhere has the abolition of capital punishment increased the number of murders.

- From year to year thousands of children grow up in the filth – material and moral – of our great cities, completely abandoned amidst a population demoralised by a life from hand to mouth, the incertitude of tomorrow, and a misery of which no former epoch has had even an apprehension.
- We cannot wonder that our big cities chiefly supply prisons with inmates.
- At the other end of the social scale, money is squandered in unheard-of luxury, very often with no other purpose than to satisfy a stupid vanity.
- Money-worship tends to develop an insatiable thirst for unlimited wealth, a love for sparkish luxury, a tendency towards spending money foolishly for every avowable and unavowable purpose; when there are whole quarters in our cities each house of which reminds us that man has too often remained a beast.
- Man is a result of the conditions in which he has grown up.
- Two-thirds of all breaches of law being so-called "crimes against property", these cases will disappear, or be limited to a quite trifling amount, when property, which is now the privilege of the few, shall return to its real source – the community.
- Prison cannot be an environment that reforms the criminal. The man who is shut up in a prison is so far from being bettered by the change, that he comes out more resolutely the foe of society than when he went in.

- All legislation within the state has always been made with regard to the interests of the privileged classes. Law originated in primitive superstitions and was developed by the decrees of conquerors. Human relations were originally regulated by custom. The dominant minority used law to make customs immutable which were to their advantage. Law made its appearance under the sanction of the priest and the club of the warrior.

Kropotkin divided laws into three categories:

1. The protection of property. This is intended to appropriate the product of labour or to deal with disputes between monopolists. These laws have no object other than to protect the unjust appropriation of human labour.
2. The protection of governments. This is constitutional law which aims to maintain the administrative machine and almost entirely acts to protect the interests of the governing classes.
3. The protection of persons. This is the most important because such laws are regarded as indispensable to the maintenance of security in society. These laws developed from useful customs but they have been modified by rulers to serve their own interests.

Punishment is not appropriate for anti-social or violent persons. The severity of punishment does not reduce the amount of crime. On the basis of his own experience of Russian and French prisons Kropotkin criticised prisons for killing physical energy, destroying the individual will and encouraging society to treat released prisoners as something plague-stricken. Prisons could not be improved. The more they are reformed, the worse they become.

People without political organisation, and therefore less depraved than ourselves, have perfectly understood that the man who is called criminal is simply unfortunate. The remedy is not to flog him, to chain him up, to kill him on the scaffold or in prison, but to help him by the most brotherly care, by treatment based on equality, by the usages of life amongst honest men.

Kropotkin on the origin of the state:

Laws were made to protect private property and were enforced by a special group of soldiers. The state dates from the sixteenth century when it took over the free towns and their federations. The state resulted from a triple alliance of lords, lawyers and priests who dominated society. They were later joined by capitalists who strengthened and centralized the state.
Consider what corruption, what depravity of mind is kept up among men by the idea of obedience, the very essence of law; of chastisement; of authority having the right to punish, to judge irrespective of our conscience and the esteem of our friends; of the necessity for executioners, jailers and informers – in a word, by all the attributes of law and authority.

French illegalists: theory of revolutionary criminality

The Bonnot Gang, active in France following the crushing of the Paris Commune, acted in accordance with the theory of *la reprise individuelle*: individual acts of re-appropriation of bourgeois property. This theory, never fully formulated, included the following:

- Theft exists only through the exploitation of man by man, that is to say in the existence of all those who parasitically live off the productive class.
- There is, therefore, a “right to steal”.
- The natural right to free existence is denied to workers by the bourgeoisie’s monopoly ownership of the means of production.
- The immoral bourgeois is the real thief, both in history and the present. The anarchist re-appropriation is superior in morality: it is part of a rightful restitution of wealth robbed from the working class, done with moral conviction.
- The isolated individual has the right to partial re-appropriation of the collective produce.

The illegalists advised unemployed working men to take food for themselves and their families wherever it was to be found, to help themselves to shoes at the shoe shop when the spring rains wet their feet, and to overcoats at the clothier’s when the winter rains ripped them.

Working men should appropriate the factories; farm labourers should take possession of the farms; miners should seize the mines and offer picks to shareholders in case they showed a willingness to work; conscripts should emigrate rather than perform military service; and soldiers should desert or shoot their officers.

It is fair to comment that this movement degenerated into gangsterism.

Emma Goldman (1869-1940)

The young Emma Goldman, introduced above in Chapter 2 (Class), was instructed to pour scorn on the inadequacy of campaigning for an eight-hour day. She aimed to expose the capitalist system and demanded its complete overthrow. The eight-hour day was a diversion. An old worker said that he understood her impatience with such small demands of a few hours less a day, or a few dollars more a week. It was legitimate for young people to take time lightly. But what were men of his age to do? They were not likely to live to see the ultimate overthrow of the capitalist system. Were they also to forgo the release of perhaps two hours a day from the hated work? That was all they could hope to see realised in their lifetime. Should they deny themselves even that small achievement? Should they never have a little more time for reading or being out in the open? Why not be fair to people chained to the block?
Goldman realised that specific efforts for improvement – higher wages, shorter hours and the rest – were part of the revolutionary transformation of society which she believed necessary.

Strong State theory

The Strong State theory, developed in the nineteen-seventies, saw political and economic forces generated by the recurring crises of capitalism moving Britain in the direction of the 'Strong State'. The main characteristic of this 'Strong State' was the strict regulation of political activity, involving tight control over education and the mass media, a secret police force and brutal suppression of opposition to the regime. These measures were not taken overnight, but authoritarian rule was achieved by a series of steps. Recent changes in United Kingdom law had amounted to moves towards the Strong State. The effectiveness of English common law as a means of Strong State political control stemmed from three factors. First, its flexibility enabled threats to be met without recourse to Parliament. Second, when state strategy was clothed with a 'legal' appearance, it had the advantage of legitimacy and could be backed up with an appeal to the 'rule of law'. Third, the sheer complexity of common law doctrines meant that few people knew what is happening.

Jessica Mitford

Jessica Mitford (1917-1996) was an English author, journalist and political campaigner who became an American citizen. She identified, in the American context,

... manufacturers of unsafe cars which in the next year will have caused thousands to perish in flaming highway wrecks, absentee landlords who charge extortionate rents for rat-infested slum apartments, Madison Avenue copywriters whose job it is to manipulate the gullible into buying shoddy merchandise, manufacturers of napalm and other genocidal weapons – all operating on the safe side of the law, since none of these activities is a violation of any criminal statute. Criminal law is essentially a reflection of the values, and a codification of the self-interest, and a method of control, of the dominant class in any given society.

Mitford took her argument further by asking her readers to imagine a prison system populated primarily by well-to-do people, convicted of offences like price-fixing, political corruption, industrial pollution, criminal neglect of safety standards at work, fraudulent share dealing and the manufacture of arms. Her conclusion was:

...that this notion seems like the wildest flight of fancy is already a commentary on the class character of the prison system. After all, no one would expect that those who command political power and control the criminal justice system would use these in such a manner as to make themselves the likeliest candidates for imprisonment.

Nelson Mandela

Working as a lawyer in South Africa meant operating under a debased system of justice, a code of law that did not enshrine equality but its opposite.

In 1963 Mandela and 15 leaders of the African National Congress were charged with 221 acts of sabotage designed to foment violent revolution. This is known as the Rivonia Trial. Mandela was sentenced to life imprisonment. His plea in mitigation involved an explanation that as a lawyer he was often forced to choose between compliance with the law or accommodating his conscience. His plea involved the following points:

I would say that the whole life of any thinking African in this country drives him continuously to a conflict between his conscience on the one hand and the law on the other. This is not a conflict peculiar to this country. The conflict arises for men of conscience, for men who think and who feel deeply in every country. Recently in Britain, a peer of the realm, Earl (Bertrand) Russell, probably the most respected philosopher of the Western world, was sentenced and convicted for precisely the type of activities for which I stand before you today – for following his conscience in defiance of the law, as a protest against the nuclear weapons policy being pursued by his own government. He could do no other than to oppose the law and to suffer the consequences for it. Nor can I. Nor can many Africans in this country. The law as it is applied, the law as it has been developed over a long period of history, and especially the law as it is written and designed by the Nationalist government is a law which, in our views, is immoral, unjust and intolerable. Our consciences dictate that we must protest against it, that we must oppose it and that we must attempt to alter it ... men, I think, are not capable of doing nothing, of saying nothing, of not reacting to injustice, of not protesting against oppression, of not striving for the good society and the good life in the ways they see it.

I was made, by the law, a criminal, not because of what I had done, but because of what I stood for, because of what I thought, because of my conscience. Can it be any wonder to anybody that such conditions make a man an outlaw of society?

I do not believe that this court, in inflicting penalties on me for the crimes for which I am sentenced should be moved by the belief that penalties will deter men from the course that they believe is right.

Albie Sachs

Sachs is a South African lawyer who was imprisoned and tortured by the authorities for his work in the freedom movement. In 1988 he was seriously injured when his car was blown up by South African security agents. He became a judge of the South African Constitutional Court in 1994.

Sachs has written extensively about the role of law and lawyers in the apartheid system. His comments include:

One of the many dismal things that racist South Africa proves is that law and tyranny can well go hand in hand. The law places a double lock on the population. In the first instance it distributes rights and duties on the basis purely of race. Secondly it imposes fearsome penalties on those who challenge this system. Legislation thus has to be seen as the authorisation, sometimes in advance, sometimes retroactively, of violence against the mass of the people.

The unjust social system requires a repressive legal system; the overthrow of the one will require the total overthrow of the other.

EP Thompson

Thompson was a leading English historian, writer and peace campaigner. His leading work is generally recognised to be *The Making of the English Working Class* (1963). A former member of the Communist Party, he left the Party in 1956 following the Soviet invasion of Hungary.

In Thompson's opinion, there is a difference between

arbitrary power and the rule of law. We ought to expose the shams and inequities which may be concealed beneath this law. But his view was that the rule of law itself, the imposing of effective inhibitions upon power and the defence of the citizen from power's all-intrusive claims, is an unqualified human good. To deny or to belittle this good is, in this dangerous century when the resources and pretensions of power continue to enlarge, a desperate error of intellectual abstraction. More than this, it is a self-fulfilling error, which encourages us to give up the struggle against bad laws and class-bound procedures, and to disarm ourselves before power. It is to throw away a whole inheritance of struggle about law, and within the forms of law, whose continuity can never be fractured without bringing men and women into immediate danger.

It is difficult to believe all this today (1979), argued Thompson, when the nation is being co-opted firmly to conservative ideology, when the "rule of law" passes silently to the "rule of existent capitalist law", when politicians and some lawyers are continually thinking of new ways to law us all into subordination. The temptation grows for us to react by unmasking all law and to speak of abolishing it, of exposing the rule of law. Thompson's view was that, in this country, the successive constitutional and legal rights of the citizen, from habeas corpus and the jury system onwards, rights of the press and of speech, rights of trade union organisation, cannot be seen as the products of bourgeois cunning, but as the products of successive struggles. The jury system originated when the bourgeoisie was not yet a glint in feudalism's eye!

Thompson stated that law matters. He commented that much law is now a very nasty business, in the service of money and property, and that some of the best-paid lawyers in London were in effect paid for finding out ways of breaking the law, finding loopholes for money to run through.

Law, Thompson wrote, matters very much to a historian. The struggle to change class-bound laws and corrupt or class-bound procedures, and to preserve and extend the real gains of the practical struggles of the past, and to defend not only the trade union and labour movement but also the individual from the new pretensions and resources of state power, remains on the daily agenda.

Thompson, Writing by Candlelight

Thompson commented further as follows:

- Under the common law an Englishman is to be tried by his peers. These peers are to be selected at random, without respect to their beliefs or opinions, and to be subject to no influence of state.
- When jurors enter the box, they enter also upon a role which has certain inherited expectations, and these expectations are inherited as much from our culture and our history as from books of law. There have been occasions in our history when that anonymous Gang of Twelve has withstood the whole awful pressure of both court and Crown.
- The jury is the last place in our institutions where the people take a hand in administering themselves.
- In the old days the profession of the law attracted many members of an uppish middle class. Lawyers might have Whiggish propensities, as advocates of

the people against the Crown. Or they might have propensities which, while Tory, were profoundly paternalist, in which they could posture as fathers and protectors of the poor.

- All this has long gone away (1980). There have been in this century, and there still are, outstanding and liberal-minded advocates. But this minority, for the purposes of promotion, put themselves out of court. A few have been permitted to pupate, but scarcely a single one to blow in ermine as a judge.

Thompson referred to lawyers employed in the service of those who are working out means of avoiding tax and estate duties, setting up evasive trusts, engineering property-development and outwitting planning officers, promoting and merging companies in dubious ways, scrutinising complex legislation to find the pin-hole of unsealed logic through which money can make its leaky way.

Law today, commented Thompson, can be a profoundly corrupting profession.

In Thompson's view, the rule of law is an unqualified human good. The rule of law must always be historically, culturally and, in general, nationally specific. It concerns the conduct of social life, and the regulation of conflicts, according to rules of law which are exactly defined and have palpable and material evidences – which rules attain towards consensual assent and are subject to interrogation and reform. That this itself is an ideal definition, which takes little account of social and ideological determinants of property and class, and which has never been matched by social reality, does not mean that the aspiration towards that state is not a human good.

Harold Barclay, People Without Government (An Anthropology of Anarchism)

A shock for lawyers – law is not universal – there are societies which have managed very well without wigs, gowns, advocates, courts, prisons and gallows.
Barclay sets out an anthropological analysis of societies which have functioned without government, which do not accept the idea of authority as natural.
His key points include:

- Legal sanctions involve expressions of disapproval of the behaviour of an individual where:
- Such expressions of disapproval are delegated to persons holding defined roles.
- These persons have authority to threaten the use of violence and use it to carry out their job.
- Punishments are imposed in relation to the infraction and are defined within certain limits and in relation to the crime.
- Examples of persons holding these defined roles include police, judges, jailers, executioners and lawmakers.
- The state declares that it has a monopoly on the use of violence.
- Legal sanctions are not universal, but are characteristic of only some types of human society.
- Law and government are invariably associated with rule by an elite class.
- The employment of violence to enforce the law is fundamental to both government and to the state. The

government may use a variety of words to describe this violence: lawful arrest, reasonable force, detention, etc., but it all involves, in the end, physical violence.

Barclay's views must be subject to the argument that societies without laws have functioned at a primitive stage of sophistication, and that more developed societies need legal systems. This is subject to the counter-argument that current society has reached a stage of development and sophistication where justice is for sale, where children and the mentally ill are put to death in the United States and other countries, and where war criminals avoid prosecution.

Thoreau, Henry David, On the Duty of Civil Disobedience

If a person considers that a law is wrong, he has no obligation to obey it. He has a duty to disobey it. Law never made men a whit more just: by means of their respect for it, even the well-disposed are daily made the agents of injustice.

Proudhon, Pierre-Joseph

No one should obey a law unless they have consented to it themselves. Law in a parliamentary democracy can have no legitimacy because individuals are not directly involved in its making.

All law is inevitably coercive and restricts the choice and action of the individual.

The true judge for every man is his own conscience, a fact which implies replacement of the system of courts and laws with a system of personal obligations and contracts.

Summary of anarchist views:

- The legal system in modern states is the cause, rather than the remedy, for disorder.
- Most laws in western democracies protect private property and economic inequality rather than civil rights.
- Authoritarian societies with a repressive morality encourage psychological disorders which result in rape, murder and assault.
- Punishment, by its nature, tends to alienate and embitter rather than reform or deter.
- The best remedy for antisocial behaviour is to be found in common human sympathy.
- To solve disputes, regularly rotated juries drawn from the local community would be able to consider each case in the light of its particular circumstances. The aim would be not to apportion blame or to punish the guilty but to restore social harmony and to compensate the victim.
- Public opinion and social pressure would act as deterrents and traditional techniques of influencing anti-social people through boycott and ostracism would operate as sanctions.

D. N. Pritt

Pritt was a Communist barrister and MP who described himself as a traditional Marxist socialist. His four volumes on Law, Class and Society analyse English law as seen through the eyes of a Marxist socialist.

Pritt's overall aim was to discuss how English law came to be as it is, what forces had shaped and re-shaped it, and what use was made of it, in the service of their own particular interests, by the various elements which hold power in the modern state.

Pritt states that his work is a justification of the Marxist assertion that the law is one of the weapons of the ruling class in the class struggle.

He also makes the point that not all law is designed to further class interests directly by imposing the will of the ruling class on the mass of the people.

Pritt also states that he has not sought to draw up a programme of law reform. He is convinced that what is needed is not reform of the existing system but a fundamental change in our political and economic structure, carrying with it a corresponding change in our law and legal system.

Haldane Society of Socialist Lawyers

The Haldane Society was founded in 1930 and is a body, mainly of lawyers, interested in law reform.

The objects of society were stated in 1978 to be:

- To uphold the principles of justice and liberty in the UK and elsewhere.
- To promote reforms in law and the legal system in

the interests of the working class movement and of democratic and socialist advance within the UK.

- To give advice and assistance to the labour movement and other progressive organisations on legal matters.
- To provide a forum for discussion on and analysis of law and the legal system from a socialist perspective.

For many years the Society has published books, pamphlets and memoranda, given evidence before Royal Commissions, and called conferences and meetings in support of its aims and policy.

It has attracted continually growing support from the labour and trade union movement, and now has affiliated to it over 100 organisations, including 8 national unions, many trade councils, union branches and local Labour Parties. The Society organises conferences on employment and housing law, and in many other ways seeks to assist the promotion of law reform and to provide legal advice of a general character to working class and progressive organisations.

It holds frequent public meetings and conducts educational programmes. The Haldane Society is independent of any political party. Membership comprises lawyers, academics, students and legal workers as well as trade union and labour movement affiliates.

Socialist Lawyer is the magazine published by the Haldane Society. It analyses law and the legal system from a socialist perspective.

American radical lawyers

The editor of *Radical Lawyers: their role in the movement and in the courts* (United States, 1971) made the following points:

- Among radicals and revolutionaries, there is mounting contempt for the courts and the legal system. The courts, they say, are the courts of the capitalist system. They uphold the law – written and unwritten – of that system.
- It is futile to hope that a racist society will produce non-racist courts. It is a wishful fantasy to believe that a society that daily, and quite methodically, victimises its poor will treat them charitably, let alone justly, in its courts… the courts are the realm of the enemy. The enemy will not give up its power happily, or reform itself out of existence. The courts and the law will make concessions to maintain a façade of fairness to keep optimism alive, but as rebellion sharpens into reality the courts cannot be expected to protect that rebellion with a civil libertarian shroud.
- The label "radical lawyer" may not add up to the sum of its parts. It is impossible to be a political radical while playing the games of the system in court. The confines and biases of the lawyer's role are a continuing damper on his activity as a radical…. his traditional commitment to the system is fairly solid. Whatever his politics, a lawyer is responsive to rules of legal decorum, rituals of the bar, and a realm of operation defined by precedent, casebooks and history. The object of his tool of persuasion is frequently a hidebound old man whom a radical will

attack outside the courtroom as a racist and fascist. The rebel lawyer is faced with constant scrutiny by an often reactionary Bar Association, and once admitted to practice must continue to restrain his speech and behaviour or face the threat of disbarment.

Tony Serra

Tony Serra, described as a "ponytailed, potsmoking criminal defense attorney famous for fighting the government", was sentenced to 10 months imprisonment in 2007 for tax evasion. Serra's reaction was to comment that he could do ten months standing on his head. The blacks loved him the whites loved him, the Hispanics and Asians loved him. He talked law 24 hours a day and he found that people in custody were far more interesting than the bourgeois people who populated society. He would prefer to get down with inmates. They were interesting and dramatic. They had overstepped the bounds of society. Some of it was high principle; some of it was low principle.

Serra served four months in prison in 1976 for failing to file tax returns as a protest against the Vietnam War.

Serra is reported to have no savings and no health insurance. Any money he earns is used to pay for the cases which he takes on free of charge.

When he missed a plane and a key hearing in a trial, the judge was unimpressed when he blamed his absence on "bad karma".

Jeffrey Haas

In 1969, Haas set up the People's Law Office where clients included the Black Panthers, the SDS (Students for a Democratic Society) and other political activists.

Haas refers to the need to protest, expose and hold accountable those in power who violate our laws and personal liberties. This need continues and remains a fundamental struggle of our society and any society.

Fighting injustice and inequality is the struggle of our lives, and perseverance in this struggle is what makes our lives valuable.

George Monbiot

Lawyers have an instinctive love of new laws, as this is how they derive their power over the rest of us.

I have met quite a few lawyers – not always voluntarily – and some of them are able to perform a passable impression of human beings. Like teenagers, they are generally quite harmless by themselves. But sensible voters would ensure that they are never let loose in a representative chamber. People of the same trade seldom meet together but the conversation ends in a conspiracy against the public. Lawyers are no exception.

Up Against The Law

Up Against The Law (UPAL) described itself as the magazine for moderate extremists. The UPAL collective, which was active during the early nineteen-seventies, stated the following:

- We are a revolutionary socialist bunch with a lot of experience of the law from various sides of the dock

- defendant, lawyer, and on the picket line. Our mag tries to tell it like it is – THE LIE OF LAW – how the system is bent something rotten, and the way the likes of us is being savaged by a ruling class full of crooks and gangsters.

- Our magazine is by and for criminals, defendants, radical lawyers and people like us who have been "up against the law", who are pissed off with the farce of British "justice" and who are angry about getting pushed around by cops and lawyers playing legal games at our expense.... the courtroom is the gentle façade of the violence of the state: the laws are meant to justify the bosses and rulers having stolen the land, the resources and the product of our labour from us. In that situation, they cannot afford to have the people beating the state at its own game – so they make the law complicated; they surround it with mystery and misery; they say only a lawyer can know about the law – so everyone remains in ignorance about how to fight the illegality of the law. We aim to destroy that misery, to spread the knowledge so that people can fight it. The law holds us in chains – if we can't begin to see the chains, how can we begin to free ourselves?
- The law defends the thieving of the rich against the thieving of the poor … this is what capitalism is about … calling one sort of crime honesty and another sort of honesty crime.
- Lawyers are in general ill-equipped, unprepared and incapable (for reasons of fear, ambition and incompetence) to challenge the tyranny of the bench. A judge can interrupt with impunity, humiliate

defence lawyers, insult witnesses and intimidate defendants.

- All this can be achieved with little or no opposition from defence lawyers, who in the final analysis always have their careers to think of. They normally defend themselves as honourable gentlemen at the Bar, rather than defend the full interests of their clients ... this means that any real expression of conflict between the prosecution and the defence in terms of emotionally charged heated exchanges are carefully prohibited by common agreement, and defendants are left on their own in the dock to stew in their own feelings of resentment … the courtroom is the ultimate arena of concealing the class struggle, such that even the drama of a riot case can be reduced to a tedious bore in front of a jury. Lawyers argue around remote legal technicalities and procedures and around points of law, and the real concerns of defendants are either hopelessly confused or ignored. Every trial is a conspiracy to silence the real life interests of people in the dock.
- Most lawyers are completely out of touch with the lives we lead. They come from the world of Savile Row suits and public schools, defending the working class of which they are unbelievably ignorant. They belong to the legal club, good for deals, bad for justice.

McLibel

The McLibel case is inspirational for critics of English law.

In *Steel and Morris v United Kingdom (2005)* the

European Court of Human Rights (ECHR) ruled that the denial of legal aid to the McLibel Two (Dave Morris and Helen Steel) deprived them of the opportunity to present their case effectively before the court and contributed to the unacceptable inequality of arms in libel proceedings brought against them. The proceedings had been unfair, in breach of Article 6 of the European Convention on Human Rights.

Morris and Steel were refused legal aid and represented themselves throughout the trial and appeal, with some help from volunteer lawyers. They argued that they had been severely hampered by lack of resources, not just in the way of legal advice and representation, but also when it came to administration, photocopying, note-taking, and the tracing, preparation and payment of the costs and expenses of expert and factual witnesses.

The ECHR ruled that the question whether the provision of legal aid was necessary for a fair hearing had to be determined on the basis of the particular facts and circumstances of each case and depended upon, among other things, the importance of what was at stake for the applicant in the proceedings, the complexity of the relevant procedure and the applicant's capacity to represent him or herself effectively.

The trial at first instance lasted 313 court days, preceded by 28 interlocutory applications. The appeal hearing lasted 23 days. The factual case which the applicants had had to prove had been highly complex, involving 40,000 pages of documentary evidence and 130 oral witnesses.

The background to the case is that, in 1990, Morris and Steel were served with a writ from McDonalds over a leaflet being handed out in the street by London

Greenpeace. The leaflet listed “hidden facts” about McDonalds which they believed that the public should know. These “hidden facts” criticised the effects of the fast food chain on the human body, the environment, animal welfare and the company’s employees.

McDonalds expected a quick apology. Instead, the case developed into a fifteen-year fight. Steel, a gardener, and Morris, a single parent and ex-postman, were denied legal aid. They raised £35,000 through the McLibel Support Campaign. The case involved a succession of witnesses, expert testimony, legal arguments and secret meetings with members of the McDonalds board of directors.

At the end of what was labelled as the longest trial in English history, the court ruled that McDonalds’ marketing pretended to provide a positive nutritional benefit which their food did not match, that they exploited children with their advertising, that they were culpably responsible for animal cruelty and paid low wages, helping to depress wages in the catering trade.

The court also ruled that Morris and Steel had libelled McDonalds and ordered them to pay £40,000 damages.

Steel and Morris announced that they would go to prison rather than pay compensation. McDonalds did not seek to enforce the award, nor did the company proceed with an application for an injunction preventing further leafleting in front of their restaurants.

Speaking in August 2005, Morris made the following points:

- London Greenpeace had initially focused on McDonalds not only because it was a powerful and influential corporation but because it was pioneering business practices which were being adopted by other companies.

- He and Steel decided that they had to stand up for the public's right to criticise. They were advised that the laws were stacked in favour of the rich and powerful.
- Effectively, they had turned the tables and put McDonalds on trial in front of the world.
- They were part of a collective. Experts of all kinds, campaigners, and ex-employees all came forward to be witnesses. Others helped in court, helped Morris at home with childcare, and sent in money and messages of support.
- The campaign was one of the pillars of the modern global anti-capitalist movement. People could see massive protests against the G8, the IMF, the World Bank and so on. This exciting upsurge of global protest against the most powerful organisations didn't come from nowhere. It had roots which went back 10 to 20 years through the patient day-to-day local work, regional and international work of specific struggles and movements – the McLibel campaign was one of these.
- When people are organised and determined, and armed with the truth, they can take on the most powerful, entrenched opposition and win.
- Multinationals and governments dominate our lives and our planet, resulting everywhere in the exploitation and oppression of people, animals and the environment.

The McLibel case is inspirational for alternative lawyers because it shows that lawyers' belief in their own indispensability is misplaced. Determined, articulate and motivated non-lawyers can take on the system and win. No matter how depressing the money-grip over the legal system in England, no matter how hopeless the struggles of those who seek justice, McLibel shines out as a beacon for the following reasons:

- The use of libel actions as tool of the rich and powerful to stifle public debate suffered a severe setback.
- Steel and Morris showed the world that committed non-lawyers, buttressed by a clear and strongly-held political analysis and with professional support, could beat the system.

In May 2008 McDonalds was fined £17,000 after a young worker was scalded by hot oil.

In February 2005 a seventeen-year old employee was working at the McDonald's restaurant in Eastgates, Leicester. She slipped and plunged the whole of her arm into a fryer full of scalding hot oil. She suffered partial thickness and superficial burns to her left arm and forearm. She had to have plastic surgery and missed five months at college because of her injuries.

The filtering machine and fryer vat extension pipe had been leaking oil onto the floor. Employees had placed cardboard underneath to soak it up. This made the slip hazard worse because of the floor's inadequate slip resistance.

McDonald's pleaded guilty to not having a safe system of work for preventing spillages and cleaning the floor. Cardboard did not count as a suitable means of removing oil and employees had not been properly trained in their cleaning duties. The maintenance history card on the

leaking machine had not been completed for more than a year.
The restaurant's risk assessment failed to identify suitable control measures for the contamination of floors, the condition of the flooring and employee footwear. Records showed that the branch had not investigated the causes of more than half of all reported accidents in the year before the scalding incident. McDonalds had failed to follow its own accident investigation procedure.

McDonalds was fined £12,400 in August 2001 after pleading guilty to 20 charges of illegally employing children. The children were working late at night in the Camberley branch of the company's restaurant on school days in the restaurant. One 15 year old girl worked for 16 hours on a Saturday. Another worked from 5 p.m. to 2 a.m. on a school day. McDonalds placed the blame on the franchisee.

CHAPTER 4

RIGHTS

Human rights? What could be more indifferent to the rights of any form of life than an H-bomb?

(Kurt Vonnegut, Timequake)

You can't eat and drink freedom of speech, and it doesn't produce regular electricity and clean water.

(Baghdad taxi driver, January 2010)

This Chapter deals with the following aspects of human rights:

- Human Rights Act 1998
- Individual and collective human rights
- The human rights industry
- International law of human rights
- Extreme examples of individual human rights cases
- The torture "debate"
- Human rights in Cuba
- The South African Constitution
- Identity cards.

The following material is highly critical of certain aspects of human rights law and practice in the United Kingdom. These preliminary points should be noted:

- These criticisms should not be taken as in any way supporting the semi-literate and populist abuse directed at human rights organisations by a number of journalists.

- The general argument is that human rights in the UK need to be extended, rather than restricted.
- The UK has developed a profitable and expanding human rights industry. Human rights have developed into a commodity, including career paths for lawyers, academic career development and increased profits for multinational publishing companies.
- Human rights law has become so complex, largely because of the involvement of lawyers, that it is now extremely difficult for non-lawyers to access the law. Victims of human rights violations are largely dependent on individual lawyers in private practice to enforce their rights.
- In common with other areas of law, human rights law is in desperate need of demystification and simplification. There is a basic human right of access to laws set out in understandable language. For example, the law dealing with the right to a fair trial is now so complex that very few non-lawyers, and not many lawyers, can negotiate a route through it. You need a lawyer to explain how you can get a fair trial, and if you can't afford a lawyer, or can't get someone else to pay, you will never understand the law of human rights. This is examined in detail in Chapter 6 (Mystery).
- British human rights organisations should, at the very least, engage in discussions as to the incorporation of social and economic rights into UK human rights law and should press for this expansion.
- UK human rights law has developed without any serious or searching theoretical analysis. This contrasts, for example, with the extensive analyses

carried out by the South African Constitutional Court.

- Human rights organisations should disclose the levels of fees received by lawyers who act in human rights cases, whether through public funding or funding from those organisations or through public funding. Lawyers' earnings are fully discussed in Chapter 1 (Money).
- As a longstanding member of Liberty, and its predecessor, the National Council for Civil Liberties, I have always supported organisations which campaign for individual civil human rights. This does not prevent me from criticising the current English preoccupation with such rights and to argue that there is an almost total lack of discussion, in academic and practising circles, of the theory of human rights and the need for collective social rights to receive equal protection with individual rights. In 2010 Liberty issued a publicity poster asking "What not to love?". The poster featured a heart-shaped statement of the rights protected by the Human Rights Act 1998. Economic and social rights were not mentioned. This lack of discussion may be peculiar to Western neo-liberal democracies.

Human Rights Act 1998

The Human Rights Act 1998 incorporated the provisions of the European Convention on Human Rights into UK law in the face of strong opposition. For example, Lord Denning voiced the widely-held view that we should not be bound by the decisions of judges who do not know our way of life, nor anything of our common law.

The main rights covered by the Act are as follows:

- Article 2: Right to life
- Article 3: Prohibition of ill treatment
- Article 4: Prohibition of slavery and forced labour
- Article 5: Right to liberty and security
- Article 6: Right to a fair trial
- Article 7: No punishment without law
- Article 8: Right to respect for private and family life
- Article 9: Freedom of thought, conscience and religion
- Article 10: Freedom of expression
- Article 11: Freedom of assembly and association
- Article 12: Right to marry
- Article 14: Prohibition of discrimination. This leads to the impenetrable maze of UK discrimination law, the opaqueness of which is fully analysed in Chapter 6 (Mystery).
- Article 1, Protocol 1: Protection of property.

These principles have been developed by a large mass of case law in the European and UK courts. Human rights law has become a huge subject in its own right. Its scheme of a basic statutory framework, developed by case law to become a sprawling and incomprehensible mass, is indistinguishable in concept from, for example, tax law.

The clarity and simplicity of the European Convention on Human Rights is now submerged in a lawyer-created mesh of endless interpretation and sophisticated analysis. Major human rights textbooks are large, expensive and highly technical. They are indistinguishable in style and layout from other technical law textbooks.

Individual and collective human rights

For an ex-miner in Blaenau Gwent, suffering from a terminal lung disease, who develops a raging toothache, and cannot afford dentistry, it is of great solace to know that a Queen's Counsel in chambers in Lincoln's Inn has worked night and day to ensure that he has freedom of religion.

When my own father was dying, and no ambulance could be found to take him from hospital to a hospice, so that I had to pay a private ambulance to travel fifty miles, it was most reassuring for me to know that it was unlawful for me to be discriminated against on the grounds of my ethnic origins and that this right would be protected by a coterie of London QCs.

The rights protected by the Act of 1998 are generally recognised as civil and political rights, largely aimed at the protection of individuals. Social and economic rights are not covered. There is no right to work and no right to healthy and safe working conditions.

While the current trend towards the protection of human rights in relation to, for example, freedom of speech and the right to a fair trial, is without doubt desirable, progressive and moving towards human emancipation and social justice, these are essentially individual civil and political rights. They do not address social and economic issues. It is, for example, of little comfort to those living in the most deprived circumstances that

liberal lawyers from London are willing to earn huge sums to protect their right to freedom of religion.
The human rights industry in England is rarely criticised from the left. It is normally selected for abuse by populist politicians and journalists. But this does not mean that it is beyond criticism. It should be realised that there is a substantial body of academic opinion, particularly in developing countries, which is highly critical of the Western emphasis on individual civil and political rights.
This has been described as the little magic territory of human rights which is just civil and political. It has also been pointed out that before people get to political rights they want to know what to do about Aids and what to do about food and water.
In 1986 Tony Gifford made the following points:

- The most profound injustices in our society stem from political and economic, rather than legal causes.
- Legal rights can do little to enrich the lives of those who have no jobs.
- If no money is spent on building new homes, then the theoretical rights of homeless people and slum dwellers are not of great value.
- If the opportunity for a good education and good health is a perquisite for the wealthy, then the idea of equality before the law becomes a fraud.

Lord Bingham has pointed out that there is no universal consensus as to fundamental rights and freedoms. In some developing countries, a higher premium is put on economic growth than on the protection of human rights.

Contents of current English textbooks on human rights

An examination of current English human rights textbooks gives some indication of the coverage of individual as opposed to collective rights in the main source material. English law does not, as a rule, deal with collective human rights.

Social and economic rights are mentioned only in passing, for example:

- Clayton & Tomlinson, The Law of Human Rights: The list of contents has one reference to social and economic rights, which is a chapter on the right to education. The subject index has three entries for economic rights and three for social rights. A total of 4 pages out of 1600.
- Starmer, European Human Rights Law: 15 pages on the right to education. 10 pages on welfare benefits. No index references to economic and/or social rights.
- Simor and Emmerson, Human Rights Practice: 3 index entries on economic rights.
- Feldman, Civil Liberties and Human Rights in England and Wales: 11 pages out of 1100 on social and economic rights.

Never mind, Nan, it's a shame you have to go cleaning houses for £6 an hour with your varicose ulcer, but don't forget there are QCs in London fighting every day for your right to religious freedom, and they only charge £1000 an hour.

It has also been commented that if you look globally today and want to talk about human rights, for the vast majority of the world's population they don't mean very much. To talk about freedom of expression to a man who can't read the newspaper, to talk about the right to work to someone who has no job: "human rights" means nothing to them unless it brings some change on these particular issues.

Western countries have not given economic, cultural and social rights the same priority as individual political and civil rights. The view of many Asian countries is that Western human rights elevate the individual above his community.

For example, in 1991 the Singapore government identified the core values of Asian society as placing society above self, upholding the family as the building block of society and the obligations of the community towards the welfare of less advantaged persons.

Some Asian countries also take the view that individual human rights are Western ideas imposed upon Asia as a form of neo-colonialism.

Chronic underdevelopment, grinding poverty, mass unemployment, homelessness, widespread illiteracy, systematic inequalities of income and opportunities and lack of healthcare can be seen as gross violations of human rights. Poverty is not simply a matter of material deprivation. It is a matter of human dignity, justice, fundamental freedoms and basic human rights.

Economic, social and cultural rights have no less priority than political and civil rights. They should be acknowledged as full legal rights which must be taken as seriously as civil and political rights. People whose economic rights are infringed are the majority. More children die of lack of food or water than people who are killed by torture or the death penalty.

In Western countries economic and social rights are treated as welfare state or socialist programmes, not as fundamental human rights. There has been academic discussion as to whether socio-economic rights can qualify as human rights. Cranston, for example, takes the view that social and economic rights are not true human rights because they do not meet the test of practicability, universality and of being of practical importance.

There are said to be very real doubts about whether socio-economic rights can qualify in principle as human rights. The argument goes that even if social and economic rights can be properly asserted on behalf of all human beings, they do not give rise to universal human rights. One reason for this is that the extent to which a society can provide economic goods for its members must depend upon the availability of resources within that society.

This implicitly accepts the universality of freedom of expression – an individual civil right: This is clearly not so – in the United Kingdom, for example, limitations on freedom of expression include libel, discrimination laws, incitement; contempt of court; hate speech, breach of copyright and official secrets. Freedom of expression fails Cranston's three tests.

In relation to the test of practicability, Cranston's argument applies to individual rights as well as to social and economic rights. Individual rights are often not enforceable in practice because of the cost of legal services. This is a significant counter-argument to that of Cranston.

The Human Rights Act 1998 protects property rights but not social welfare. For those with a small stake in the property economy, this is simply irrelevant. English applications of the law of human rights have done nothing to narrow the gap between rich and poor. Since 1998, for example, child poverty has not reduced. Despite the plethora of case law, the rich have got richer and the poor have got poorer. Legal assistance for poor people has become less and less attainable. Without the financial resources for their application, individual human rights are purely abstract. For most people, they have no concrete existence. They are illusory, a chimera.

Bill Bowring's discussion of human rights includes the following:

- There is a clear conflict between the Western conception of rights as liberal conceptions of human rights, and social justice.
- In the United States individual rights, especially freedom of expression and property rights, will always trump social policy considerations.
- Everyone is entitled, as a right of citizenship, to be able to meet their basic needs for income, shelter and other necessities.
- The Human Rights Act 1998 does not protect the full range of rights contained in the UN Declaration on Human Rights.

- There is nothing inherent in social and economic rights that prevent judicial determination of their content.
- There is a deep antipathy in the United Kingdom to collective or group rights.

The human rights industry

Human rights law has become a commodity which generates its own professional niche and attendant service industries. One example of this is the law publishing industry. This can be illustrated by the following examples of the current prices of human rights textbooks:
Human Rights Practice (Sweet & Maxwell): £540.00
Human Rights: Law & Practice (Lexis Nexis): £310.00
Law of Human Rights, The (Oxford University Press): £350.00
Human Rights & Civil Practice (Sweet & Maxwell) £510.00
Information Rights (Sweet & Maxwell) £300.00
Practitioner's Guide to the European Convention on Human Rights (Sweet & Maxwell) £159.00.
In this connection, it is interesting to note Lord Bingham's view that accessibility of the law is an essential aspect of the rule of law. The law must be accessible, intelligible, clear and predictable. Expensive source books are in conflict with this principle.

International law

Although collective social and economic rights are not protected by English and European human rights law, there are a number of international instruments which do deal with rights other than individual civil and political rights. For example, the Universal Declaration of Human Rights 1948 states the following key points:

- The universal nature of human rights norms is beyond question.
- Human rights are universal, indivisible, interdependent and interrelated.
- Economic and social rights are real rights.

The Declaration states that everyone has the right to work, to free choice of employment, to just and favourable conditions of work and to protection against unemployment. Also, everyone has the right to rest and leisure, including reasonable limitation of working hours and periodic holidays with pay and the right to an adequate standard of living including food, clothing, housing and medical care.

War Resisters International and Amnesty International have argued that a right to refuse to kill should be added to the Declaration. This would recognise a legal right to conscientious objection to military service.

Whether these rights are enforceable through the United Kingdom courts is a question with no easy answer. The case law is unclear.

Part III of the International Covenant on Economic, Social and Cultural Rights 1977 (a multilateral treaty) recognises:

- The right to work
- To enjoy just and favourable conditions of work
- To rest and leisure
- To form and join trade unions

- To strike
- To social security
- To special protection for the family, mothers and children
- To an adequate standard of living including food, clothing and housing, physical and mental health
- To education and to scientific and cultural life.

Another example is the European Social Charter (1996 version), which includes the following:

- All workers have the right to safe and healthy working conditions.
- Children and young persons have the right to special protection against the physical and moral hazards to which they are exposed.
- Workers have the right to take part in the determination and improvement of the working conditions and the working environment.

Parties to the Charter undertake to formulate, implement and periodically review a coherent national policy on occupational safety, occupational health and the working environment. The aim of this policy shall be to improve occupational safety and health and to prevent accidents and injury to health arising from workplace conditions. Specifically, the Charter provides the following:

- Right to work
- Right to work under fair and safe conditions
- Fair remuneration
- Right to collective organisation and bargaining
- Special protection for women, children and young persons

- Right to education and vocational training
- Rights to health care, social security, welfare services and care for the disabled
- Protection for the family, especially for mothers and children.

These rights are to be secured without discrimination on the grounds of race, colour, sex, religion, political opinion, national extraction or social origin.

The Charter has no enforcement mechanism and does not confer enforceable rights on individuals. Proposals for reform of the enforcement system have not been ratified. The Charter was signed by the UK in 1997 but has not been ratified.

The European Social Charter and other conventions dealing with economic and social rights do not have direct effect in English law. Their status in English law is unclear.

The Social Chapter of the Maastricht Treaty 1992 committed the European Community and Member States to the objectives of promoting high employment, improved living and working conditions, social protection, equal pay for equal work, dialogue between management and labour and the development of human resources. The Chapter was accepted by the UK in 1997.

International Labour Organisation (ILO)

The ILO was created in 1919 with the aim of advancing social justice in the belief that universal and lasting peace can only be established if it is based on social justice.

The ILO Declaration of Aims and Purposes 1944 included the following:

- Labour is not to be regarded as a commodity.
- Poverty constitutes a danger to prosperity.
- The war against want must be carried on with unrelenting vigour within each nation and by means of concerted international efforts.
- All human beings have the right to pursue both material well-being and spiritual development in conditions of freedom and dignity, economic security and equal opportunity without discrimination on the ground of race, creed or sex.

The ILO has obligations to promote programmes with the aim of achieving:

- Full employment
- Rising standards of living
- Worker satisfaction
- A minimum wage
- A basic income for all in need
- A just share in the fruits of progress for all
- The right to free collective bargaining
- Adequate protection for the health and safety of workers
- Child welfare and maternity protection
- The provision of adequate nutrition, housing and facilities for recreation and culture
- Equality of educational and vocational opportunity.

The law relating to these areas of international law is unincorporated and vague. Their influence on English courts is not settled. They should be incorporated into

English domestic law, just as the Human Rights Act incorporated the European Convention on Human Rights.

In the context of European human rights law, it is interesting to note the decision of the European Court of Human Rights in the McLibel case. The court ruled that the denial of legal aid to the McLibel Two (Dave Morris and Helen Steel) had deprived them of the opportunity to present their case effectively before the court and contributed to the unacceptable inequality of arms in libel proceedings brought against them. The proceedings had been in breach of Article 6 (the right to a fair trial). The McLibel case is discussed in detail in Chapter 3 (Dissent).

Extreme examples of individual human rights

In *James v United Kingdom (1986)*, a chartered surveyor, the Sixth Duke of Westminster, a chartered accountant and a banker were trustees of the will of the Second Duke of Westminster. The Westminster family owned 2000 houses in Belgravia.

The trustees complained that their right to public property was violated by the Leasehold Reform Act 1967 which gave the right to purchase freeholds to his tenants in Belgravia. 215 properties had been enfranchised. The trustees claimed £2.5 million compensation. The European Court of Human Rights ruled that the provisions of the 1967 Act were not in breach of the European Convention on Human Rights because the Act was within the limits that a national legislation has in implementing social policies. The elimination of social injustice by leasehold reform

legislation was a legitimate aim and could not be characterised as unreasonable. The taking of property in pursuance of a policy calculated to enhance social justice within the community could properly be described as being “in the public interest”.
The lawyers’ fees have not been disclosed.

Another example of extreme individualism as opposed to the protection and enforcement of collective rights is the case of two English motorists, Francis and O’Halloran, who complained to the European Court of Human Rights in 2007 that their right to silence, and not to incriminate themselves, had been violated. Francis had been photographed by a speed camera driving at 47 mph in a 30 zone. O’Halloran was photographed doing 69 mph in a 40 zone on the M4. English law requires car owners to disclose the identity of drivers whose vehicles have been photographed exceeding speed limits.
O’Halloran admitted being the driver but later revoked this confession on the grounds of the right to silence and not to incriminate himself. Francis refused to state whether he had been the driver. Both were convicted and complained to the European Court of Human Rights.
That court rejected the complaints. It ruled that the protection against self-incrimination was not absolute. Drivers of motor vehicles accept responsibilities and obligations. In the United Kingdom, these obligations include informing the authorities about the identity of the driver.
Francis and O’Halloran were supported by Liberty. That organisation later accepted that its commitment of resources in this case had been a serious mistake.

The first health and safety related case involving an express application of human rights law was reported in August 2009.

In *R v Nottinghamshire Healthcare NHS Trust (2009)*, the Court of Appeal gave judgment in a case involving smoking and human rights.

The facts, in summary, were that E, a patient at Rampton high security psychiatric hospital, complained that a smoking ban introduced at the hospital, as a consequence of the NHS Trust's policy and the Smoke-Free (Exemptions and Vehicles) Regulations 2007, was a breach of his rights under Article 8 of the European Convention on Human Rights.

The 2007 Regulations prohibited smoking within enclosed spaces and permitted smoking to continue in outside spaces. The NHS Trust's policy banned smoking both inside and out, subject to very limited exceptions. The basis for this ban was that security reasons prevented the Trust from allowing patients to smoke outside.

On behalf of the claimant, it was argued that Article 8 protected a person from interference by the state with that which he chose to do within the privacy of his own home. If that was right, then the claimant's life, detained in Rampton, could be equated to life at home.

The claim was rejected by the High Court. The claimant appealed to the Court of Appeal.

That court dismissed the appeal and made the following points:

- The freedom protected by Article 8 was not the same as the freedom to do whatever a person chose to do.

- Rampton was the claimant's home, but it was not the same as a private home and the distinction was significant. It was a public institution, operated as a hospital. For safety and security reasons, supervision was intense. It was a public and not a private place.
- Freedom from interference by the state was already significantly constricted within the confines of a secure hospital. There was no basis for distinguishing the loss of freedom in such an institution to choose what to eat or drink, and the ban on smoking.
- Although Article 8 did apply to closed institutions, it applied to a far more limited extent than it would to activities in a person's home.
- Difficult as it was to judge the importance of smoking to the integrity of a person's identity, it was not sufficiently close to qualify as an activity deserving the protection of Article 8.
- Article 8 did not protect a right to smoke at Rampton. The prohibition did not, in such an institution, have a sufficiently adverse effect on a patient's physical or mental integrity.
- A policy of prohibiting smoking in the premises of an NHS Trust, which had the consequence of a ban on smoking for those detained in a high security psychiatric hospital, did not violate the patients' human rights and was lawful.

The Health Act 2006 required, in summary, that all premises used by the public must be smoke-free by July 1, 2007. Rampton was a place of work and had to be smoke-free unless exempted by regulations. The 2007 Regulations permanently exempted prisons but only gave temporary exemption to mental health units.

Article 8 of the European Convention on Human Rights states that everyone has the right to respect for his private and family life, his home and his correspondence. It also provides that there shall be no interference by a public authority with the exercise of this right except such as is in accordance with the law and is necessary in a democratic society in the interests of national security, public safety or the economic well-being of the country, for the prevention of disorder or crime, for the protection of health or morals, or for the protection of the rights and freedoms of others.

The Rampton case can be seen as an exemplar of a lengthy and expensive legal process involving individual human rights. The process failed. Again, the lawyers' fees have not been disclosed.

In this connection, it is interesting to note that the general ban on smoking in public places does not generally apply to the House of Commons.

The torture "debate"

A recent, sinister development in the human rights industry has been the preparedness of mainly American, but also some English academics, to "debate" the legality of torture. The prospect of academic lawyers "debating" the proposed legalisation of torture is appalling. There should be no "debate". Torture is non-negotiable. This is beyond discussion in most civilised countries.

Article 3 of the European Convention on Human Rights states that no-one shall be subjected to torture or to inhuman or degrading treatment or punishment. This provides absolute protection. In no circumstances can such treatment be made legal. States are never able to argue that such treatment is acceptable or justifiable. The drafters of the European Convention had experience of legalised torture under the Nazi regime. They were determined that this would never be repeated.

The definition of torture, and its distinction from inhuman or degrading treatment, is problematic. Article 1 of the UN Convention against Torture gives the following definition:

Torture means any act which by severe pain or suffering, whether physical or mental, is intentionally inflicted on a person for such purposes as obtaining from him or a third party information or a confession.

In 2005, in the case of *A and Others v Secretary of State for the Home Department*, seven Law Lords decided unanimously that evidence which may have been obtained by torture is inadmissible in English courts, regardless of where or by whom the alleged torture has been perpetrated.

This judgment was described as the leading judgment on torture which would reverberate around the world, putting beyond doubt that the ban on torture was absolute in civilised countries.

Lord Bingham commented that from its earliest days, the common law set its face firmly against the use of torture. The principles of the common law, standing alone, compelled the exclusion of third party torture evidence as unreliable, unfair, offensive to ordinary standards of humanity and decency, and incompatible with the principles which should animate a tribunal seeking to administer justice. Torture was prohibited by statute in 1640 in England and in 1708 in Scotland.

Those who seek to "debate" the legalisation of torture have introduced, as justification, the "ticking bomb hypothetical". This is a devised scenario involving a large number of lives at stake in the immediate future, where the torture of suspects is the only means of dealing with the threat. It has been suggested that there is anecdotal evidence that this scenario has some basis in reality. Those who put forward this argument have never produced independent evidence to support their claims.

Academic discussions of legal torture conveniently avoid the realities of the torture chamber. For example:

- Who will be the torturers? The police? Prison officers? It is to be hoped that their trade unions would have some points to make in this connection. How will the torturers be trained? Will there be accredited courses in torture techniques, with diplomas awarded for successful trainees?
- How will the torturers deal with the health and safety aspects of spattered blood from the victims' wounds?
- Will there need to be risk assessments for torture workers who use electric drills to pierce victims' bones?
- Will judges be delegated to sit in on torture sessions? It is to be hoped that the English judiciary would have nothing to do with this.
- Presumably, doctors would have to be present at legal torture sessions to ensure that victims do not die. Again, it is hoped that the medical profession

would find itself precluded, on the grounds of professional ethics, from assisting in the torture chamber.

- What kinds of torture will be legalised? Pliers to extract fingernails? The rack? Electric batons? Wall handcuffs? Beatings? A more recent example of a torture technique is to make incisions in the victim's penis with a scalpel and then to pour hot and irritating liquid onto the wounds. Any proposal to legitimise torture must face up to these disgusting realities.
- Will licences be granted for the manufacture and supply of instruments of torture?

Apparently, there is a huge body of academic research into the legalisation of torture. It should be asked whether these researches, presumably funded in part by the taxpayer, are more worthwhile than, for example, the reasons why there are only two Law Centres in the Southeast of England outside London, or the effects of the abolition of legal aid in most civil cases on the most vulnerable and deprived members of society.

The appalling realities of the torture chamber have been examined by the European Court of Human Rights in a number of cases. For example in the *Greek* case (1969) torture took the form of *falanga* (the beating of the soles of the feet with a wooden or metal stick or bar) which, if skilfully done, breaks no bones, makes no skin lesions and leaves no permanent and recognisable marks, but causes intense pain and swelling of the feet; severe beatings of all parts of the body; the application of electric shock; mock execution and threats to shoot or

kill the victim; squeezing of the head in a vice; pulling out of the hair from the head or pubic region; kicking of the male genital organs; dripping water on the head and intense noise to prevent sleep.
This illustrates the horrific reality of the torture chamber. If *falanga* is to be "skilfully" applied, then its practitioners will have to be trained. Torturers must develop the skills of extracting information by the use of very severe and cruel suffering without killing the victim or, in an ideal world, leaving no permanent and recognisable marks. Can anyone seriously contemplate a legalised training school for torturers in Britain?

In 1949, during discussion on the proposed Universal Declaration of Human Rights, the British representative at the United Nations is reported to have made the following comment:
All forms of torture, whether inflicted by the police, military authorities or members of private organisations, are inconsistent with civil society, are offences against heaven and humanity and must be prohibited. This prohibition must be absolute and torture cannot be permitted for any purpose whatsoever, either for extracting evidence, to save life or for the safety of the state. It would be better for society to perish than for it to permit this relic of barbarism to remain.
The last word on torture should go to Albie Sachs, who was subjected to torture by sleep deprivation by the South African security forces. He makes the point that his experience was not the hypothetical situation of the kind discussed by some academics in relation to the costs and benefits of governments using torture. In his

case, as in 99.9 per cent of torture cases, there was no ticking bomb. The object of the torturers was not to obtain information but to humiliate and degrade their victim so as to achieve power and dominance.
In 1988, Sachs lost an arm and the sight of an eye when his car was bombed by South African security agents. It appears that he was bombed because he was an intellectual who challenged the claim of the South African apartheid government that no political system could be found to enable black and white to live together as equals in South Africa.
Sachs makes the point that when the African National Congress was a liberation movement in exile, a Code of Conduct was drawn up which prohibited torture in any circumstances.

Lord Bingham has pointed out that the Bush administration rewrote the definition of torture to mean "physical pain of an intensity akin to that which accompanies serious physical injury such as death or organ failure". This excludes "enhanced interrogation techniques".
Recent disclosures have indicated that the United Kingdom has been involved in torture. In January 2010 the UN Human Rights Council declared that the UK had been complicit in the rendition, unlawful detention and torture of terror suspects.
In the case of Binyam Mohamed (a torture victim), the Court of Appeal stated that MI5 had failed to respect human rights, deliberately misled Parliament and had a culture of suppression which undermined government assurances about its conduct. The lawyer acting for the

government demanded that the Court of Appeal should change the wording of its judgment to be less critical of MI5.

Cuba

Reports of the theory and practice of the Cuban legal system give clear examples of contradictions between collective and individual human rights.

Anyone with an interest in human rights should look to the Cuban model, not as an ideal to be achieved, but as a comparative and alternative model for a legal system with an emphasis on social and economic rights.

The Cuban legal system is discussed further in Chapter 2 (Class).

In November 2009 the Human Rights Watch report on Cuba, entitled "New Cuba, Same Cuba" made the following points:

- There is a provision in the Cuban criminal code allowing people to be convicted for "dangerousness", defined as behaviour which contradicts socialist norms. This would appear to have some similarities to the English concept of the Anti-Social Behaviour Order (ASBO), except that the ASBO does not require a criminal conviction. ASBO proceedings are civil proceedings. An ASBO is a civil order containing conditions prohibiting specific anti-social acts or entering defined areas. "Anti-social behaviour" means behaviour which causes or is likely to cause harassment, alarm or distress. This includes writing graffiti (unless it is deemed artistically acceptable), begging and prostitution. It does not include war crimes, arms manufacturing or health and safety violations.

- According to Human Rights Watch, there have been at least 40 cases of "dangerousness" in Cuba, which include:
- Distributing copies of the Universal Declaration of Human Rights
- Staging rallies
- Writing articles critical of the government
- Trying to organise independent trade unions
- Failing to attend pro-government rallies
- Not belonging to official party organisations
- Being unemployed.
- Cuban prisons are overcrowded, unhygienic and unhealthy. This can be compared with the position in the United Kingdom and the United States. For example, in *Napier v Scottish Ministers (2005)*, N was a remand prisoner in Barlinnie Prison. He had to share a cell which was designed for one person. The cell had poor washing and toilet facilities and human waste had to be "slopped out". He was confined to the cell for an average of 20 hours a day. The cell was described as small, overcrowded, gloomy and stuffy. N developed severe eczema and psychological problems. The Scottish court decided that he had suffered degrading treatment in breach of Article 3 of the European Convention. He had been exposed to conditions of detention which were such as to diminish his human dignity and to arouse in him feelings of anxiety, anguish, inferiority and humiliation.

- Political prisoners are routinely subjected to solitary confinement, beatings, restriction of visits and denial of medical care.

Human Rights Watch acknowledged advances in education and healthcare for the general population but lamented that they were not matched by respect for civil and political rights. It concluded that Cuba had the worst human rights record in the region.

The Cuba Solidarity Campaign responded to these allegations with the following:

- Cuba had 40,000 doctors providing healthcare in 80 developing countries.
- 1.5 million people had received sight-saving operations.
- Thousands of students from poor countries were in receipt of free medical scholarships.
- Cuban priorities were health, education and literacy.

In October 2009 the UN Development Program's Human Development Report, which measures and compares development status in 182 countries, made the following points about Cuba:

- Cuba's education index is the equal highest in the world, ranked with Australia, Finland, Denmark and New Zealand.
- Its adult literacy rate is 99.8%.
- School enrolments are 100%.
- Public expenditure on education is higher than that of Australia.
- Cuba has the highest ratio of female to male enrolment in education.
- Life expectancy is 78.5 years.

- 43% of seats in Parliament are held by women. This is the third highest level in the world.

In January 2007 the Independent reported the following:

- Against the background of the United States trade embargo, criticisms of the Cuban regime for human rights violations met the response that Cuba was more interested in social and economic rights than in bourgeois individual rights.
- A Law of 2004 forbade Cuban private citizens to access the Internet. It is reportedly illegal to buy a computer without government approval, which is rarely granted to ordinary Cubans. Similar restrictions apply to the ownership of mobile telephones.
- In 2003, three men were executed by firing squad. According to Amnesty International, there are more than 30 persons on death row.
- Guantanamo: this comprises 45 square miles of Cuban territory ceded in perpetuity to the United States. According to Amnesty International: "The detention facility at Guantanamo Bay has become the gulag of our times".

In summary, there are about 500 internees, mainly arrested in Pakistan. They are subject to a chaotic system far short of international standards. No international monitors can attend military tribunal hearings at Guantanamo.

In relation to healthcare, the following has been reported:

- Life expectancy in Cuba is equivalent to that in the US. It could be argued that, as the ultimate expression of the right to life, this is the most fundamental of all human rights.
- The infant mortality rate is lower than that of the US.
- The HIV/AIDS prevalence rate is lower than that of the US.
- There are, proportionally, twice as many doctors in Cuba than in the US.
- There are, proportionally, more hospital beds in Cuba than in the US.
- 25,000 Cuban doctors are on humanitarian missions outside Cuba.
- 20,000 Cuban doctors were sent to Venezuela to provide for healthcare.
- Emergency planning for hurricanes is detailed, sophisticated and effective.

Matters for which citizens have been reportedly prosecuted and imprisoned include:

- Publishing articles or giving interviews said to be critical of economic, social or human rights matters in Cuba.
- Communicating with international human rights organisations.
- Having contact with those viewed as hostile to Cuba's interests.
- Cubans must obtain official permission to leave or return. This is often punitively denied.
- Amnesty International and Human Rights Watch are not allowed to visit.

The United Nations has described food and hygiene levels in Cuban prisons as substandard and medical care as either unavailable or inappropriate.
The International Committee of Red Cross has been denied access to Cuban prisons.

Amnesty International: human rights concerns in Cuba (2007)

- Severe restrictions on freedom of expression and association affect thousands of people in Cuba.
- All broadcast and print media are controlled by the state. Access to the Internet is severely limited outside educational institutions and governmental offices. In this connection, it is interesting to note the Prince Harry media conspiracy. In 2007 the Ministry of Defence and British news outlets agreed that the deployment of Prince Harry in Afghanistan would be kept secret. The secret was revealed by the Drudge Report, an American political news blog. Since the Prince Harry agreement to withhold information, the British press and broadcasting media must have some difficulty criticising foreign media outlets for being "state-controlled". The Prince Harry deal illustrates the frailty of human rights in Britain when the establishment and the media collude to restrict freedom of information. It also raises the question of what other matters have been kept secret by collusion between the press and the state.
- Critics of the Cuban government are frequently arrested and imprisoned, sometimes for "pre-criminal dangerousness".

- There are at least 67 prisoners of conscience in Cuba, including journalists, teachers and human rights activists detained for peaceful dissident activities.
- Amnesty receives frequent reports of dissidents being arbitrarily arrested and imprisoned awaiting trial.
- A number of persons are detained with trial or charge on suspicion of counter-revolutionary activities.
- Dissidents are often sentenced for "social dangerousness", a pre-emptive measure defined as proclivity to commit a crime.
- Dissidents are publicly intimidated and harassed by "acts of repudiation". These are public demonstrations by organized groups who hurl insults.
- Cuba retains the death penalty for serious crimes. This was last applied in 2003. It is estimated that 40 people are currently on death row.
- The US embargo against Cuba should be lifted. It affects a wide range of economic, social and cultural rights including the right to food, health and sanitation.

Cuban Constitution

The Cuban revolution of 1959 was based on humanistic and egalitarian aims. These included gender and race equality, the redistribution of wealth, land reform and the realisation of social and economic rights to housing, health care and education. The central, general aim of the revolution has been the creation of a system of economic well-being founded on the equitable distribution of resources.

The legal system was of minor relevance to these aims. During the early part of the Castro regime, law comprised a large number of decrees made by the revolutionary leadership.

In 1976 a new Constitution came into force, together with new codes dealing with, for example, the legal profession, the judicial system, employment law and criminal justice. Legislation came to be seen as a primary instrument for social change.

The Cuban Constitution of 1976 includes the following:

- The obligation of the state to assure the economic and social well-being of the collective.
- Positive social and economic rights: the right to work, right to social security, free health care and free education.
- Equality of rights and duties and the prohibition of discrimination.
- Individual liberties, for example freedom of speech in keeping with the objectives of a socialist society.

The 1976 Constitution sets out all the rights recognised by the Universal Declaration of Human Rights.

The Cuban view is that US and UK jurisprudence puts individual autonomy and property rights above group rights and collective economic and social well-being.

Socialist legality, in the Cuban context, is concerned with collective well-being based on egalitarian values. It imposes limitations of individual liberties for the collective good. Political expression is restricted where it conflicts with state policy.

All efforts to organise internal dissent are linked, by the Cuban authorities, to US efforts to destabilise the government.

Achievements in universal free education, health care and equality are now regarded in Cuba as fundamental rights. It is generally recognised that individual freedoms have been subordinated to these collective aims. It is clear that those who oppose the socialist system are subject to limitations on their freedom of expression and association.

The question of human rights in Cuba can only be properly considered in the context of the fact that the United States has continuously attempted to undermine and destabilise Cuba's government. These attempts have included an invasion, assassination attempts, an economic embargo and travel restrictions. Some aspects of the Cuban system are viewed as "draconian" by human rights organizations. These are justified by Cubans as being national security measures necessitated by US aggression. Cuba has repeatedly stated that the US economic embargo, which in itself can be seen as a form of human rights abuse, impedes Cuba's ability to adopt more permissive policies in the area of political freedoms.

The British government has, on a number of occasions, been prepared to suspend individual human rights in perceived emergencies. An extreme example of this is the role of law during the First World War. The Defence of the Realm Acts 1914 and 1915 gave the King in Council "such powers as may be necessary for the efficient prosecution of the war". This meant the imposition of a comprehensive system of state control over industry and agriculture, with the extension of the jurisdiction of courts-martial and the effective supremacy of military law. Britain was governed almost exclusively by statutory powers from 1914 until 1919. Ireland was governed under martial law from 1919 until 1921.

HIV/AIDS in Cuba

Another extreme example of the contradiction between collective and individual human rights is the reported action of the Cuban government in response to the anticipated HIV/AIDS epidemic.
The Cuban approach was the compulsory testing and quarantining of persons with HIV symptoms. The result of this has been that Cuba now experiences a very low incidence of HIV/AIDS, particularly in comparison with other developing countries. It can be argued that the collective rights of the majority have been safeguarded by breaches of individual human rights of the few. In England, those subject to compulsory quarantine would no doubt have been represented by batteries of QCs earning thousands of pounds a day, probably financed by the taxpayer. Meanwhile, HIV/AIDS marches on.

South Africa

Albie Sachs considers whether the obligation on the state to promote socio-economic advance should be made a constitutional duty. He comments that where the struggle for survival is overwhelming, the freedom to vote and the right to criticise the government risk becoming devoid of practical meaning. Individual human rights can

guarantee to people dying of hunger the inalienable right to use their last breath freely to curse the government.
In South Africa, the judicial enforcement of socio-economic rights poses the question of whether social and economic rights can be regarded as fundamental rights enforceable directly by the courts, and if so, how?
Sachs tells how a group of black South African students set up an Anti-Bill of Rights Committee. They regarded the Bill of Rights as a document established by the privileged white community to block future moves towards social and economic transformation. Whites owned 87 per cent of South African land and 95 per cent of its productive capital. Property rights guaranteed by the Bill of Rights meant that the poor would remain poor and the rich would get richer.
Sachs was detained in solitary confinement for 90 days without charge, trial, or access to lawyers on suspicion that he had information which could help security forces in dealing with anti-state activity. Following the 90 day period, he was immediately detained for another 90 days. Sachs states that the law created a vacuum, a space with a totally extralegal area, with only the conscience or system of command of the authorities to prevent abuse if people were locked up. Basic decisions on guilt or innocence were made by the security police. The exceptional became the normal.
Sachs' practical experience is that, once the door is opened to diminishing respect for the rule of law, the door is closed to the rule of law, to habeas corpus, to standards of interrogation, to the right to a fair trial. The opening or the closing of the door is never enough for the security people.

During the drafting of the South African constitution, a question for discussion was whether social and economic rights, for example the right to health, housing, food and education, should be included as fundamental rights.
This discussion centred on whether "bread rights" should be on a par with "freedom rights".
The 1996 Constitution of the Republic of South Africa sets out, in simple and transparent terms, a number of social and economic rights. It has been described as the most progressive Constitution in the world.
For example:

- Everyone has the right to have access to adequate housing.
- Everyone has the right to have access to health care.
- The state must take reasonable legislative and other measures, within its available resources, to achieve the progressive realisation of these rights.

This has been considered by the South African Constitutional Court in a number of cases, including the following:

- *Soobramoney v Minister of Health, KwaZulu Natal (1998).* S suffered from chronic renal failure. He complained that the state's failure to provide him with continued dialysis amounted to a failure to take active measures to protect his right to life under the Constitution. The Constitutional Court decided that there had been no breach of the Constitution because chronic conditions were not to be given the same priority as emergency medical cases. S died. Justice Albie Sachs later commented that access to resources, unlike the right to free speech or to vote, had to be rationed. The queue for resources must be fairly established and non-discriminatory. The Court could not say that S should go to the head of the queue.

- *Government of the RSA v Grootboom (2001)*. G and others were squatters on privately owned land. The owner applied to the local authority for their eviction. The Constitutional Court was asked to interpret the sections of the Constitution which guaranteed the right to access to adequate housing and gave children the right to shelter. The Court ruled that the state had an obligation to establish a coherent and coordinated housing programme. This obligation had to be concentrated on people in crisis. Those whose needs were most desperate had a right to emergency relief and shelter.

- *Minister of Health v Treatment Action Campaign (2002)*. The South African Health Department refused to generally supply Nevirapine, a drug for treating HIV positive pregnant women. The Constitutional Court ruled that the Health Department was in breach of its obligation under the Constitution to provide access to health care in a reasonable manner and taking account of pressing social needs. The Department was ordered to supply the drug at all public hospitals and clinics.

Crucially important issues like these have not been discussed in the English courts or by the human rights industry.

Generally, individual human rights in the UK are individually enforced and protected. The involvement of a number of "celebrity" solicitors and barristers can sometimes be seen to approach a cult of personality.

The Human Rights Act is incomplete. It should be amended to include social and economic rights, following the South African model.

The protection of human rights, and the enforcement of the 1998 Act, should not be the prerogative of individual lawyers.

Identity cards

Without going into the details of the current arguments for and against identity cards, which may seem to have reached the level of a sixth-form debate, the historical context may be useful:

The United Kingdom had an identity card system between 1939 and 1952. Under the National Registration Act 1939, a National Register was set up. This contained details of all citizens and National Identity Cards were issued to all persons on the Register. The following information was entered on the Register:

- Names
- Sex
- Age
- Occupation
- Residence
- Marriage status

- Membership of the armed forces.

The Act of 1939 stated that the police had power to require the production of the National Identity Card and created a number of offences.

This law was justified by three reasons:

- The need for central planning in a national emergency.
- The likelihood of rationing being introduced.
- The need for detailed statistics about the population.

The Act was introduced without any real scrutiny by Parliament. It gave very wide powers to the police, which did not cease at the end of the war. Identity cards were not abolished until 1952.

Aneurin Bevan was reported to have commented that he believed that the requirement of an internal passport was more objectionable than an external passport, and that citizens ought to be allowed to move about freely without running the risk of being accosted by a policeman or anyone else, and asked to produce proof of identity.

CHAPTER 5

WAR: The Iraq War

I don't give a shit about international law.
(Thomas Foley, appointed in 2003 as head of private sector development in Iraq)

At the heart of the British nation is still the horrible, exploitative, violent, colonial past. We've never got rid of it. So we go into Iraq and think "these Iraqis, they're savages. Forget about Iraq being the cradle of civilisation. As a nation, we don't really care".
(Phil Shiner, Public Interest Lawyers)

Any resort to war – any kind of war – is a resort to means that are inherently criminal. War inevitably is a course of killings, assaults, deprivations of liberty and destruction of property. An honestly defensive war is, of course, legal and saves those lawfully conducting it from criminality. But inherently criminal acts cannot be defended by showing that those who committed them were engaged in a war, when war itself is illegal. The very minimum legal consequences of the treaties making aggressive war illegal is to strip those who incite or wage them of every defense the law ever gave, and to leave the war-makers subject to judgment by the usually accepted principles of the law of crimes.
(Justice Robert H Jackson)

This Chapter deals with war, specifically the Iraq War. It argues that the legality of the Iraq War is the most important issue which currently faces English lawyers. It examines the legal issues arising from the War and considers English case law connected with the War. The Chapter analyses the effect of the Iraq War on the relationship between law and morality. It discusses the Nuremburg principles and examines the death penalty as illustrated by the "squalid lynching" of Saddam Hussein. It concludes with a critical comparative analysis of health and safety in a war context.

The economic implications of the Iraq War

In 2008 Joseph Stiglitz, former Chief Economist at the World Bank, and Linda Bilmes, a leading American economist, published *The Three Trillion Dollar War: the true cost of the Iraq conflict.* Their book examines the true financial, economic and social consequences of the Iraq war. They conclude, in summary, that the US government's early estimate of $50 billion for the cost of the war was underestimated by sixty times. They make the following points:

- The invasion of Iraq was a terrible mistake.
- The decision to go to war was based on a number of false premises.
- The total cost to the US will be $3 trillion.
- The total cost to Britain will be £20 billion.
- Estimates of violent deaths of Iraqi citizens are disputed. They range from 100,000 to more than 150,000, with 700,000 deaths from other causes.
- Civilian casualties in Iraq since the invasion have been estimated at between 68,796 (Iraq Body Count) and 650,000 (Lancet October 2006). More bombs

were dropped in the initial 'shock and awe' attack on Iraq than in the whole of the first Gulf War.

- The main alleged "benefit" of the War – the destruction of weapons of mass destruction – had no validity.
- The Iraq War has resulted in a humanitarian catastrophe.
- 2.8 million Iraqis have fled their country.

Stiglitz and Bilmes do not deal with the legality of the War. Their economic analysis confirms the apocalyptic nature of the war in human and economic terms. In the light of a humanitarian and economic disaster of this magnitude, the legal implications have less significance for those who have suffered as a direct result of the invasion of their country. The projected cost of the War can, of course, be compared with the cost of providing a nationwide network of fully staffed and resourced law centres in the United Kingdom.

It can be argued that British lawyers have an overwhelming professional duty to examine and analyse the legal aspects of the War and to express their views on its implications for the UK legal system.
For example, in 2007 a leading international lawyer, a Cambridge University professor with outstanding expertise in his field, was asked if it was true that most international lawyers thought that the invasion of Iraq was illegal. He replied that he only knew one lawyer who thought that it was legal.

The prohibition of the use of force by one state against another is one of the most fundamental principles of international law. Article 2 of the United Nations Charter states that war is unlawful. This is so basic a principle that the burden is on those seeking to show authorisation to use force, to show that it has in fact been authorised.

Legality of the War

First, war is illegal under international law. Second, the British government's case for war was fatally flawed, from legal, practical and humanitarian points of view. Third, there are allegations of war crimes on the part of political leaders who planned and ordered the invasion of Iraq. If English lawyers believe, as they so often declare, in justice and the rule of law, then they have an overriding duty to speak out loudly and often against the War in Iraq and to take action in accordance with the principles of justice and the rule of law.

In terms of the legality of the War, which is not a fundamental issue in humanitarian terms, but is the most significant for lawyers, it is clear that the great majority of international lawyers – practising and academic – are of the opinion that there was no justification in law for the invasion of Iraq.

In the light of the overwhelming legal and humanitarian disaster which resulted from the War, lawyers should treat the Iraq War as their first priority.

Not all lawyers share these views. For example, recent comments by academics on the legality of the Iraq War have included the following:

- Even if the War was illegal, there are few if any legal implications.

- The War was lawful under UK law because its legality has not been successfully challenged in any UK court.
- To claim that the War was a serious violation of the rule of law should not be taken at face value.
- The legality of the War could be tested by litigation brought by a state to the International Court of Justice. This process would be deeply affected by politics.
- Even if the War was illegal, this does not necessarily mean that it was a crime in itself.
- There is no prospect of anyone ever standing trial for the Iraq War in any national or international court.

In response to these views, senior members of the UK judiciary have made it clear that they regard the War as illegal and that this is a significant issue.

For example, Lord Bingham commented that the issue of legality has enhanced the importance of international law in the public mind. It is perhaps unlikely that states chastened by their experience in Iraq will be eager to repeat it. Although they have not been brought before any court, they have been arraigned at the bar of world opinion with resulting damage to their standing and influence.

Leading opinions on the legality of the War

In October 2003 Robert Alexander QC, Chairman of Justice, published an article in The Times headed *Scrutiny by the courts could put a stop to this military adventurism.*

The article, in summary, made the following points:

- Article 2 (4) of the United Nations Charter specifically prohibits an armed attack on another country unless it is either in self-defence or under the aegis of the United Nations.
- UN Security Council Resolution 1441 did not authorise war and stated that the UN was to remain in control. This was recognised by the British and US governments when they promoted a second resolution in March 2003.
- The UK government invoked the sophistry of arguing that UN Security Council Resolution 678, passed in 1990 for the express and limited purpose of expelling Iraq from Kuwait, had "revived" to permit an invasion.
- The Attorney-General published his advice in summary form in a parliamentary answer in March 2003. Essentially, this relied on Resolution 678.
- The Attorney-General refused requests to disclose the details of his advice on the basis that there was a convention that law officers were not obliged to disclose advice which they had provided to the government.
- This meant that the following questions had not been answered in public:
    1. What were the factual assumptions upon which the Attorney-General's advice relied?
    2. How did he deal with the clear wording of Resolution 1441?
    3. What arguments were used to deal with those of the majority of international lawyers who took the view that an invasion would be unlawful?

4. Did the Attorney-General consider the doctrines of proportionality and necessity under international law?
5. What was the legal basis for asserting that an old UN Resolution could "revive"?

Legal advice supplied to the government should be open to challenge in the courts. It was logical that the courts should give a ruling on the legality of action as important as any which the government would take for years to come.

Lord Bingham

In November 2008 Lord Bingham, England's former Lord Chief Justice and senior Law Lord, gave a speech on the rule of law to the British Institute of International and Comparative Law. His comments were reported to include the following:

- The invasion of Iraq by the UK and the US had been a serious violation of international law.
- The Attorney-General's advice failed to acknowledge the lack of hard evidence of Iraq's non-compliance. Hans Blix and his team of weapons inspectors found no weapons of mass destruction, were making progress and expected to complete their work in a matter of months.
- The invasion of Iraq was not authorised by the Security Council and there had been a serious violation of international law and the rule of law.

Lord Steyn

In November 2003 Lord Steyn, a former Law Lord, made the following points:

- The treatment by the US government of 660 prisoners in Guantanamo Bay had been a monstrous failure of justice.
- Judges have a duty, in times of crisis, to guard against an unprincipled and exorbitant executive response.
- As a lawyer brought up to admire the ideals of American democracy and justice, he regarded Guantanamo as a monstrous failure of justice.
- The military would act as interrogators, prosecutors, defence counsel and judges, and when death sentences were imposed, as executioners. None of the guarantees of a fair trial need be observed.

In October 19, 2005 he stated:

- The War with Iraq had made the world a more dangerous place and London a target for terrorist attack.
- The invasion of Iraq was military folly and the government scraped the legal barrel in trying to justify it.
- It was wrong of the Prime Minister to have called the rule of law a "game". The maintenance of the rule of law is not a game. It is about access to justice, fundamental human rights and democratic values.
- After the recent dreadful bombings in London we were asked to believe that the Iraq War did not make London and the world a more dangerous place.

Surely, on top of everything else, we do not have to listen to a fairy tale.

- With reference to Walter Wolfgang, who was detained under anti-terrorist legislation for protesting about the war in Iraq at the Labour Party's annual conference in Brighton, Lord Steyn is reported to have commented that one knows, of course, that the government earnestly desires a closure on this issue. But that is not possible. Even Mr Walter Wolfgang would be free to express the opinion for which he was charged under the Terrorism Act. Possibly his name will live on when the names of some now in charge of affairs are forgotten.
- Lord Steyn agreed with Lord Alexander of Weedon that in its search for justification in law for war the government was driven to scrape the bottom of the legal barrel. Lord Alexander analysed the constantly shifting grounds for intervention. He rightly concluded that none of these grounds had any plausibility. The earlier Resolution 678, preceding the driving of Iraq from Kuwait 12 years earlier, had no relevance to the contemporary international position. The sole reason for harking back to it was that it was impossible to obtain Security Council approval for intervention in Iraq.

In a speech to the Bar Council in November 2006, Lord Steyn put forward the following views:

- President Bush was guilty of high crimes under international law. Blair backed Bush, however lawless and outrageous the means adopted.

- Members of the British government who were consciously involved in the decision to invade Iraq were subject to the universal criminal jurisdiction of international law.
- The Attorney-General's advice of March 2003 had paved the way for a disastrous war. It had been a black day for the rule of law.
- Examples of illegality were the Guantanamo prison camp, secret CIA prison camps, CIA extraordinary rendition flights of prisoners and the invasion of Iraq.
- The Bush administration had set out to undermine international institutions and refashion international law.
- The record of British troops in Iraq was far from unblemished.
- Long after the Prime Minister and his Cabinet had gone, the UK would pay the price for an abdication by our government of independent responsibility in foreign affairs and for playing a part with the Bush administration in undermining the international rule of law.

George Monbiot

In May 2008 Monbiot attempted a citizen's arrest of John Bolton, former Under-Secretary of State in the US State Department, for the crime of aggression. The international criminal law background to this action was that:

- Principle VI of the Nuremberg Principles states that crimes against peace are punishable as crimes under international law. This includes:

- Planning, preparation, initiation or waging a war of aggression or a war in violation of international treaties, agreements or assurances.
- Participation in a common plan or conspiracy for the accomplishment of any of these acts.
- Principle VII states that complicity in the commission of a crime against peace, a war crime, or a crime against humanity is a crime under international law.

Monbiot alleged the following:

- Bolton had orchestrated the dismissal of the head of the Organisation for the Prohibition of Chemical Weapons, who had offered to resolve the dispute over Iraq's alleged weapons of mass destruction and avoid the war.
- Bolton had helped to promote the false claim that Saddam Hussein had been seeking to procure uranium from Niger as part of a plan to initiate war.

Monbiot's attempt to arrest Bolton was unsuccessful. He made the following points:

- His attempt was the most serious action which could be taken by someone who was neither a Law Lord nor a legislator.
- The British state was prepared to punish petty misdemeanours with vindictive ferocity but it would not legislate against the greatest crime of all.

In October 2009 Monbiot made the following further points:

- Tony Blair has the distinction of being one of the two greatest living mass murderers on earth.

- He commissioned a crime of aggression – waging an unprovoked war, described by the Nuremburg Tribunal as the supreme international crime.
- This crime has caused the death of between 100,000 and 1 million people.
- Blair cannot be prosecuted in the United Kingdom. In 2006 the law lords decided that the international crime of aggression has not been incorporated into domestic law.

Monbiot's case against Blair

A Downing Street memo in July 2002 revealed that the decision to attack Iraq had already been taken by the US. There were three possible legal bases for the War: self-defence, humanitarian intervention or authorisation by the UN Security Council.

The conditions for a lawful war are:

- An armed attack upon the state or an imminent attack.
- The use of force must be necessary and other means to reverse or avert the attack must be unavailable.
- Acts in self-defence must be proportionate and strictly confined to the object of stopping the attack.

In January 2010 Monbiot launched a fund to reward people who attempted to arrest Blair. If the War was illegal, a question which Monbiot regards as the only one which counts, then the War becomes a criminal matter. Monbiot made the following points:

- Those who commissioned it should be committed for trial.

- An inquiry in the Netherlands found that the invasion of Iraq had no sound mandate in international law.
- Without legal justification, the Iraq War was an act of mass murder.
- The International Criminal Court should be allowed to prosecute the crime of aggression.
- There must be no hiding place for those who have committed crimes against peace.
- No civilised country can allow mass murderers to move on.

Monbiot has launched a website, www.arrestblair.org, whose purpose is to raise money as a reward for people who attempt a citizen's arrest of the former prime minister.

Peacerights

Peacerights is a non-governmental organisation established to promote peaceful conflict resolution, challenge threats to peace and to develop educational and research initiatives for those concerned with peace and justice in the world.

In 2003, a Peacerights panel of eight leading academic international lawyers held an inquiry into legal aspects of the military operations against Iraq in March of that year. The panel published its report in January 2004. It concluded that there was enough evidence for the chief prosecutor at the International Criminal Court (ICC) to investigate members of the UK government for alleged crimes against humanity and war crimes during the War and the occupation.

These alleged crimes included the use of cluster bombs

in urban areas, whether attacks had been launched on non-military targets, attacks on media targets and whether weapons were used which caused excessive loss of life or injury to civilians.

The Inquiry set out a detailed analysis of the legal implications of its work.

The terms of reference for the Inquiry were whether there was sufficient cause and evidence for the ICC to investigate members of the UK government for breaches of the ICC Statute in relation to crimes against humanity and/or war crimes committed during the Iraq conflict and occupation 2003.

This involved:

- A consideration of the issue of civilian casualties
- An examination of the weapons and methods of warfare used during the invasion
- An analysis of the possible criminal liability of UK nationals.

The panel concluded that the ICC prosecutor should initiate a preliminary investigation into the following matters:

- The individual criminal responsibility of members of the UK government and the military for the commission of war crimes.
- Whether the UK had a common purpose with the US in criminal activities.
- Whether the attacks on the Iraqi media violated international law.
- Whether attacks were made on locations or means of transport which were not military objectives, causing civilian casualties in breach of international law.

- Whether methods of warfare, weapon systems or locations of attack chosen were in breach of international law.
- Given the use of cluster bombs in urban areas, whether this was prohibited by international law.

The panel referred to these aspects of the Statute of the International Criminal Court 1998:

- The ICC has power to examine and prosecute serious violations of human rights and international humanitarian law.
- It has no jurisdiction over crimes of aggression.
- The UK government had acknowledged its use of land-based and airborne cluster bombs which open before reaching their target. The failure rate of the bomblets discharged by these weapons averages between 2 and 20 per cent.
- Cluster weapons were used against military objectives located in urban areas.
- There was evidence of the indiscriminate use of cluster bombs in urban settings.
- There were credible reports of attacks causing many civilian casualties with no manifest military advantage, for example attacks on media outlets, electricity supplies and marketplaces.
- The jurisdiction of the ICC included the individual responsibility of British troops.
- The UK could be held responsible for the commission of an intentionally wrongful act for aiding and abetting another state.
- There had been common purpose in members of the coalition in their military activities against Iraq.

- The ICC prosecutor should fully investigate the issue of the responsibility of UK nationals notwithstanding that violations might have been committed by US forces.
- The gravity of alleged crimes and the interests of the victims demanded that there should be an investigation. It was essential to establish the truth, fearlessly and without favour.
- The victims of the conflict in Iraq were owed this much at least, especially as military operations were not justified by the right of self-defence and were undertaken without the express approval of the UN Security Council.
- By promoting respect for the rule of law, and helping to deter violations of international humanitarian law, an investigation by the ICC prosecutor would serve to achieve the Court's objective of contributing to the prevention of the most serious crimes of concern to the international community as a whole.

Although this initiative may have come to nothing, it at least shows that a continuing insistence that the legal implications of the War cannot be forgotten means that the War itself cannot be written out of history.

Chilcot Inquiry

Before this Inquiry started its hearings, Public Interest Lawyers commented that the key issues should include the following:

- Examination of the role of legal advice on the legality of the invasion and the UK's international human rights obligations.

- The misleading of the public over prior commitment to regime change.
- The use of indiscriminate weaponry and tactics, including the targeting of infrastructure, the use of cluster bombs, fuel-air explosives and depleted uranium shells.
- War crimes.
- At least 650,000 deaths, four million refugees and the devastation of Iraq.
- A victim-centred approach must be fundamental.

The Inquiry hearings have been held without taking evidence under oath and have expressly excluded legal consequences. Its function was not to apportion blame.
Matters emerging during the Chilcot Inquiry hearings have included the following:

On November 29, 2009 the Mail on Sunday reported that in July 2002 the Attorney-General wrote to Blair stating that to depose Saddam Hussein would be a blatant breach of international law.
In March 2003 he gave legal backing to the War. The newspaper report suggested duress.
The letter of July 2002 is reported to have contained the following points:

- The War could not be justified purely on the grounds of regime change
- It was not self-defence: there was no threat from Iraq
- Humanitarian intervention was not relevant
- It was very hard to rely on earlier UN Resolutions.

Elizabeth Wilmshurst, a senior legal adviser at the Foreign Office, told the Inquiry that it was the unanimous view of Foreign Office lawyers that the Iraq War was illegal. She resigned in protest against the invasion. Wilmshurst stated that the invasion was illegal. The rules of international law on the use of force by states are at the heart of international law. Collective security, as opposed to unilateral military action, is a central purpose of the UN Charter. The advice of the Foreign Office lawyers was ignored by Ministers.

The Attorney-General changed his opinion after a secret briefing with American government lawyers in February 2003. The Americans told him that "the French" had told them that a second UN Resolution was not needed to sanction the War. This has been denied by "the French". Britain's decision to go to war was based on a series of private conversations and anecdotes.
Documents relating to the Attorney-General's advice on the legality of the war are not to be declassified.

Sir Michael Wood, the chief legal adviser at the Foreign Office, stated that he considered that the use of force against Iraq in March 2003 was contrary to international law. That use of force had not been authorised by the UN Security Council and had no other basis in international law.
The Attorney-General was finally consulted only at the very last minute as the troops were ready to go in.
John Prescott is reported to have commented that intelligence reports at the time were "tittle-tattle" and that his role was to support Blair and the Cabinet.

The inquiry has finished its public hearings and is currently (June 2014) preparing its final report. It is also assessing the extent to which material should be disclosed to the public.

The Iraq legacy

Iraq is now facing numerous sectarian and ethnic divides which are fragmenting the country. The US-trained Iraqi security forces are currently engaged in fighting jihadists and disaffected Sunni Muslims. Blair has reportedly stated that the removal of Saddam Hussain has contributed to this new war.

Examples of UK cases connected with the Iraq War

The following selection of Iraq-War related cases aims to show the range of issues connected with the War which have impacted on the English legal system.

R v Jones and Others (2006)

The issue in the appeals in these cases was the extent to which the international determination to prevent war was transposed into English law.

There were 20 appellants. They all committed acts in 2003 which were criminal offences unless there was a defence of legal justification. All the appeals raised the issue of whether the crime of aggression formed part of English criminal law. The appellants acted as they did because they wished to prevent the commission of that crime against Iraq.

Their actions included breaking into RAF Fairford and damaging equipment and trespass on Marchwood Military Port.

The House of Lords decided the following:

- Customary international law is part of the law of England and Wales.
- Customary international law has recognised a crime of aggression.
- Crimes recognised in customary international law are not automatically recognised and enforced by English law without the need for any domestic statute or judicial decision.
- The crime of aggression is not a crime in the domestic law of England and Wales.
- Even if aggression had been a crime in English law, the apprehension that such a crime was about to be committed could not have made it reasonable for the appellants to use force of any kind to obstruct military activities at Marchwood or Fairford.
- The International Criminal Court does not have jurisdiction over crimes of aggression.

R (on the application of Gentle and another) v The Prime Minister (2008)

The mothers of two young soldiers who were killed in Iraq tried to use the European Convention on Human Rights to make the government hold a public inquiry into the circumstances in which Iraq was invaded. Their application failed.

The House of Lords ruled that Article 2 of the Convention (the right to life) could not be used to question the legality of going to war.

Lord Bingham stated that, despite the numerous occasions on which states had gone to war in the last fifty years, and the fact that such wars inevitably caused deaths in the armed forces, Article 2 had never been applied to the process of deciding on the legality of wars. The states of Europe could never have contemplated binding themselves to set up independent public inquiries into the process by which a decision to go to war had been taken.

Lord Hoffman commented that it was desirable that the government should not act in breach of international law but this did not mean that Article 2 applied.

Lord Hope stated that it was a hard thing for a court to say to the mothers of two young soldiers who lost their lives that it could do nothing for them in the campaign to have the circumstances that led up to these tragedies investigated.

Baroness Hale is reported to have made the following comments:

- If the use of force had been lawful, it would be of some comfort to the mothers to know that their sons had died in a just cause.
- If it was not, there might at least be some public acknowledgment and attribution of responsibility and lessons learned for the future. If her child had died in that way, that was exactly what she would want.
- She wished that Article 2 did impose a duty on a state not to send its soldiers to fight in an unlawful war.

R v Kendall-Smith (2006)

In April 2006 Malcolm Kendall-Smith, an RAF doctor, was sentenced to eight months imprisonment for failing to comply with lawful orders after he had refused to serve in the Iraq War.

Kendall-Smith had refused to go to Iraq because he believed that the War was illegal. He did not want to be complicit with an act of aggression which was contrary to international law. He stated that he had evidence that the Americans were on a par with Nazi Germany with their actions in Iraq. The ongoing acts of aggression in Iraq and systematically applied war crimes provided a moral equivalent between the US and Nazi Germany.

He also refused to take part in training and equipment fitting before deployment to Iraq because they were preparatory acts which were as criminal as the act itself.

In sentencing, Judge Advocate Bayliss is reported to have made the following comments:

- The offences were so serious that only a custodial sentence was appropriate.
- Kendall-Smith would be ordered to pay £20,000 defence costs.
- Obedience to orders was at the heart of any disciplined force. Disobedience to orders meant that it was not a disciplined force but a disorganised rabble.
- Those who wore the Queen's uniform could not pick and choose which orders they obeyed and those who did so must face the consequences.
- Kendall-Smith had sought to make a martyr of himself. He had shown a degree of arrogance which

was amazing.

- He might have acted out of his moral viewpoint but his interpretation of the presence of British forces in Iraq as illegal was incorrect.

The reported statement by Bayliss that members of the military cannot pick and choose which orders they obeyed, and those who do so must face the consequences, appears to show a breathtaking disregard for the principles laid down during the Nuremburg trials, in particular the clear statement that the plea of superior orders cannot be considered as an absolute defence, but merely as a mitigating factor.

Hopps v Mott MacDonald Ltd and Ministry of Defence (2009)

H was a civilian engineer employed by MM to work in Iraq in the emergency reconstruction programme after the Iraq War in 2003. His work included the assessment of Iraqi power stations and advising on the work needed to restore electric power to Southern Iraq.
Security for MM's employees was provided by the Army. They provided ordinary, soft-skinned Land Rovers. These did not protect against sniper fire or improvised explosive devices (IEDs). H was also supplied with a helmet, body armour and an armed escort.
In October 2003 H's Land Rover was attacked by an IED. He suffered serious injuries and claimed compensation from his employer and the Ministry of Defence.

The claim was dismissed. The court made the following points:

- It was not negligent to transport civilian employees in unarmoured vehicles in southern Iraq in 2003.
- This decision took into account the level of risk and the urgency and desirability of the emergency infrastructure projects.
- MM and the Army were continuously reassessing the security situation. In any event, the absence of a recognisable risk assessment would only be significant if, had such an assessment been made, it would have resulted in a decision to provide armoured vehicles.
- H had failed to prove that an armoured vehicle would have prevented or reduced his injuries in the context of this particular attack.
- The emergency reconstruction of Iraq was a "desirable activity" for the purposes of section 1 of the Compensation Act 2006. The court's decision took into account the possible deterrent effect of a finding of liability on future activities of this type.

This was thought to be the first decision of an English court in a case involving a claim by a civilian for personal injury suffered in an attack in Iraq while working after the war. It also appears to be the first case in which a judge has applied section 1 of the Act of 2006.

Section 1 of the Compensation Act 2006 states, in summary, that a court considering a claim in negligence or breach of statutory duty may, in determining whether the defendant should have taken particular steps to meet a standard of care, have regard to whether a requirement to take those steps might prevent a desirable activity from being undertaken at all, to a particular extent or in a particular way, or may discourage persons from undertaking functions in connection with a desirable activity.

The expressed aim of the Act of 2006 was the protection of volunteer sports organisers from legal action by participants injured in recreational activities. It was accepted that such organisers had a disproportionate fear of litigation and this had resulted in risk-averse behaviour. The Act was not intended to provide a yardstick for the desirability of the Iraq War.

Davies v Global Strategies Group (2009)

D's husband was shot and killed in Iraq. He was employed by G, which was a company supplying defence and security services. G had been contracted by the United States after the Iraq War to provide convoy escort services for commercial vehicles. D's husband was driving to meet a convoy in northern Iraq. His vehicle came under fire. The vehicle was soft-skinned. All doors except the driver's door had been removed from the vehicle. G's personnel were equipped with weapons, helmets and body armour, but no collar for neck protection.

G's tactics involved vehicles being highly manoeuvrable, personnel and weapons being highly visible, and personnel being able to leave their vehicles quickly.

D's husband was shot through the windscreen of the vehicle in which he was travelling. A bulletproof windscreen would have prevented this, but it was stated that collar protection would have made no difference because the bullet struck the deceased just below his left ear.

D claimed compensation from G for the death of her husband.

The claim failed. The court stated that G's tactics had been reasonable.

The deterioration in the security situation between the time when the contract with G was signed, and the death of G, had not been such as to call for the wholesale change of tactics in favour of armoured vehicles. Also, at the time of the operation when D's husband was killed, armoured vehicles were not available. The wearing of a collar would have made no difference. The stage had not been reached when the operation should have been called off.

On the evidence, it had not been reasonably practicable to have fitted a bulletproof windscreen to the vehicle. There was no causative breach of duty on G's part.

B-52 Two

In May 2007 Phil Pritchard & Toby Olditch, known as the B-52 Two, were acquitted of conspiracy to cause criminal damage. They had broken into RAF Fairford shortly before the invasion of Iraq with the aim of immobilising B-52 bombers to prevent them from bombing Iraq.

The two men were arrested inside the perimeter fences at RAF Fairford in the early morning of 18 March 2003, two days before the bombing of Iraq started. They carried with them tools to damage the planes, nuts and bolts to jam the aircrafts' engines, pictures of ordinary

Iraqi civilians and paint symbolizing blood and oil. They also carried warning signs for attaching to any damaged planes which would help alert aircrew to their action. The two men acted non-violently in a way which would not result in harm to anyone, including the military personnel at Fairford. They intended to stay with the aircraft and tell the operators what they had done.

The jury at Bristol Crown Court accepted their defence that they were acting to prevent the US Airforce committing war crimes and causing damage to life and property in Iraq. The two argued that their action was reasonable because other means of protest had failed. They were acting to prevent a crime: potential war crimes against Iraqi civilians and to prevent criminal damage to Iraqi property.

The B-52 Two stated that they were nonviolent and accountable, attempting to prevent the deaths of innocent Iraqis in an illegal war. They were careful to ensure that no harm would come to anyone from their actions. They maintained that war crimes were committed in the bombing as cluster bombs, which spread unexploded bomblets that kill and maim civilians (like mines) were used, as were 'bunker busting' bombs tipped with depleted uranium which broke into fragments, spreading radioactive toxins which are harmful to civilians. During the trial the prosecution accepted that even delaying the bombers would have prevented civilian casualties, as it would have allowed those fleeing cities more time to escape. In his summing up the judge explained the legal tests that must be met for the prosecution to succeed. A document 'steps to verdict' had been provided to assist the jury.

Toby Olditch commented after the case that he and Pritchard were overjoyed, and thankful for the good sense of the jurors, for the wonderful support they had received, and for the commitment and expertise of their legal representatives. But hundreds of thousands of Iraqi people had still suffered as a result of the Government's actions. It shouldn't have come to the point that people had to take direct action to try to check the abuse of executive power.

Phil Pritchard stated that he was delighted that the jury had returned a unanimous not-guilty verdict. Their action in trying to prevent illegal attacks on the people of Iraq in 2003 had been vindicated. He hoped that war of this kind never happened again.

Al-Saadoon and Mufdhi v United Kingdom (2010)

The European Court of Human Rights (ECHR) decided that the transfer of two Iraqi murder suspects by the United Kingdom to the Iraqi authorities for trial was a breach of the European Convention on Human Rights.

A and M were Iraqi nationals, Sunni Muslims and former officials of the Ba'ath party. In 2003 they were arrested by the UK military on suspicion of having been involved in the killing of two British soldiers.

The Iraqi High Tribunal, set up to try Iraqi nationals accused of war crimes, repeatedly requested the UK military to transfer A and M to its custody. They were transferred in December 2008.

Iraq had reintroduced the death penalty in 2004.

The ECHR made the following points:

- The death penalty is inhuman and degrading and contrary to Article 3 of the European Convention on Human Rights.
- There was a real risk of A and M being executed.
- The Iraqi authorities had not given a binding assurance that they would not execute A and M.
- A and M had been subjected to a well-founded fear of execution which had given rise to a significant degree of mental suffering, which must have intensified and continued after they were transferred into Iraqi custody.

Comparative health and safety in a war context

Reports of health and safety prosecutions cover, with depressing regularity, incidents involving deaths and injuries caused by crushing. For example, an eighteen-year old worker, crushed by an unguarded industrial machine, lies dying in an English hospital. In Iraq, an eighteen-year old worker, crushed by British and American military operations, also lies dying in hospital. Physically and medically, there is no difference between the two. Both are innocent young human beings whose lives have been cut short by others.

Those responsible for the death of the first young man will almost certainly be prosecuted for health and safety offences and perhaps for manslaughter. His dependants are likely to receive financial compensation for his death. Those responsible for the second will not be held accountable in civil or criminal courts.

What is the difference? Physically, mentally and morally, none. In terms of law, it would probably be argued that the second is an unfortunate victim of an act of war. But we were under the general impression that war is illegal under international law. Not this War, those responsible would respond. But the great majority of international lawyers take the view that the Iraq War was illegal. The legal justification argument carries no weight.

Further arguments, involving political and military expediency, are also invalid. There is no justification for the second death. No justification, whether moral, ethical, legal, political or military. The fact that there is no justification debases legality and warps justice so that it becomes unrecognisable. English law has severed any connection with morality until it condemns the Iraq War and brings the war criminals to trial.

Nuremburg Trials: International Military Tribunal November 1945

Key features of the Nuremburg process

- The military, political and economic leaders of a state were tried for offences against international law and morality.
- They could not hide behind a shield of sovereignty.
- Their own laws were no excuse where such laws were unjust and contrary to recognised principles of law and morality.
- Their official capacity did not protect them.
- Crimes are committed by men, not by abstract entities, and only by punishing individuals who commit such crimes can the provisions of international law be enforced.
- The plea of superior orders cannot be considered as

an absolute defence, but merely as a mitigating factor.

- Aggressive war is a crime according to international law.
- The act of planning, preparing, initiating or waging aggressive war, or conspiring to accomplish these objectives, is illegal and individuals can be held liable for committing them.
- War crimes are violations of the laws or customs of war. Such violations include but are not limited to murder, ill-treatment of civilian populations; murder or ill-treatment of prisoners of war; killing of hostages, plunder of public or private property, wanton destruction of cities, towns or villages, or devastation not justified by military necessity.
- Crimes against humanity include murder, extermination, enslavement, deportation and other inhumane acts committed against any civilian population.

The essential lesson of the Nuremburg trials was that the officials of every state must now be aware that they too may be condemned as international criminals if they offend against international law, if they instigate or prepare wars of aggression, or if they apply laws that are in violation of the law of humanity.

The trial and execution of Saddam Hussein

Saddam Hussein was arrested in December 2003. His first appearance before an Iraqi tribunal was not until July 2004. Under international law, a defendant must be brought before a court as quickly as possible.

Amnesty International commented as follows:

- Saddam's trial was deeply flawed: there had been political interference by the Iraqi government, failure to provide protection for witnesses and lawyers and denial of access to legal advice for Saddam for a year after his arrest.
- The trial was held under a mix of statute created by the US-led Coalition Provisional Authority and the Iraqi criminal code. The court was set up, funded and provided with security by the US.
- The trial of Saddam Hussein was described as a show trial to justify the invasion of Iraq. On this view, both Blair and Bush condemned Saddam in advance, in possible breach of contempt of court rules.
- The Iraqi Special Tribunal was created under the Coalition Provisional Authority. It was believed that the process was guided by US policy, and the tribunal was described as a puppet court.

Questions were raised about the experience and impartiality of the five judges. Only the identity of the presiding judge has been disclosed. There were also concerns about the competence of the judges, only two of whom had ever sat as judges before. The first judge resigned because of government pressure. Judges were appointed by the Coalition Provisional Authority.

The tribunal was able to convict Saddam on a lower standard of proof than the generally recognised international standard of proof beyond reasonable doubt. Witnesses gave evidence from behind the screen in fear of retaliation.

US pressure resulted in the trial being held in Iraq, not before the international tribunal at The Hague.

The Iraqi, US and British governments all ignored criticisms of the trial.

It was pointed out by Robert Fisk that America, Germany and the UK had supplied material for Saddam's atrocities. During his trial, Saddam was not allowed to comment on the sources of his material.

Fisk also stated the view that Iraq was swamped with mass murderers, guilty of rape, murder and torture. Many worked for the Iraqi government which we were supporting. In some cases these war criminals were paid by us. They would not be tried or hanged.

The British government commented that the decision to execute was a matter for the Iraqi authorities. The Sunni Arab response to the trial was that the verdict was unfair and illegal under the occupation.

Albie Sachs has expressed the view that the effective prosecution of war crimes and the rights of the accused to a fair trial are not antagonistic concepts. Both stem from the same constitutional and humanitarian foundation, namely the need to uphold the rule of law and the basic principles of human dignity, equality and freedom.

Judicial killing

On November 5, 2006, Saddam Hussein was sentenced to death by hanging for crimes against humanity.

The following points should be noted:

- The death penalty is contrary to the European Convention on Human Rights. When Saddam Hussein was executed, this ran against sixty years of European jurisprudence. Article 1, Protocol 6 of the European Convention on Human Rights

(ECHR) states that the death penalty shall be abolished. No-one shall be condemned to such penalty or executed. This was incorporated into English law by section 1 of the Human Rights Act 1998. Of course, the ECHR does not apply to Iraq – nor to the United States with its record of mass judicial killing.

- A consensus has emerged in international human rights law that the use of a mandatory death penalty in times of peace constitutes an inhuman and degrading form of punishment.
- To justify hanging Saddam, Bush and Blair needed moral ascendancy, which they had forfeited. Saddam's execution would appear to be merely another dirty deed in the endless succession which had taken place in Iraq since 2003.
- The matter of principled opposition to the death penalty, to which there can be no exceptions.
- The manner of Saddam Hussein's execution has been described as "unfortunate". This implies an element of bad luck. To imply that such an event was "unlucky" is so far removed from reality as to be disgusting.
- According to the Times, commenting on the execution of Saddam, it does not matter what we think, and we have no reason to intervene in a decision which depends on the culture of Islam rather than of Britain. This interpretation can be characterised as racist.
- My own view of judicial killing is that we debated capital punishment in school; we stood in silence in sixth-form lessons when the last hanging was

carried out (and were punished for this act of rebellion) and we foolishly thought that it was all over. We were under the false impression that we had advanced to a liberal, humanistic society where judicial murder was a thing of the past, where the beating of children for the sexual satisfaction of schoolmasters was dead and buried, where we were safe in the cocoon of the UN Charter and the European Convention on Human Rights.

And now, the reality. The return of barbarism which never really went away. The images of what George Galloway has described as a squalid lynching remind us of the eggshell thinness of our progressive liberal traditions. English lawyers, safe in their priesthood, assuming that the sophisticated web of procedure protects them, should be aware that we have fallen off the tightrope.

Philosophical and moral objections to judicial killing

These include the following:

- George Orwell's description of an execution in colonial Burma: the condemned man stepped aside to avoid a puddle on his way to the gallows. Orwell saw what he described as the mystery, the unspeakable wrongness, of cutting a life short when it is in full tide. Orwell concluded that there can be no exceptions: either one executes or one does not. Either the hangman places the noose over the condemned's head, or the electric chair operator throws the switch, or he does not. There cannot be degrees of capital punishment.
- Albie Sachs' view of judicial killing is that the

death sentence violates the right to human dignity and the right not to be subjected to cruel, inhuman or degrading punishment. If a killer is executed, in Sachs' opinion, he/she achieves a perverse moral victory because by killing the killer, the state effectively reduces public abhorrence at the idea of the deliberate taking of human life.

- Albert Camus stood apart from his contemporaries in post World-War II France through his refusal to accept the death penalty. He opposed his former resistance comrades' approval of the execution of collaborators. His opposition to capital punishment contributed to his split from the Stalinists and resulted in his refusal to endorse the use of terrorism by Algerian nationalists. During his childhood in Algiers, public executions by guillotine were carried out.

Camus' views on judicial killing included the following:
There is not a writer who ignores the value of human life and I suppose that this is one of the honourable definitions of that profession. It is perhaps for that reason that I have always detested the justice of men in power.
We must serve justice because our condition is unjust, add to happiness and joy because this universe is unhappy. In the same way, we must not sentence to death because we have been given death sentences.
Any death sentence is a denial of morality.
Inside existing nations men must strive for a new social contract; on the world level, an international convention should abolish the death penalty.

The world is divided between those who agree to be murderers when necessary and those who refuse with all their strength.

The effect of the Iraq War on the relationship between law and morality

If we accept the opinion of most practising and academic international lawyers, including the Foreign Office's legal advisers, that the Iraq War was illegal, a number of consequences must flow. Not least, a government responsible for such extreme illegality, causing unknown numbers of deaths and injuries, must have forfeited any claim to moral and legal legitimacy.

If we say that, as a matter of law, the government has committed mass murder, then its pronouncements on any legal issue can be seen as hypocritical and invalid. This can be compared with a serial killer criticising groups of youths for noisy behaviour, or a millionaire tax fraudster condemning a shoplifter who stole food to feed her family.

How is it possible to teach children that they should obey the law, that killing is morally wrong and that war is a crime against humanity, when the very people who make the laws have, in the opinion of many lawyers, committed this crime?

Those who assert the basic and fundamental importance of the rule of law must apply that rule as much to the rapist as to the tax evader, the arms trader and the government which carries out war crimes.

For example, if one were to tell an intelligent six-year old that killing is morally wrong, how does one react if the child's response is that some political leaders have never been prosecuted, or even investigated, for waging an illegal war? Should the reply be that politicians are exempt from the normal rules of criminal law and from generally accepted ethical principles?

How can we lecture young people who make their neighbours' lives a misery when our leaders have avoided prosecution for mass murder? The war-wagers have devalued and corrupted concepts of criminal law and morality. Thou shalt not kill except when it is in your own interests and when you are confident that you will never be prosecuted for it.

We now appear to be in the position where the most vicious criminals, for example rapists and the extremely violent, having been convicted and sentenced to long prison sentences, can say with some justification that their crimes are not that serious after all – at least, they have never burnt children alive. And those who have committed the worst crimes are unlikely ever to stand trial. This twists, debases and warps any concept of justice.

The Iraq War: the role of the lawyer

Faced with the reality of an illegal and disastrous war, the lawyer is on the sidelines. The best that can be done is to persist in stating the opinion that the state has acted, and continues to act, in breach of its own legality.

Most lawyers believe that the rule of law was ignored before, during and after the invasion of Iraq. The consequence of this is that lawyers can help to prevent the state persuading people that the Iraq War is yesterday's news, best forgotten, and that normal business should be carried on.

The horrors of the Iraq War dwarf all academic arguments about the nature of law and lawyers. The reality of children maimed and burned alive, whatever the theoretical political and/or legal justification, puts all other concerns in the shade. The ***legality*** of the Iraq war may be a minor consideration compared with its moral and political implications, but for lawyers it should remain a central issue. Monbiot takes the view that the legality of the invasion of Iraq is of central importance, because if it was illegal, then those responsible for it are mass murderers. The seriousness of these allegations, and their potentially devastating consequences, are not generally recognised.

Lawyers with an awareness of the War's illegality, regardless of the wider political and ethical issues, have a professional duty to ensure that it is not business as usual. They should make the point, repeatedly, that most legally qualified people believe that the War was illegal.
The Iraq War continues to override all other current issues. The state desperately seeks closure. Those of us who have opposed the War from its start, who have unsuccessfully used all peaceful and democratic methods to stop it, still have one weapon and one continuing duty. We can and should do our best to make sure that it is not relegated to one short paragraph on the inner pages of the national press. We can try to keep it in the forefront of the national consciousness.

Why is the Iraq War, and its aftermath, so important for English law and lawyers?

1. Although arguments have been put forward by some members of the British government for the legality of the War, it is absolutely clear that most expert opinion (that of the great majority of academic and practising lawyers) is that the war was illegal under international law. This is the narrow, legalistic approach to the significance of the War.

2. War is the single most important act that a government can undertake and one with the most terrible of consequences.

3. In a broader sense, the actions of the UK government in attacking Iraq, and the subsequent conduct of the War, can be seen to have resulted in a significant and possibly irreversible warping and twisting of the relationship between law and morality. The unimaginable horrors unleashed by the war have changed the perspective for viewing serious crimes committed by individuals. The state can no longer argue that it occupies the moral high ground.

4. If English law is impotent in the face of an illegal war, then its whole moral basis becomes questionable.

5. English prosecuting authorities appear to be preoccupied with the relative trivia (when compared to alleged war crimes) of administrative reform, victim support and transparency. It seems that they have failed to address the war crimes issue.

6. We are now (2014) in the astonishing position where the national press openly and regularly accuses the former Prime Minister of the United Kingdom of war crimes. One of these accusations stated that Blair has the distinction of being one of the two greatest mass murderers on earth. These allegations are so serious that they should dominate the agenda for any discussion on the role of English law and lawyers.
7. This leads on to the point that those responsible for waging the War are guilty of criminal acts. Although it may be unrealistic to press for the prosecution of such people, we can argue that the impunity with which they have carried out such crimes has the effect of slewing other criminality out of focus.
8. The issue of collective responsibility may also arise. This involves considering the possible criminal liability of those members of the government who supported the decision to invade Iraq. The criminal liability of Cabinet members and senior civil servants may need to be considered.
9. It has been stated that more human rights abuses have taken place in Iraq since the invasion than when Saddam Hussein was in power. There is evidence of the widespread use of torture by the US military.
10. The Iraq War is often described as being "controversial". This labelling of any issues as "controversial" is a device often used by politicians with the aim of blurring and distorting moral issues. The Iraq War is no more "controversial" than any other act of mass murder.

The details of specific areas of law, so complex that no-one can really understand them apart from lawyers who charge obscenely high fees, become simply irrelevant when compared with the scale of killing in what has been characterised as a colonial war. For example, the "proceeds of crime" has become a hugely detailed and complex topic in its own right. We are in a position where the amount of tobacco and alcohol which can be brought into the UK has generated a costly and impenetrable system of law and procedure. Most of the offenders under this system are small-time smugglers, but we are told that the rules are important because of "organised crime".

This poses the question of the identity of the organised criminals and what steps are taken to deal with the arms manufacturers, the senior military officers and the governments which bomb and kill?

The moral imperatives appear to have been reversed. We can no longer take "serious organised crime" seriously when those accused of truly serious organised crimes govern us and appear to be immune from the law. The Crown Prosecution Service has made no move against war criminals involved in the Iraq War.

CHAPTER 6

MYSTERY

Laws are like cobwebs, which may catch small flies, but let wasps and hornets break through.
(Jonathan Swift, A Critical Essay upon the Faculties of the Mind)

All of us know that there is no better way of exercising the imagination than the study of law. No poet has ever interpreted nature as freely as a lawyer interprets reality.
(Jean Girardoux, La Guerre de Troie n'aura pas lieu)

The have-his carcase, next to the perpetual motion, is vun of the blessedest things as has ever been made.
(Sam Weller, Pickwick Papers)

Reading a law book is like eating sawdust.
(Franz Kafka)

Many law books should be hailed as the finest cure for insomnia since opium was first extracted from the unripe seed head of papaver somniferum (the opium poppy).
Anon

To reach a conclusion on this matter involved the court in wading through a monstrous legislative morass, staggering from stone to stone and ignoring the marsh gas exhaling from the forest of schedules lining the way on each side. I regarded it at the time, I must confess, as

a Slough of Despond through which the court would never drag its feet but I have, by leaping from tussock to tussock as best I might, eventually, pale and exhausted, reached the other side.
(Harman LJ in *Davy v Leeds Corporation (1964)*)

It is too often suggested that the intelligibility of a statute to the general public is a prime consideration in drafting. I do not believe that this is so. I am firmly of the opinion that however we draft our statutes, the British public, except perhaps for the remote lunatic fringe, never read the statutes nor are likely to.
(First Parliamentary Draftsman for Scotland, 1986)

This Chapter attempts to unravel the mysteries of English law. It sets out a list of words and phrases in common use by lawyers which form a sort of secret code. The Chapter considers the reasons for obscure legal language, discusses legal Latin and sets out examples of clarity in the law. Examples of extreme mystery are also considered. Aspects of employment law are analysed in detail as illustrations of unnecessary mystification. Recent examples of judicial comments on demystification are set out.

In August 2010 research published by Public Legal Education Network reported the following:

- 65 per cent of UK citizens do not know their legal rights
- 70 per cent have no knowledge of basic legal processes.

Mystery jargon

The terminology of the profession can baffle those of us who qualified many years ago, so we can only wonder how it appears to non-lawyers. What, for example, do the following mean? How are they different from their non-legal meanings?

Actus reus
Bands
Bear Garden
Bench wig
Bencher
Black bag
Blue bag
Breeks
Bundle
Cab rank principle
Call
Case law
Chambers
Chambers tea
Civil action/proceedings
Client
Collarette
Counsel
Damages
Devil
Discovery
Entail
Eructation
Ex parte
Full bottomed wig
Green bag
Guinea
Habeas corpus
In camera
Inner Temple
Inns of Court
Junior
Junior QC
Ladies' collar
Libel
Lightweight pincetta gown
Lord
Master
Master of the Rolls
Mens rea
Middle Temple
Neckband shirt
Novus actus interveniens
Ogden Tables
Party
Pecunia non olet
Perpetuities
Practice
Pro bono
Pro hac vice
Punter
Pupil

Pupilmaster
Quantum
Quantum meruit
Queen's Counsel
Red bag
Refreshers
Res ipsa loquitur
Rogue and vagabond
Royal Bencher
Senior barrister
Senior junior
Senior QC
Silk
Table/Tabling
Temple
Tenant in tail
Tippet
Touting
Treasury Devil
Trousering
Tunic shirt
Vest, vesting

Answers are given in the Glossary at the end of this book.

The language of the law

For those of us who often find the language of the law incomprehensible, it is worth noting the comments of Jeremy Bentham in the early nineteenth century. Bentham, a campaigner for the demystification of English law, made the following points:

- Laws are expressions of the will of the human lawgiver. This is disguised by the fact that many laws are not expressed in imperative language.
- The use by lawyers of language so complex and different from normal use serves three purposes:
  (1) It forms a bond among legal professionals, setting them apart from society and reinforcing their complacency and resistance to reform;
  (2) it increases their fees;
  (3) it creates an atmosphere of awe.

- Lawyers' instruments of mystification are devices used to make judges and lawyers appear more than life-size. The use of formal methods of address, robes and traditional apparatus obscures the fact that lawyers and judges are all mere human beings.

In 1973 Hart, writing on Bentham and demystification in the Modern Law Review, commented that the words "mystification" and "demystification" had recently appeared in the literature of the radical New Left. Hart points out that the idea that harmful social institutions are protected by a veil of mystery is not new and was most thoroughly examined by Bentham.
The complexity and obscurity of legal language can form a barrier between articulate non-lawyers and the content of law which affects everyday life. Bentham's analysis of the reasons for this mystification is as relevant today as they were almost two hundred years ago.

Francis Bennion is reported to have commented in the Times, in 1995, that it might be positively dangerous to encourage non-lawyers to think they can understand legal texts unaided by expert advice. Unexplained terms of art and references in legal texts could not be fully understood by non-experts in law, any more than medical language could be fully understood by non-experts in medicine.
In response to this view, it could be argued that competent doctors do their best to explain to patients exactly what their problems are, in understandable English. And doctors are paid by the state, not by their patients. Their patients do not have to rely on charitable handouts from professionals with time on their hands.

It has also been commented that the moral and professional duty of the highly-educated, highly-trained lawyer should be to interpret and explain the law to those without legal training who need to know, in plain English, the meaning of laws and legal procedures which affect their everyday lives.

Lord Bingham makes the point that accessibility of law is an aspect of the rule of law. Law must be accessible and, so far as possible, intelligible, clear and predictable. Citizens are entitled to know the extent of their legal rights and obligations. The rule of law requires that the rules laid down should be clear. The traditional practice of British parliamentary draftsmen depends very heavily on cross-referencing between provisions in a number of different Acts and statutory instruments. This often results in a long paper chase for those who need to know the law. In many cases, even the courts are unable to find out what the law is.

An American attorney has commented as follows:

- *The lawyer as priest: the acceptance by lawyers of their role as interpreters of the dogma and the rituals of the law. On one side of this contradiction is the law's insistence on the isolation of its subject. Kafka, Camus and Dylan have written about the alienation suffered by the criminal defendant. Others have described the hopelessness felt by those who come into contact with the law. The lawyer actively acquiesces in this system by making his clients feel that only he, the lawyer-priest, can adequately understand the law, and only he can lead them safely through its tangle.*

- *The judiciary is an integral part of the enslavement drama and requires some attention. With its robes, enforced deference, demanded linguistic superiority and unintelligible jargon, the judiciary cloaks the bases of law, the realities of equity, in myths of fairness. The show never stops. The armour of mystification creates and supports the values of hierarchy and authority and the interests of rulers.*
- *The power of the lawyer-haves is partly maintained by the use of jargon, symbols and procedures which are aimed at being mysterious. The mystery of jargon is a powerful means of preserving privilege and excluding those who are not in the know.*

It can be argued that English law has been made deliberately complex and obscure with the aim of preserving the 'us-and-them' gap between lawyers as insiders and non-lawyers as outsiders. Further, some legal language is incomprehensible even to most lawyers and its secrets are known only to a small group of elite insiders. This area of mystification involves the most highly-paid of all lawyers – tax practitioners. The laws which govern the collection of money for use by the state are some of the most abstruse of all laws. A recently published book dealing with tax law has been proudly hailed by the publisher as the longest law book ever.

The point needs to be made that people who are not trained lawyers have the right to know exactly what laws control their lives. Any literate person (and the right to literacy can be characterised as a human right) should be able to know the law. This demand was put forward by the Levellers in the seventeenth century and is discussed further in Chapter 3 (Dissent).

Legal Latin

Customs and Excise Commissioners v Polok and Another (2002)

P and others ran an escort agency. The Customs and Excise Commissioners stated that they should be registered for value added tax. A tribunal ruled that they were not registrable because their business activities were unlawful, consisting of the procurement of women for the purposes of prostitution.
On appeal, Mr Justice Jacob allowed the appeal and ruled that the supply of escorts was lawful. The activities of the escorts and their customers were separate from the service of the taxpayers.
As the Latin poet (Vespasian -Titus Flavius Vespasianus – Roman Emperor from AD 69) said, *pecunia non olet* (money doesn't smell). The principle of fiscal neutrality prevents any general distinction in the levying of VAT as between lawful and unlawful transactions. The mere fact that conduct amounts to an offence is not sufficient to justify exemption from VAT.

English law is littered with Latin words and phrases. Many of these survive from the middle ages. Latin was the language for official documents and a number of Latin expressions were created by medieval lawyers. In 1730 an Act was passed which abolished legal Latin.

Two years later this was repealed and legal Latin has remained with us ever since.

Examples of often-used Latin words and phrases include:

Et cetera: and the rest

Bona fide: good faith

Ex parte: on behalf of

Mens rea: guilty mind

Nemo dat quod non habet: No-one can give what he does not have

Quantum meruit: as much as has been earned

Causa causans: A judicial statement of 1940 made the following points:

> Counsel has strenuously contended that the master's action was *novus actus interveniens*, which broke the nexus or chain of causation, and reduced the unseaworthiness from *causa causans* to *causa sine qua non*. I cannot help deprecating the use of Latin or so-called Latin phrases in this way. They only distract the mind from the true problem, which is to apply the principles of English law to the realities of the case.

Another example is land law, which has its origins in the feudal system. Student land law textbooks continue to quote "bad" Latin maxims, for example:

Cuius est solum eius est usque ad coelum et ad infero

Quicquid plantatur solo, solo cedit

Durante minore aetate.

The use of legal Latin has been the object of sustained judicial criticism. Examples of this in the context of health and safety are the concepts of *res ipsa loquitur* and *volenti non fit injuria.*

Res ipsa loquitur (the thing speaks for itself) is a rule of evidence which may lead to liability for negligence without further evidence.

For example, in the case of *Fryer v Pearson (2000)* F, a gas fitter, was working at P's house. As he knelt on the floor, the point of a needle buried in a deep-pile carpet pierced his knee. He claimed compensation from P. It was argued on his behalf that *res ipsa loquitur* applied, that the incident spoke for itself, and that he therefore did not have to prove negligence. His claim was dismissed. The court ruled that this had been a freak, unfortunate accident. Lord Justice May commented that people should stop using maxims or doctrines dressed up in Latin, such as *res ipsa loquitur,* which are not readily comprehensible to those for whose benefit they are supposed to exist.

Volenti non fit injuria (the consent to the doing of a harmful act will prevent the recovery of compensation for damage resulting from the harmful act) is reputedly a principle which dates back to Aristotle. An example of its application in the context of health and safety is the case of *ICI v Shatwell (1965).* Two brothers were employed in a quarry as certified shot-firers. They agreed to ignore their employers' orders and safety regulations when preparing for blasting. This resulted in one of the brothers being injured in an explosion. He claimed compensation from the employers. The House of Lords ruled that *volenti non fit injuria* applied. The employers were not liable.

This was the high water mark of the application of the doctrine in employment cases. For two centuries, the doctrine was repeatedly applied in relation to injuries suffered by manual workers. The courts ruled that knowledge of a risk in employment inferred consent to that risk. The doctrine is no longer applied in the context of health and safety.

Mens rea and actus reus

In relation to criminal liability (including health and safety offences) crimes are traditionally divided into *mens rea* (the guilty mind) and *actus reus* (broadly, the action forbidden by the law). Despite judicial criticism of this use of bad Latin, the phrases continue to be of crucial significance for the criminal law. The general rule is that the prosecution must prove both *actus reus* and *mens rea.*

All current criminal law textbooks analyse crimes according to these concepts.

Lord Diplock commented that it would be conducive to clarity of analysis of the ingredients of a crime if we were to avoid bad Latin and instead to think and speak about the conduct of the accused and his state of mind at the time of that conduct, instead of speaking of *actus reus* and *mens rea*.

It is always tempting for lawyers with some knowledge of legal Latin to slip an obscure phrase into their documentation with the aim of confusing or intimidating the other side. This practice is now strongly discouraged by some judges. For example, in *Williams v J. Walter Thompson Group Ltd (2005)*, the Court of Appeal stated that the use by an employment tribunal of breaking down a long decision into numbered paragraphs, using small roman numerals running up to lxxiii, was not the most user-friendly method available.

The use of legal Latin can also be seen as a manifestation of intellectual laziness, for example the continued description of charitable legal work as "pro bono". This is discussed in more detail in Chapter 1 (Money).

In my experience, in the council estates of South Wales, little else but the perpetuity rule is the topic of conversation.

In Liswerry in 1951 we liked nothing better than to sit before the fireside and discuss, over a glass of dry sherry and a charcoal biscuit, the implications of *novus actus interveniens.*

I well remember in Liswerry in 1950 how I used to pop next door to number cxxii to borrow a cup of sweet Sauternes, or how I cheered when Newport County won iii to i.

My father worked the night shift in the aluminium works from x to vi. *Actus non facit reum nisi mens sit rea,* my father would cheerily remark when he came off the night shift reeking of sweat and machine oil.

Alienatio rei preferatur juri accrescendi, my grandmother would quip as she bandaged up her varicose ulcer before setting off to work as a cleaner.

An even more extreme example of the use of ancient Classical languages in modern English law is a recently published law book which breaks its paragraphs down into Arabic, Roman and ancient Greek numerals. Everyone understands Arabic numerals, some people understand Roman numerals, but very few can translate ancient Greek except, possibly, those readers who have had the benefits of a public school education.

Court dress

Practice Direction (Court Dress) (No. 5): from October 1, 2008, judges in civil cases would wear a new civil robe, without a wig, and would be distinguishable by different coloured tabs.

The Direction includes the following: circuit judges would wear their existing gown and lilac tippet without a wig, or bands, wing collar or collarette.

Counsel will wear the following:

- In the Commercial Court and Admiralty Court: business suits
- In the Technology Court: business suits
- In the Family Division: business suits save for contested divorce/nullity petitions when court dress will be worn
- In the Administrative Court: court dress
- In the Queen's Bench Division: court dress for trials and business suits on all other occasions
- In the county court: business suits for applications and court dress for trials
- Before Masters, Registrars and District Judges: business suits
- In any case where the liberty of the subject is in issue: court dress (except the magistrates' court and Crown Court bail applications held in Chambers).

The profession indicated its strong preference for the maintenance of the prevailing position.

Those who argue in favour of separate court dress for advocates – wig, gown and bands - must deal with the fact that there are no dress requirements in the employment tribunal or the Employment Appeal Tribunal (EAT). Can they seriously argue that the quality of justice in these tribunals is somehow diminished by the fact that lawyers wear normal clothes? How many miscarriages of justice have been reported from employment tribunals? These tribunals and the EAT deal with complex and arcane points of law, procedure and evidence. They can, in some cases, award millions of pounds in compensation. Can it really be argued that these legal discussions, or the quality of justice dispensed, are devalued because the advocates have no horsehair on their heads?

Lord Gifford argued in 1986 that wigs and gowns should no longer be worn. In his opinion, the wig and gown are intended to convey a message: that we, judges and barristers, are different and superior; that we have more in common with each other than with you, the litigants; that we practise a craft which you can never understand.
It may be of interest to note a recent case where an impostor barrister was unmasked by a judge who noticed that he was wearing a solicitor's, rather than a barrister's gown. It was not reported whether the quality of his advocacy was affected by this lack of dress sense.

An English barrister has commented that many of those

who appear in the courts on a daily basis, who enjoy the dressing up and the eighteenth-century formality so much that they are prepared to put up with the bullying and the poor pay for criminal work, have a crucial interest in preserving the mysteries and myths of advocacy. The reality is that any articulate, literate and determined person can do at least as good a job as a supposedly trained advocate. In many cases, non-lawyers actually have advantages because, if they are up against trained advocates, judges may interpret the rules to help them. Courts and tribunals may also make allowances for their lack of detailed knowledge of evidence and procedure. The McLibel case operates as a template for alternative lawyers and as an inspiration to non-lawyers preparing their own cases. (See McLibel documentation: Chapter 3 - Dissent).

The Bear Garden

The index to the Civil Court Practice contains the following entry: "Bear Garden" lists.

The entry refers to the Queen's Bench Guide 2000, paragraph 6.3: Listing before Masters.

The Masters' lists consist of:

The ordinary list – short applications in Rooms E102 and E110 ("the Bear Garden lists"). Masters will sit each day at 10.30 a.m. in the Bear Garden to hear applications in the Bear Garden lists.

Masters deal with interim and some pre-action applications and manage the claims so that they proceed without delay. Short hearings only take place in the Bear Garden.

What is this mysterious place?

The apparent origin of this phrase in the legal context can be found in evidence given to the Common Law Procedure Commission in 1831 by Thomas Lott, an attorney:

The rule office on the first day of term is a perfect bear garden and where there has been a great pressure of business, and those dirty little holes, the judges' chambers, much crowded, I have seen oaths administered through the window to deponents in the courtyard, and persons excepting to bail compelled to make their exit through a back window rather than encounter the crowd.

Dickens refers to Judges' Chambers, then situate in the Rolls Gardens, and vulgarly known as the "Bear Garden"

The Oxford English Dictionary defines a bear garden as a place set apart for the baiting of bears, a scene of strife and tumult.

The position appears to be that unrepresented claimants appearing before Masters in the Queen's Bench Division are consigned to a Bear Garden. The origin of this may be the chaotic nature of the place. In any event, how can it be acceptable to name a suite of rooms on the Royal Courts of Justice after a cruel and illegal practice? Perhaps it might be renamed "The Cockpit"?

The Bear Garden is clearly signposted in the Royal Courts of Justice. One might, unrealistically, expect some element of suppressed guilt, or at the least embarrassment, at this label. But no, there is a proud boast of this continued use of early Victorian metaphor based on a viciously cruel baiting of animals.

The Bear Garden is a suite of rooms and antechambers, richly carpeted and decorated, at the far reaches of the Gothic temple known as the Law Courts in the Strand.

Examples of incomprehensible legal language

This is an easy target. It is probably easier to find examples of incomprehensible language in statutes than to discover examples of clarity.

Rent Act 1974, Schedule 2, paragraph 4:

"In any case where (a) a tenancy which, by virtue of only section 5A of this Act, was precluded from being a protected tenancy, and (b) before it became a protected tenancy was registered for the dwelling concerned under Part VI of this Act, the document which is so registered shall be deemed to be registered under Part VI of this Act as the rent for the dwelling-house which is let on that tenancy, and that registration shall be deemed to take effect on the day the tenancy becomes a protected tenancy".

The rule against perpetuities

This is a sort of mental torture for law students and a means of generating income for practitioners. It is one of many areas of impenetrable law with no relevance for the propertyless.

Thomas W. Hopes, in his authoritative book on perpetuities, states that he has never acquired the faculty of brief and concise statement. He has certainly acquired the faculty of understatement. Hopes states that the perpetuity rule can be split into 32 separate rules, for example:

1. Any provision restraining a tenant in tail from barring the entail or limitations thereto is void.
2. A life estate to an unborn person or to a person who may be unborn will not if it vests support a contingent remainder.
3. Any future executory interest legal or equitable or equitable contingent remainder whose vesting in interest is subject to a condition precedent which will not necessarily happen within a life or lives in being and twenty-one years is void.
4. The general rule is that no interest in property is good unless it must vest, if at all, not later than 21 years after some life in being at the creation of the interest, allowance being made for gestation only when it actually exists.

Immediate questions:

- What is a tenant in tail?
- What is an entail?
- What is a vest?
- What is an equitable contingent remainder?

This Victorian conveyancing language is so far removed from normal English that it might as well be Martian.

These rules are of no interest or significance to anyone who is not a property owner.

They exist as a sort of deliberately impenetrable code, designed to mystify property rights for the material benefit of lawyers.

Section 78(1) Law of Property Act 1925:

"A covenant relating to any land of the covenantee shall be deemed to be made with the covenantee and his successors in title and the persons deriving title under him or them, and shall have effect as if such successors and other persons were expressed. For the purposes of this subsection in connection with covenants restrictive of the user of land 'successors in title' shall be deemed to include the owners and occupiers for the time being of the land of the covenantee intended to be benefited".

What does this mean? Does anyone know? What is certain is that a conveyancing solicitor will charge at least £200 an hour to deal with it.

Disability discrimination

The Disability Discrimination Act (DDA) is a good example of the modern mystification of a new area of law. The aim of the Act (now replaced with minor amendments by the Equality Act 2010) appears, at first sight, to be useful. It is a clear example of good, useful law in that its purpose is to protect the weak and vulnerable. But I defy you to find a lawyer who can tell you, off the top of his head, which sections of the Act were ever in force. Then we come on to the contents of the Act, which were so opaque and convoluted that non-lawyers and lawyers alike had extreme, almost insuperable, difficulty in grasping their meaning.

There are an estimated 6.5 million people in the United Kingdom who may come within the meaning of "disabled". There is evidence of widespread discrimination against such people. If ever there was a need for a clear set of rules, it is in the context of protecting the rights of the disabled.

A disabled person who took the view that he or she had been discriminated against, and who sought to discover what the law was, faced a study of at least the following sources:

- The body of the Disability Discrimination Act 1995.
- Complex rules set out in the Schedules to the Act.
- Disability Discrimination (Employment) Regulations 1996.
- Disability Discrimination (Meaning of Disability) Regulations 1996.
- Disability Discrimination (Exemption for Small Employers) Order 1998.
- A mass of commencement orders which stated the date at which different parts of the Act came into force.
- A Code of Practice issued by the Department of Education and Employment.
- Guidance on matters to be taken into account in determining questions relating to the definition of disability.
- An increasing body of case law.

Thus a ten-year old body of law became fragmented and less and less accessible to disabled people. The parliamentary draftspersons responsible for the DDA created what can only be described as a monster - a set of rules which placed access to the law outside the reach of non-legally qualified disabled persons.

The result of an overview of disability discrimination law is the depressing conclusion that it is not realistic for disabled persons who are not lawyers to bring their own proceedings. Even highly-trained lawyers find the law difficult to grasp. A totally new area of law which should have provided a rare opportunity to demystify the rules has been wasted. The meaning of "disability" should not be a complex matter of law.

In a recent case, *O'Hanlon v Commissioners for HM Revenue & Customs (2007)* (a complex case dealing with the application of "reasonable adjustment" principles), Lord Justice Sedley said that the DDA in its amended form is not at all easy to follow. This is a particular misfortune in an Act which it ought to be possible for employees and managers to read, understand and implement without legal advice or litigation.

Harvey on Industrial Relations and Employment Law, the six-volume looseleaf leading text on employment law, has 50 pages of closely printed, closely argued text in Volume 2, in a section headed "People with disabilities".

The editors of Harvey refer to "subtle and obscure legal difficulties" and describe the DDA legislation as an unusually complex piece of legislation which poses novel questions of interpretation.

A proper understanding of the DDA, according to the editors of Harvey, requires a close study of its structure and technical detail. A commonsense approach is simply not sufficient and, in many cases, is likely to be positively dangerous if taken as a guide to proper behaviour.

For example, it is not necessary to show that in a case when what is in issue is not direct discrimination but disability-related discrimination, that there is a comparator whose relevant circumstances are the same,

or materially different.
The terminology of the disability discrimination legislation must be understood as having a variety of shades of meaning, for example “long-term”, “substantial” and “normal”.
Case law interpreting the legislation has added complexity. There are many EAT and Court of Appeal decisions of great complexity, for example those dealing with the concepts of reasonable adjustment and justification.
The incomprehensibility of disability discrimination law may itself be seen as a form of discrimination against the disabled.
The Equality Act 2010, which has been described by its proponents as a codification of the whole of English discrimination law, has not improved the accessibility of disability discrimination law. An opportunity to demystify the rules governing the position of some of the most vulnerable and deprived members of society has been lost.
Disabled persons who are non-lawyers, for whose protection the law of disability discrimination exists, are effectively prevented from understanding the rules. They are obliged to seek legal advice, often at ruinous cost, in order to understand their rights.

Employment Tribunal procedure

In 2014, the employment tribunal has the same basic structure as its predecessors (the industrial tribunal and the National Industrial Relations Court).
The Report of the Donovan Commission in 1968 stated that the aim of the industrial tribunal should be to make

available an easily accessible, informal, speedy and inexpensive means of resolving employment disputes. Increased legalism, which has inevitably accompanied the expanding role of lawyers in the employment tribunal, is difficult to reconcile with the expressed expectation that employment tribunal hearings have always been suitable for self-representation or assistance by non-lawyers including trade union officials, members of employers' associations or advice workers.

Current problems with Employment Tribunal applications

- Fees. From April 2014, the following fees have been introduced:
  For a Type A claim (for example, unpaid wages): £160 to lodge an application and £230 for a hearing.
  For Type B claims (for example, unfair dismissal): £250 to lodge an application and £950 for a hearing.
  Remission of these fees, though available, has rarely been granted.
- Additional cost. Solicitors charge at least £150 per hour. Cheap or free advice may be available from trade unions, advice centres, the Free Representation Unit or the Bar Pro Bono Unit. This raises the question of why the enforceability of employment rights should depend on charitable initiatives.
- Unbalanced or unequal hearings where one party (normally the employer) is represented whereas the other party is not.
- Efforts by lawyers to characterise employment tribunals as courts, for example the publication of the "Employment Court Practice", an attempt to create a

parallel to the Civil Procedure Rules and to characterise the employment tribunal as a court. There is, in reality, no such creature as an employment court. A judicial view of these efforts to assimilate employment tribunals into the civil procedure system was stated in *Neary v Governing Body of St Albans Girls' School and Another (2009)*, where Lady Justice Smith made the following points:

- Parliament deliberately did not incorporate Rule 3.9(1) of the Civil Procedure Rules into employment tribunal practice when it chose to incorporate the overriding objective.
- Employment tribunal proceedings were intended to be as short, simple and informal as possible. High Court and county court practice accordingly differed from that of employment tribunals.
- An over-rigid approach was not required when an employment tribunal was considering an application.
- We all know that that intention has not been fulfilled and that employment law and practice have become difficult and complex.

- The complexity of substantive employment law. It is difficult for full-time employment lawyers to keep abreast of the flow of statutes, regulations, cases and European materials which have swelled employment law to fill an expensive five-volume loose leaf encyclopaedia. Significant reported cases are currently running as at least four or five a week. This volume of legal development makes it almost impossible for non-lawyers, without access to source material, to keep abreast of changes, some of which may have crucial implications for their claims.

Employment law statutes have become more and more complex. For example, section 33(2) of the Employment Relations Act 1999 states the following:

> "In s.117(3)(b) of the Employment Rights Act 1996 (amount of additional award) for 'the appropriate amount' there shall be substituted 'an amount not less than 26 nor more than 52 weeks' pay, and subsections (5) and (6) of s117 shall cease to have effect."

Anyone looking at this section, which is part of a statute aimed at protecting the rights of employees, has to refer backwards to the 1996 Act and forwards to the 1999 Act in order to make any sense at all of the wording. And this is merely a first hurdle: section 33(2) did not come into force until October 25, 1999. The subtleties of commencement orders, which may give Parliamentary draftspersons great intellectual satisfaction, cause almost insuperable difficulties for lawyers and non-lawyers alike. Even the most articulate and well-informed claimant faces great difficulty in finding out exactly what the current law says.

The role of the employment tribunal as a cheap, quick and informal means of settling employment disputes looks set to become a footnote in employment law textbooks. Political pressure to reduce the number of applications appears to have fundamentally changed the ethos of the tribunal. By imposing fees for applications and hearings, the government has created a financial hurdle in addition to a substantive one. Not only does this fly in the face of the original aims of the tribunal, it undermines the rule of law. Employment tribunal claims are reported to have fallen by 80 per cent.

Employment tribunals remain, marginally, a maverick element of English legal system. Despite desperate and calculated efforts by lawyers to bring them into the mainstream, they continue to retain residual elements of the tribunal rather than the court, with the aim of providing a quick and cheap resolution of employment disputes.

It is not clear for how much longer this can continue. At present there is no dress code, no advocacy monopoly and relative informality.

Employment law

In the context of general employment law the rules have become so detailed, complex and obscure that non-lawyers have little chance of understanding them.

Suffolk Mental Health Partnership NHS Trust v Hunt and Others (2009)

This case involved the level of detail which should be included in a written grievance relating to an equal pay claim.

Lord Justice Pill made the following comment:

- The encouragement of negotiation, conciliation and settlement might be frustrated if the grievance procedure led to satellite litigation on technical issues about whether a statement amounted to a grievance.

Lord Justice Wall added the following:

- Employment-related issues which were designed to be simple and understood by ordinary working people had become overlaid with degrees of sophisticated argument which at times render them unrecognisable.
- Employment tribunals were set up as *fora* in which ordinary working men and women could bring claims which they had been unable to resolve in the workplace with a view to swift and straightforward resolution. To this end, the rules relating to representation were very relaxed, case management powers are wide and costs were only to be awarded in extreme circumstances.
- His experience was that these essentially worthy aims were in grave danger of being frustrated by over-elaborate and sophisticated argument unintelligible to the layman.
- His layman's plea was that there should be a return to the clear intentions underlying the establishment of the employment tribunal system; that lawyers should strive for clarity and simplicity and that unions and employers should strive to make the system work in the interests of ordinary working people.

Fixed-term employment contracts

Some employers have tried to get round the rule that employees have to work for two years before being able to complain of unfair dismissal by employing them on a series of fixed-term contracts, often for 364 days at a time.

It was recognised that something should be done about this attempted evasion of employment protection law. What eventually emerged was the familiar result - a scheme of such obscurity and complexity that no-one without access to a law library could possibly understand it. This has caused real hardship to those who try to assert their employment rights.

The lawmakers (and, no doubt the parliamentary draftspersons) tried to deal with the issue by the use of procedural requirements and fictions. These are so far removed from the realities of people's day-to-day working lives that they achieve a kind of abstract, illusory fascination comparable to a hard-fought game of chess. One aspect of this is that a person whose fixed-term contract comes to an end is deemed to have been "dismissed". This immediately imposes a legal fiction upon a crucial everyday reality. The employee has not been "dismissed" or sacked, as most workers would say. She will certainly not tell future prospective employers that she was dismissed, but rather that her fixed-term contract expired.

If employers are using fixed-term contracts to avoid legal protection for their employees, there are two simple ways of dealing with this which everyone could understand:

1. Make fixed-term contracts unlawful.
2. Give employees the right to complain of unfair dismissal as soon as they start work.

Employment Act 2002 (Dispute Resolution) Regulations 2004

Regulation 13: Extension of time limits

"(1) Where a complaint is presented to an employment tribunal under a jurisdiction listed in Schedule 3 or 4 and

(a) either of the dismissal and disciplinary procedures is the applicable statutory procedure and the circumstances specified in paragraph (2) apply; or
(b) either of the grievance procedures is the applicable statutory procedure and the circumstances specified in paragraph (3) apply;

the normal time limit for presenting the complaint is extended for a period of three months beginning with the day after the day on which it would otherwise have expired ....

(3) The circumstances referred to in paragraph (1) (b) are that the employee presents a complaint to a tribunal –

(a) within the normal time limit for presenting the complaint but in circumstances in which section 32(2) or (3) of the 2002 Act does not permit him to do so; or
(b) after the expiry of the normal time limit for presenting the complaint, having complied with paragraph 6 or 9 of Schedule 2 in relation to his grievance within that normal time limit ..."

This is very difficult for experienced employment lawyers to understand, and needs access to statutory source material. For even the most determined, articulate and highly-educated non-lawyer, it is impenetrable. This sort of convoluted draftsmanship takes employment law even further away from the grasp of wronged employees and into the control of professional specialists.

The aim of these Regulations was to reduce the number of applications to the employment tribunal by encouraging the resolution of disputes before tribunal proceedings were started. It was, essentially, a cost-cutting exercise.

This was done in such a clumsy, obscure and legalistic way that the system was unworkable. It created more work for lawyers and moved employment law even further away from workers. The scheme has been described as disastrous and scandalous by many employment lawyers. It has now, thankfully, been scrapped but has left complex transitional provisions.

In one case, for example, an employee of a small charity lodged a grievance on a CD, comprising 500 pages of detailed complaints. This came within the definition of "grievance" for the purposes of the dispute resolution regulations (there was no definition) and the cumbersome and obscure machinery of the Regulations swung into place.

Examples of clarity: Health and safety law

The law of health and safety is in general, fortunately, relatively easy to understand and is set out in normal language which is accessible to the averagely intelligent person. The main statute, the Health and Safety at Work, etc., Act 1974, was passed as a result of the deliberations of the Robens Committee which expressly set out to codify and simplify a mass of obscure regulations.

The main provisions of the Act – sections 2 and 3 – are clear in comparison with many other statutes outside the field of health and safety. In summary, the Act of 1974 makes it an offence to fail to ensure the health and safety of employees and non-employees.

Despite this clarity, health and safety professionals, and employees who have suffered injury and disease because of workplace conditions, or the dependants of deceased workers, may be only too well aware that many of the cases which interpret statutes and regulations in the health and safety field have complicated the rules so that only trained and experienced lawyers can attempt to understand them.

This complexity and obscurity is wholly unnecessary. In relation to health and safety case law, examples of cases which deal with a complex legal issue in clear English are as follows:

Fytche v Wincanton Logistics plc (2004)

F was employed as a driver of an articulated bulk tanker collecting milk from farms. He was supplied with steel-capped safety boots to protect his feet against injury from heavy objects. During a night of very cold weather his vehicle became stuck in snow. F spent several hours digging it free. He did not know that there was a hole in one of his boots and he suffered frostbite in his toe. He claimed compensation from his employer on the basis of a breach of the Personal Protective Equipment at Work Regulations 1992. The issue in the case was whether the employers could be liable for a risk other than that for which the equipment had been issued.

The majority decision of the House of Lords was that the 1992 Regulations required employers to provide equipment suitable to protect employees against an identified risk, and that the boots had been in efficient working order and good repair for the purpose of protecting against the assessed risk. The employers were not liable.

Baroness Hale disagreed. Her judgment is generally regarded as a model of judicial analysis and clarity, and included the following:

- The 1992 Regulations were part of the "six-pack" made in response to the EU's Framework Directive. The aim of the Directive was to improve the protection of employees' health and safety.
- The overall strategy was that prevention is better than cure.
- Many of the duties imposed by the Regulations were strict in the sense that they might be broken without any negligence or other fault.
- In this case, "personal protective equipment" was the whole boot, not just the steel toe cap.
- The whole boot had to be kept in good repair.
- A boot with a hole in it is not in good repair.
- The employer rather than the employee should bear the risk that boots supplied for a particular reason turn out to have an incidental effect which causes an employee injury at work.
- There are good policy reasons for imposing strict liability on employers for many of the injuries which their employees suffer at work.
- The overall object of the legislation is to protect the health and safety of workers. If this fails and they suffer injury, strict liability means that they are compensated for that injury without the need for slow and costly litigation.
- A non-lawyer would find it odd indeed that F would have recovered damages if his employer had thought that the boots should protect against a weather risk,

but does not recover compensation because the employer had a different risk in mind.

It is also worth noting that the judgment of Baroness Hale contains not one Latin word or phrase.

Hatton v Sutherland and Others (2002)

Baroness Hale also gave judgment in this, the leading case on workplace stress. Her judgment in that case extends to almost 30 pages of the report. Again, there are no Latin words or phrases at all in the judgment. The judgment examines and analyses psychiatric illness in general, defines and describes workplace stress and goes on to explain the relevant law. In general terms, literate non-lawyers can be advised to read the judgment if they want to find out about workplace stress. Such advice can rarely be given. Judicial analyses of cases involving complex facts and difficult areas of law do not need to be obscure and littered with incomprehensible Latin terminology.

The judgment in Hatton v Sutherland examines and analyses psychiatric illness in general, defines and describes workplace stress and goes on to explain the relevant law. This is divided into the following areas:

- Principles of negligence
- Foreseeability
- Breach of duty
- Causation
- Apportionment and quantification.

The judgment includes the following:

- The dividing line between a normal but unpleasant state of mind or emotion and a recognised psychiatric illness or disorder is not easy to draw.

- The employer is or should be aware of what is going on in his own factory, school or office.
- It is in everyone's interests that management should be encouraged to recognise the existence and causes of occupational stress and take sensible steps to minimise it within their organisation.
- Some things are no-one's fault.
- Liability in negligence depends upon three inter-related requirements: the existence of a duty to take care; a failure to take the care which can reasonably be expected in the circumstances; and damage suffered as a result of that failure.
- There are no special control mechanisms applying to claims for psychiatric or physical injury or illness arising from the stress of doing the work which the employee is required to do.
- Unless he knows of some particular problem or vulnerability, an employer is usually entitled to assume that his employee is up to the normal pressures of the job.
- An employer is generally entitled to take what he is told by his employee at face value, unless he has good reason to think to the contrary.
- The employer is only in breach of duty if he has failed to take the steps which are reasonable in the circumstances, bearing in mind the magnitude of the risk of harm occurring, the gravity of the harm which may occur, the costs and practicability of preventing it, and the justifications for running the risk.
- An employer who offers a confidential advice service, with referral to appropriate counselling or

treatment services, is unlikely to be found in breach of duty.

Demystification methods

Statutes and Regulations

Many of these can be simplified by breaking them down into their essential elements, with bullet points and explanations of key words and phrases. Some statutory material, however, is totally incomprehensible and impossible to explain, even for the most highly qualified and experienced specialists. The only way forward for these rules is abolition and replacement with clearly-drafted material.

Case law

Most case law can be summarised so that non-lawyers can relatively easily understand the facts and the decision. But arcane analyses of, for example, tax law, are virtually impossible for anyone to understand and might best be consigned to history along with the thousands of dusty volumes which line library shelves, which are only ever looked at by students researching the history of particularly obscure legal concepts and which contain endless, opaque pages upon pages of incomprehensible judicial deliberation.

In legal proceedings, the classes speak different languages. Even the most basic legal concepts can be misunderstood by those victims of the system unfortunate enough to have missed out on a legal education. For example, the following conversation was

recently overheard in an inner-city magistrates' court:
Justices' clerk - Do you plead guilty or not guilty?
Accused - I never done it.
Justices' clerk - Is that guilty or not guilty?
Accused - I never done it.
Justices' clerk - Is that guilty or not guilty?
Accused - Guilty.

Civil Procedure Rules

The legal establishment recognises an obligation to simplify legal rules. The overriding objective of the Civil Procedure Rules is to enable courts to deal with cases justly. This includes ensuring that the parties are on an equal footing and saving expense. Ensuring that the parties are on an equal footing should include an equal understanding of the law as it applies to their case. This should mean clarifying legal rules so that they can be understood by any reasonably-educated person.

European Convention on Human Rights

Article 2 of the European Convention on Human Rights states that everyone charged with a criminal offence has the right to be informed promptly, in a language which he understands and in detail, of the nature and cause of the accusation against him. An accused person has the right to understand the evidence and argument. He also has the right to the free assistance of an interpreter if he cannot understand or speak the language used in court. If these principles were to be applied generally, not only to criminal proceedings, this would be a significant move towards the demystification of English law.

Litigants in person

Most intelligent, reasonably articulate, literate and averagely educated people can make a start on legal proceedings themselves. They can draft letters of claim, fill out forms and prepare witness statements. But as court or tribunal proceedings roll along, they find themselves increasingly trapped in a fog of procedural technicalities. These technical rules are less complex than they used to be, but they remain hugely difficult to cope with, especially when the litigant in person is up against ruthless and experienced lawyers. As a judge is reported to have commented to an unrepresented claimant in an industrial injury case, you have plunged into the icy waters of English legal procedure.

Eructation

In *Ng v Director of Public Prosecutions (2007)*, Ng argued that an intoximeter reading had been affected by eructation, in common parlance belching. The High Court ruled that the presence of a driver's elevated mouth alcohol caused by eructation went directly to the commission of the offence and was capable of amounting to a special reason in relation to disqualification from driving.

Rogue and vagabond

In *JL (A Youth) v Director of Public Prosecutions (2007)*, a youth was convicted of being found in an enclosed yard for an unlawful purpose, contrary to section 4 of the Vagrancy Act 1824. The Court of

Appeal quashed the conviction and made the following points:

- Hiding from the police was not an unlawful purpose because it was not a criminal purpose. The case against the defendant was flimsy in the extreme.
- Section 4 was preventive in nature and was intended to prevent conduct escalating into mainstream criminal conduct. It should be resorted to with caution.
- The case's headnote states that an accused was deemed a rogue and vagabond where he had been discovered in an enclosed yard and had criminal conduct in mind.

The Mystery of the Gavel

A gavel is a small wooden mallet with a matching block. It can be bought from a specialist legal accessories dealer (made from Mexican rosewood). The gavel appears as a clichéd image on many law-related websites and quasi-legal advertisements. Like the scales of justice and the wig, the gavel image achieves meaninglessness and significance at the same time. It has no meaning because gavels are not used in English courts. Its contextual irrelevance is not the point. Its imagery, like the wig and the scales of justice, is an essential part of the mystique of English law.

The obscurity of law is unnecessary. From an academic and intellectual point of view, obscurity is useless. Obscurity is anti-intellectual. There are many examples of complex laws which can be understood by any reasonably educated person. The European Convention on Human Rights, for example, is easily understood. In a community governed by the rule of law, citizens must be able to find out, in their own language and from sources accessible to the general public, what the state expects of them.

Orwell's principles of good English could profitably be adopted by Parliamentary draftspersons, who do not need to be legally qualified, for example:

- Clear thinking
- Fearlessness
- Avoid dead metaphors
- Avoid foreign words
- What am I trying to say?
- What words will express it?
- What image or idiom will make it clearer?
- Is this a fresh image?
- Could I put it more shortly?
- Have I said anything avoidably ugly?
- Avoid familiar metaphors
- Avoid words which the averagely intelligent person cannot understand
- Use short words
- Use active not passive tense
- Exclude Latin
- Thoughts only have meaning if they are expressed in such a way that they can be understood
- Theory constructed in an obscure way is meaningless to readers and makes sense, if at all, only to the writer

- Bad writers are nearly always haunted by the notion that Latin and Greek words are grander than Saxon ones.

The use of incomprehensible language to express legal rules is not only wrong in terms of preventing people from understanding the law, but is, quite simply, bad English.

Parliamentary draftspersons need look no further than the Bible as an example of clear English.

The King James version of the Bible succeeded in its aim of making the text accessible to ordinary people. It clearly demonstrates that archaic language can be clearer than modern legal jargon. Compare, for example, the 21st Psalm with the employment dispute resolution regulations.

The linguistic impact of the King James Bible has given us, for example:

- A thorn in the flesh
- Beat swords into ploughshares
- The wages of sin is death
- The fly in the ointment
- Man does not live by bread alone
- Blessed are the peacemakers.

It has been commented that we are fortunate that the translation of the Bible in the seventeenth century was not entrusted to teams of parliamentary draftspersons. The King James Bible remains a model of clarity compared with current English disability discrimination law.

Some areas of law are of crucial significance to everyday life. Examples are family law, employment law, housing and welfare rights. These areas cry out for simplification. It is an affront to the intelligence that such key areas have to be interpreted by a priesthood. Mystery jargon is not a charming tradition to be preserved but deliberate obscurantism to maintain the privileges of rich lawyers.

CHAPTER 7

PRACTICE

No thinking person can but be embarrassed by the lack of provision by the state of the means for access to the courts. I have seen litigants and their families broken by the process and the cost of litigation. It is the duty, in particular, of the law and lawyers to avoid this scenario whenever possible.
(Mr Justice Lightman).

Washing one's hands of the conflict between the powerful and the powerless means to side with the powerful.
(Che Guevara).

There are currently approximately 100,000 solicitors and 15,000 barristers working in England and Wales. The former would fill Wembley Stadium and the latter would fit into a provincial rugby ground. These are truly frightening images.

This Chapter discusses current legal practice. It considers the advocacy monopoly and suggests methods of alternative practice. The Chapter examines the apparent contradictions between the public perception of lawyers and the image which the profession aims to project. The Queen's Counsel system is analysed. Barristers' public access rules are examined. The Chapter continues with a consideration of the nature of advocacy, the position of unrepresented litigants and the process by which lawyers qualify.

The generally accepted view is that the English Bar plays a vital role in our society ... so long as our democracy survives, and so long as disputes between citizens, or between citizens and the state, continue to be resolved after each side has had its say, there will be a need for presentational skills, for drafting skills and for objective advice ... the forms of expertise which the Bar, both employed and self employed, routinely displays.
(Anon)

The advocacy monopoly

The monopoly over advocacy and the conduct of litigation is central to the powers and privileges of the legal profession. This was recognised in the seventeenth century by the Levellers who declared:
Any man may plead his own cause or call in whom he will to plead for him (the lawyers' monopoly is broken) (Third Agreement of the People). This is discussed in more detail in Chapter 3 (Dissent). It is worth noting that a proposal put forward by the Levellers that practice as a lawyer would be a crime has reportedly been in effect in Cuba since shortly after the Revolution.

The advocacy monopoly is partly based on the fact that it is a criminal offence for an unqualified person to "conduct litigation". Section 13(2) of the Legal Services Act 2007 requires individuals wishing to provide "reserved legal activities" to be authorised to do so by the relevant approved regulator. "Reserved legal activities" are, basically, rights of audience in courts and the right to conduct litigation. This does not apply to tribunals. Some lawyers are keen, in their own interests, to extend their advocacy monopoly to tribunals. Recent moves, for example, to redesignate the employment tribunal as a "court" could have the effect of extending the advocacy monopoly to that tribunal, where it does not currently apply.

Image and perception

There is an extreme contradiction between lawyers' perception of their own image and public perception of the profession. The lawyer in his professional role can be perceived by the public as devious and manipulative, perhaps hypocritical or dishonest, and sometimes unconcerned with the harm done to others or to society in general. Other recent general comments include:

- *The Bar is perceived as elitist, in the sense of exclusive. This is a damaging perception because it breeds hostility towards a profession that exists predominantly to serve the public interest.*
- *The Bar is simply not discussed as a career option in families from lower socio-economic groups.*

Lawyers know that the public does not hold the profession in high esteem. The public attitude to English lawyers has been described as "unfortunate and understandable".

A recent example of this image and perception is of a junior criminal barrister who was seen to be carrying a Mulberry handbag, valued at £1100, during a picket of the courts in protest against the legal aid cuts.

The profession is currently making desperate efforts to change this image.

There is a significant gap between theory and practice and serious contradictions between the cultural practices of the profession and its attempts to modernise and diversify. The contradictions are between intense efforts by the legal profession to present itself as modern, enlightened, accessible and classless and the reality of its own culture.

The Bar has been forced to change by outside bodies, for example the Office of Fair Trading. In 2001 the Office of Fair Trading issued a report – Competition in the Professions – which warned the legal profession that unless prompt action was taken to change the professional rules which restricted competition, it would use its available powers with a view to the removal of those restrictions.

A former Chairman of the Bar was reported to have commented that the justice system is a critical element in our society … it is essential that an independent and impartial tribunal is available to provide a just adjudication of legal disputes … those of us who have the temporary custody of these traditions are only too well aware of the responsibility which lies upon our shoulders.

The Bar, while constituting an essential element of the money-worship legal system, also struggles to present itself as altruistic. It is making desperate attempts to modernise and to present an acceptable face.

The cultural divide between the legal profession and non-lawyers is illustrated, for example, by recent issues of Counsel magazine. This publication, for practising barristers, contains the following:

- A leading member of the profession who has an apartment in the Temple is described as "living above the shop".
- An unconfirmed anecdote about another leading barrister who ordered his clerk to serve him with a glass of champagne on a silver plate at six o clock each evening.
- A barrister describing himself as a "total cad".

In April 2008, Counsel magazine carried an article which looked at what the well-dressed barrister was wearing in 2008. Among the points made were the following:

- Go to Savile Row and get yourself kitted out like a successful barrister.
- Prices for hand-made suits start at £2,200.
- Younger barristers, who would like to be more adventurous without offending judges, can show their colours by their choice of lining.
- At Gieves & Hawkes, a bespoke suit starts at £3,400.
- A Savile Row tailor said that he could provide anything a man needs for his wardrobe from business suits to tweed sports jackets, shooting and riding clothes, summer jackets, blazers and smoking jackets.
- If you want to exude an elegant aristocratic air, wear a Chesterfield overcoat which was designed by the dandyish Earl of Chesterfield in the nineteenth

century and is one of the top winter coats.

The contradiction between the traditional public perception of barristers and current efforts to present a modern, classless image is also illustrated by a supplement to Counsel, issued in 2007, entitled *Open Road – an essential guide to motoring for the Bar.*
Open Road, we were told, will have you lusting over several exceedingly sumptuous cars. The supplement included the following:

- The Ecurie 25 Supercar Club, annual subscription £9500, gives 40 days of driving supercars.
- Mercedes-Benz GL Class: £59,038.
- A personalised service for sourcing luxury and performance cars.
- Bentley Continental Flying Spur: £117,500.

The Inner Temple Yearbook 2007-2008 includes the following:

- A full page colour advertisement for a Savile Row tailor, offering suits from only £795.
- A double page colour advertisement for a car dealer offering to supply Rolls Royce, Lamborghini, Ferrari, Bentley and Bugatti.
- A double page colour advertisement offering bespoke homes – the opportunity to build a home of architectural grandeur.
- A full page colour advertisement offering handmade platinum earrings with natural pink sapphires and pear-shaped diamonds.
- A full colour one page advertisement for motor yacht brokerage.

A leading radical barrister has commented that the legal profession is seen as whining fat cats, only concerned about their own welfare and that nothing could be further from the truth. The reality is that the vast majority of criminal legal aid lawyers, both barristers and solicitors, are highly-committed, industrious and long-suffering individuals. Their concern has always been to ensure, both in the civil and criminal arenas, that there is proper and adequate access to the means of redress where injustice has occurred.
On the other hand, it has been reported in the legal press that potential pupils at a large set of Chambers were given "a slap-up lunch, after which they are told whether they have made the cut".

This cultural divide is also illustrated by obituaries of barristers, for example:

- "The affetato misto in the Jager-Stubli in the Bernese Oberland was transformed by his description from a decent, if ordinary, platter of charcuterie to the most mouth-watering fare in the world."
- "Away from court, no dressing down for him. One might occasionally see a flash of red braces but on the whole he saw himself as keeping up standards of sartorial elegance in an increasingly shabby world."

There have also been reports of "a popular and eminent QC" who, while working on a case in Croydon, could not find anywhere which served a decent lunch. He was photographed holding a cigar in one hand and a bag of fish and chips in the other. His instructing solicitor commented that this was how he liked his QCs: extravagant on the one hand, down to earth on the other. Language used in legal practice includes sporting metaphors, for example a successful prosecution is described as "potting" the accused, and a trial can be described as a "fight". Cases are "won" or "lost". This use of language illustrates the highly competitive and adversarial nature of current mainstream legal practice.

During a barristers' conference some years ago, where the matters being discussed included the possibility of direct access to the public without the intervention of a solicitor, one barrister hissed loudly every time the word "solicitor" was mentioned.

These types of comment illustrate a cultural context which is very far removed from a profession which is strenuously trying to rebrand itself as modern, caring and in touch.

The changing rules of professional etiquette are illustrated by Boulton's Conduct and Etiquette at the Bar (1965), which included:

- Any form of advertising or touting by a barrister is contrary to professional etiquette.
- No QC should accept a fee of less than £3.5s.6d for any work and no junior counsel less than £2.4s.6d.
- A barrister who has retired from practice may write memoirs of his experiences at the Bar, using his discretion in regard to cases in which he has been engaged and always remembering the confidences which have been reposed in him and the feelings of

the persons who were concerned in the case, or their relatives.

The cab-rank rule (whereby barristers are, subject to exceptions, obliged to accept all cases sent to them falling within their expertise) is said to be crucial to the Bar as it ensures representation of all parties regardless of the desirability of their case. All barristers know that the cab rank rule can be flouted with impunity. Clients can be turned down for a number of reasons, including:

- The case is outside the scope of the lawyer's expertise
- The lawyer is too busy to deal with the matter properly
- The client cannot afford fees of £500 per hour (or any figure which the client cannot afford).

Albie Sachs and Joan Hoff Wilson, Sexism and the Law: A study of male beliefs and judicial bias

This book, published in 1978, documented for the first time the judicial response to attempts by feminists to use the courts to secure full citizenship. It also questioned the structural sexism which is so closely connected with the professional elitism of the legal system, and proposed ways to eliminate it. Sachs and Wilson argued that such sexism is not only unjust to female litigants and women lawyers but is also harmful to the men who remain entrenched within an archaic male-dominated profession.

Sachs and Wilson stated the view that sexism is all-pervasive in legal life. Their comments included, for example:

- The legal profession and the judiciary are overwhelmingly dominated by men. Clerical work is feminised – women are generally employed to do secretarial and reception work.
- The current structure of the profession is such that highly talented and fully qualified persons queue in vain for a chance to exercise their talents.
- The club-like character and mannered quality of the legal profession.
- British lawyers have cultivated a characteristic mode of speech, bearing and appearance, which manifests itself in a distinctive legal style. This style includes well-elocuted speech, carefully considered language and a detached manner with the aim of creating an aura of integrity.
- These qualities are praised by supporters as hallmarks of erudition, objectivity, intellectual strength and moral trustworthiness. On the other hand, they are criticised by their opponents for their pomposity, complacency, dessication and lack of contact with the real world.
- The created mystique of professionalism disguises the fact that professionals deal mostly with routine matters. Special knowledge is frequently merely information supplied to them by ancillary workers.
- In terms of professional style, accents, impulses and modes of dress which jar against accepted standards are rapidly eliminated.
- Features of professionalism involve the imparting of a stamp of special status.
- A grouping together of people who compete fiercely with each other for income and prestige, but who

stand firmly united against encroachment on their territory from the outside world.

- A combative camaraderie is characteristic of lawyers.
- Males of the English middle and upper-middle class are trained to suppress feelings, to accept formalised modes of conduct, to be intellectually aggressive and emotionally restrained.
- Lawyers feed on deference. The lawyer is in control and the client is subservient.
- The legal profession displays stereotypical masculine characteristics of rational thinking, competitiveness, aggressiveness, strength and seriousness.

Wanted

The January 2009 issue of Counsel magazine carried a full-page advert in the style of a Wild West wanted poster. It stated that a man, who was pictured, wanted a pupillage and was prepared to offer a reward of experience, dedication, loyalty, commitment and tenacity.

The February 2009 issue of the same magazine carried a statement from the Bar Standards Board pointing out that the advert had been inappropriate and out of line with the Board's pupillage advertising requirements. Any set of Chambers which made a direct offer of pupillage on the basis of such an advertisement would be in breach of the provisions of Annexe R to the Code of Conduct and the Board would almost certainly refuse to register any such pupillage.

Counsel magazine stated that it would not be accepting any such advertisements in future.

Barrister's clerk

A recent article in the legal press has discussed the relationship of the clerk with a barrister – he was at once his clerk, his good servant, dresser, his friend, his flapper, his guide, stopwatch, auditor, treasurer. One of the clerk's tasks was to send a barrister's summer reading books to his hotel in Davos. He also booked the train ticket. No, no, no, said the barrister. He never sat with his back to the engine.

The clerk could be compared with a public school fag. (For those fortunate enough to have avoided an English public school education, a "fag" is a young boy who acts as an unpaid servant for an older boy. The benefits of this system are said to include an appreciation of the service ethos and respect for one's elders).

In theory, the role of the barrister's clerk has developed into management and administration, and clerks are now often described as practice managers. It is not clear how far this modern terminology reflects the reality of the barrister-clerk relationship. Clerks, who do not need formal qualifications, can exercise significant power over members of chambers, particularly in relation to the arrangement and distribution of work. In reality, practice as a barrister can be efficiently managed without the services of a clerk.

Queen's Counsel

The rank of QC (Queen's Counsel) has been awarded, for at least 400 years, to advocates (mostly barristers) who have been recognised, within their own profession, as having shown particular skill and expertise in the conduct of advocacy.

This rank, known as “silk” because QCs wear silk gowns, casts light on a number of features of the legal profession and the English legal system.

The reality is that senior barristers (and a few solicitors), predominantly white, male, public school and Oxford or Cambridge educated, are selected to become QCs (or KCs if the current occupier of Buckingham Palace is a male).

These are the chosen elite of the Bar, who line themselves up for judicial appointment. But the most important point about taking silk is that the barrister’s income can double overnight. This was expressly recognised in the Office of Fair Trading Report of 2001.

It is very difficult to find hard evidence of QC’s earnings. For example, Part 48 of the Civil Procedure Rules sets out a table of guidelines for counsel’s fees. It states that the table does not include any figures in respect of leading counsel (QC)’s fees, since such cases would self-evidently be exceptional.

Anecdotal evidence about QC fees includes a charge of £5000 for an hour’s telephone advice in an insurance-funded commercial dispute.

The QC appointment system, which is regarded with incredulity outside the United Kingdom, was based for centuries on an opaque series of informal soundings. In 2001 the Office of Fair Trading called for the abolition of the rank. It stated that it did not operate as a genuine quality accreditation scheme but rather as an informal quota which raised fees. The OFT went on to make the point that, even if it could be shown that the QC appointment system was transparent, objective and non-discriminatory, and operated as a genuine quality mark, it was of questionable value to consumers. The Malleson Report on QCs concluded that the selection process was riddled with indirect race and sex discrimination.

In November 2004 the Bar Council and the Law Society concluded an agreement on the reform of the QC system. The following points emerged:

- The new process served the public interest by offering a fair and transparent means of identifying excellence in advocacy in the higher courts.
- The title QC was an important reference mark for those who chose to purchase the highest quality advocacy services.
- The rank of QC was the recognition of excellence for advocacy in the higher courts.
- In April 2003 the award of Silk was suspended. The Lord Chancellor commented that if Silk disappeared, those receiving the award would be the last in an illustrious line of leading counsel recognised by the state as leaders of the profession.
- There was wide acceptance that abolition of the QC title would damage the international reputation of English law, would close a route to diversity and would weaken the administration of justice. It was not explained exactly how the abolition of the QC concept would "close a route to diversity" or affect the reputation of English law.
- Key features of the new system included an independent selection panel and letters patent from the Queen.

One expressed aim of the new selection system was to increase diversity. An application for silk now costs £1950 plus VAT, with a further £3500 plus VAT fee for acceptance of the award if it is granted.
Another aim of the new procedure was to deal with "mischiefs about the tap on the shoulder and that it all happened in smoke-filled rooms". One view of the new procedure is that the old, informal system has been replaced by a financial hurdle. On the other hand, it has been argued that people seeking appointment as QCs should be able to afford this, and that there was no evidence that people would be deterred from applying by the cost.
One effect of the new procedure for applying for the QC designation is that it has generated, as is common in the English legal system, another layer of profit-making. Consultancy services have been set up to coach applicants through the "long and daunting" application and interview process. One such consultancy offers detailed advice on how to fill in the application form, the selection of assessors and referees, coaching on the interview process and in-depth training and coaching on all competency areas.
The consultancy company offers, for a fee, a tailored programme to prepare and coach applicants for QC status. The programme includes advice on preparing the application form, the choice of referees, a template for referees, coaching on the interview process and training on all competency areas including integrity and diversity. The company's publicity states that 100 per cent of applicants who took part in this scheme were

successful with their applications. It includes the following:

- Do you want to have a successful QC interview, make more money and gain the respect of your peers and clients?
- We provide CONFIDENTIAL results-focused coaching.
- We will help you with your interview preparation.
- We will help you answer the very difficult questions on DIVERSITY. 40 per cent of applicants fail because they give the WRONG answers on DIVERSITY.
- The interview is a MINEFIELD.

One of the most disillusioning aspects of the radical edge of the legal profession is that the soundest, ablest, most courageous and sympathetic progressive lawyers all seem to accept the offer of Silk. Like Herbert Read (the anarchist who said yes to a knighthood), it is very hard to turn down.

The late John Mortimer QC repeatedly ridiculed the pomp, ceremony and fancy dress surrounding the formalities of becoming a QC. His Rumpole stories included the description of QCs as “Queer Customers” and referred to the wearing of silk stockings and suspender belts. It would be interesting to know why he was prepared to go through with the pantomime. But very few people can resist the lure of £200,000 a year.

Recent efforts to reform the QC appointments procedure have been hailed as moving the system away from a closed cabal populated by chaps who were at school, university and chambers together.

The main practical significance of the status of Queen's Counsel was, and remains, the doubling of fees.
The rank of honorary QC – known as Queen's Counsel honoris causa – is awarded to lawyers who have made a major contribution to the law of England and Wales outside practice in the courts. Traditionally, it has been awarded to distinguished legal academics and some lawyers in public service for achievements beyond their normal responsibilities. It is not a working rank. It cannot be used in practice as a lawyer and holders are strongly discouraged from exploiting the rank to attract business.
The Law Society Gazette commented that perhaps it was time to take another step towards modernity and consign Silk to the history books.
Peter Herbert, the Chair of the Society of Black Lawyers, is reported to have commented that the increased fees would make it harder for ethnic minority lawyers and women to apply because they often had lower earning capacity than their white or male comparators.

My pupillage

In 1970 there were no central controls, no formalities and no set procedures dealing with pupillage.
Acceptance as a pupil involved nothing more than a payment of 100 guineas to the pupilmaster and 10 guineas to the clerk.
This was a hole in the wall set of provincial chambers with an alcoholic head who had been expelled from a mainstream set for drunkenness.

The reason for my acceptance was that I owned a van which would take the head to outlying courts and weekly auction sales where he would successfully bid for numerous items.

The clerk, a chain smoker, used an ashtray decorated with the motto “Rest your weary ash” and kept his cigarettes in a case labelled “Smoke like Helen B. Merry”.

The members of Chambers were a strange collection of individuals who could find nowhere else to go. All were white males except for one Asian man. One member treated Chambers purely as a social venue and would call in every morning before playing golf. He only ever had one brief and, sadly, he died of a heart attack shortly before the court hearing.

There was a significant flow of work, mainly from the head’s solicitor drinking companions. The work, of dubious quality, included a wide range of crime, family and property. The width of this work meant that there was little chance of developing expertise in any specialisation and no chance whatever of anyone progressing to QC or the judiciary.

This was the setting for a steady career as a small-time provincial lawyer in dead-end Chambers.

Public access

Until recently, barristers could only be approached through solicitors. When this rule was carried to its most extreme and absurd conclusion, cases arose where barristers refused to speak to their clients (who were often paying them large sums of money) except when a solicitor was present in the room.

Following years of pressure from inside and outside the profession, and the opinion of the Office of Fair Trading that this was an unfair and illegal restrictive practice, the rule was changed to allow limited public access to the barrister.

In 2004 changes required by the Office of Fair Trading, following the Clementi review of legal services, allowed direct public access to barristers. This reform was carried through in the teeth of determined opposition from the Bar.

The Office of Fair Trading Report 2001 – Competition in the Professions - warned the legal profession that unless prompt action was taken to change the professional rules which restricted competition, it would use its available powers with a view to the removal of those restrictions.

The OFT took the view that the restriction on barristers having direct access was anti-competitive.

The new rules allow members of the public to go directly to a barrister, but only in limited circumstances.

The public access barrister can do most of the work which would normally be carried out by a solicitor.

From the public access barrister's point of view, the main advantage of the new regime is, unsurprisingly, money. The client pays the barrister direct and the previously financially crippling experience of waiting for months, and sometimes years, for solicitors to pay fees, is a thing of the past for public access barristers. The downside of direct access, in the view of the mainstream profession, is that it is harder for the barrister to retain the distance from the client required to maximise objectivity.

Public access practice can involve contact with highly vulnerable and disadvantaged people, many living in extreme poverty, who have a misplaced faith in the fairness of the English legal system and a naïve belief that justice will prevail.

The Westminster School of Law reported that almost 90 per cent of users found that directly instructing a barrister was better value for money than going through a solicitor.

A solicitor is reported to have made the following comments:

- The Bar was not geared up for direct access except in very limited circumstances.
- Barristers did not have the ability to deal with the administration of litigation.
- Solicitors were used to dealing with clients, questions which clients have about the process and the day to day relationship which they have with clients. The Bar is not up to speed with these areas.
- The Bar works in a particular way which does not involve direct access by clients seeking information, often on a fairly constant basis.

These comments do not deal with the undoubted fact that, before public access, clients seeking specialist legal advice had to pay twice because the case had to be passed through a solicitor.

In the case of *GE Capital Bank v Rushton & Jenkin (2006)*, which involved a hire purchase dispute, the bank, which had instructed a solicitor and a barrister, claimed costs of £68,000. The defendants had instructed a barrister direct. They claimed £6,400 costs.

Qualification as a barrister by accident of birth

In July 2009 it was reported that Prince William had been made an honorary barrister. He is the sixth member of the royal family to be made a Royal Bencher. Others include Princess Diana and the Queen Mother.

300 guests dined in the Middle Temple Hall for the ceremony. William was admitted as a member of the Inn, and called to the Bar, before dinner. He promised not to practise as a barrister except for the odd speeding ticket.

Meanwhile, most of those who struggle to qualify as barristers by studying for law degrees and professional examinations find themselves deep in debt by the time they are qualified. Their chances of finding pupillage, and practising in the profession, are limited in the extreme. Recently, one set of provincial barristers' chambers received 500 applications for one pupillage vacancy.

On the one hand, the Bar is seen to be making serious efforts to encourage the disadvantaged to join the profession, and to dispel its image as a club for the wealthy and privileged. For example, in February 2008 Ladders2Law was launched by the Social Mobility Foundation, a registered charity which aims to give bright students from financially disadvantaged backgrounds insight into the leading professions through internships and mentoring.

Ladders2Law is a mentoring scheme which links students with a practising barrister or solicitor. This has been described as a hugely important way of reaching bright young people who would not normally have access to relevant information about the legal profession.

On the other hand, the profession is seen to accept qualification by accident of birth.

Lawyer jokes (found on the Internet)

- What is the difference between lawyers and sperm? There's no difference: one in 50 million has a chance of becoming a human being.
- Why is it prohibited for lawyers to have sex with their clients? To prevent the client being charged twice for the same service.
- It was so cold in Aberdeen one winter's day that a lawyer was seen with his hands in his own pockets.
- The problem with the legal profession is that 99 per cent of lawyers give the others a bad name.
- What's the difference between a lawyer and an onion? You cry when you cut up an onion.
- How many lawyers does it take to change a lightbulb? Three. One to climb the ladder. One to shake the ladder. One to sue the ladder company.
- Mark Twain: *It is interesting to note that criminals have multiplied of late, and lawyers have also, but I repeat myself.*
- Legal problems? Take my advice:
    1. Don't trust lawyers.
    2. Treat lawyers as you would treat sharks.
    3. Keep away from lawyers as far as possible.
    4. Don't pay lawyers.
    5. If you have no choice but to consult a lawyer, be choosy, critical, questioning and cynical.

The commonly observed habits of the traditional lawyer:

- Drinking red wine to excess at every possible

opportunity, particularly if it's free.

- Talking loudly in public
- Wearing a period costume
- Treating employees with disdain
- Self-aggrandisement
- Casual and subconscious racism
- Contempt for the disabled
- Sexual harassment
- Falsely asserting detailed knowledge of legal topics
- Contempt for progressive social movements.

It does no good to assert that solicitors will ever achieve the levels of advocacy skills which are attained on an everyday basis by the English Bar
(Anon)

Thank God none of my sons became lawyers
(Anon)

Such is the bounteous liberality of the legal profession that its members may hold any number of opinions, just as other members of society are entitled to. If this opinion oversteps the bounds of decency to which all opinions must restrict themselves, and in particular if opinion and profession become mixed up in court, then this becomes "a gross act of discourtesy" and contempt of court.
(Anon)

Ever since the growth of central government, lawyers have been willing accessories to the political whims of the tyrant of the day and then with rat-like acumen

switch sides at the last moment: feudalism to mercantilism, laisser faire capitalism to social democracy.
(Anon)

These, and many other jokes and ironic/sarcastic comments about lawyers, can be seen as harmless attempts at humour. But it is more likely that the reality is that the viciousness of many of these jokes reflects the true public perception of the profession. Jokes about, for example, doctors, are also common, but they lack the bile and cynicism of lawyer jokes.

Law Centres

The original concept of the Law Centre was a service of salaried solicitors and legal workers who would be able to devote themselves to people's needs, choosing priorities which reflected the seriousness of the need rather than the profitability of the case. The staff were accountable to a management committee representing locaal organisations and interests. When the movement started, it was described by the Law Society as a means of stirring up political and quasi-political confrontation.
In 1979 the Royal Commission on Legal Services commented as follows:
The impact of law centres has been out of all proportion to their size, to the number of lawyers who work in them and to the amount of work it is possible for them to undertake. The value of work they have attracted shows how deep is the need which they are attempting to meet.

A spokesperson for the Law Centres movement is reported to have commented that the most important thing to know about Law Centres was that they did not just do casework. Their philosophy was that they promoted legal solutions to the problems of poverty, discrimination and social exclusion. The role of Law Centres was to campaign for wider social justice by doing strategic work, including education, test cases and group actions.

Gifford stated in 1986 that the issues dealt with by Law Centres included:

- Taking on agencies which had been a major source of oppression and injustice: uncaring central and local government departments, slum landlords and autocratic employers.
- Acting for groups of people suffering a common grievance.
- Educating people about their legal rights.
- Helping people to organise in tenants' associations and trade unions.
- Tackling acute problems which lawyers ought to be involved in but rarely are.

In terms of financial problems, one in three Law Centres are currently reported to be on the critical list and are only surviving by cutting back on more complex, time-consuming cases. Cities like Birmingham and Leeds have been left without Law Centres. They have reached the point where they are providing an extremely inferior and diminished product.

Brent Community Law Centre First Report 1972-4:

Our purpose was not merely to try to meet unmet needs

for legal services of individuals or groups but rather to meet such needs in such a way as to make a positive contribution to community development and combating deprivation. The Centre was to ensure that the actual needs and aspirations of people within the deprived areas rather than the established and perceived needs should be harnessed to determine the course of our own and public policies aimed at meeting those needs. Our work necessarily involved helping those people to organise themselves and generally to help them to help themselves...what is needed is not simply to increase the resources available to the legal aid scheme or the public enforcement agencies, although this is certainly necessary; rather it is legal services which will help the poor and powerless to organise themselves so that they are capable of negotiating and enforcing rights and obligations and of having an effective voice in the decision making processes which affect them. The service which is needed is one which can mobilise others rather than simply do everything itself.

Advocacy

A standard text on practical hints for advocacy at the Bar (Evans, see Further Reading) makes the following points:

- It is generally accepted throughout the English-speaking world that the standards of the English Bar are by and large among the best.
- Ideal wear – unless you are utterly determined to make a political statement – is still the black jacket and waistcoat with striped trousers.
- My Lord, Your Honour: there are complex rules of

etiquette in addressing different levels of the judiciary: these are conventions, not law.

- Conduct generally: for example, a barrister in robes never carries a briefcase or any other kind of bag. Barristers do not shake hands and should always address each other by their surnames.
- The public attitude towards lawyers is unfortunate and understandable.
- Give nothing away by your facial expressions.

There is an irreconcilable contradiction between this sort of advice and the professed commitment of the Bar to a modern and classless approach. The English legal system pays homage to the primacy of oral argument.

The sheer, mind-numbing boredom of courtroom advocacy is rarely admitted. The detailed, endless preparation, the waiting in draughty corridors, the tiresome repetition of evidence and counter-evidence, the predictably bad-tempered judge, the waiting for the jury to return. The interminable waiting on draughty station platforms for the train to Snaresbrook for the plea in mitigation for £50, the standing on crowded trains for the case management conference in Merthyr Tydfil for £30. The egotism of the advocates who love to be “on their feet”. The dressing-up, the dressings-down. The judge who was obviously bullied at his public school and who subconsciously returns the favour to his subordinates throughout his working life.

The mystique of oral advocacy can be a gift to those who love the sound of their own voices. It is now generally accepted that the English tradition of oral adversarial advocacy involves a massive waste of time, and therefore money.

Even the supposedly glamorous side of the trade, the Crown Court trial, has its great share of tedium. The trial process itself appears endlessly repetitive. Cross-examination, hailed as an art form, consists largely of repeating over and over again, questions to expose supposed inconsistencies in evidence.

And the waiting – nothing to do but wait – for the judge, the jury, the court. Hours of lost and wasted waiting time. Advocates in the Crown Court adopt a particular style of deference towards the judge – a deference which has been honed by convention over the centuries.

The speech to the jury – repeating everything the jurors already know and the judge's summing up which repeats it all over again. This can be more than the normal person can stand.

The "art" of the advocate is often seen to be the asking of questions of such detail and complexity, endlessly repeated with hardly noticeable variations, until everyone has lost track of reality and any answer can be challenged.

A recent scheme to assess and approve the quality of advocates has been introduced by the Bar Council – perhaps this implies that things are not so perfect as is often implied?

The supposed image of calm efficiency in the courts is very different from the chaos which can reign in reality. Documentation is often faxed through the night before a trial and if a judge demands that papers should be reorganised, advocates may find themselves kneeling on the floor outside the court to comply with this judicial diktat.

Jacques Verges is a French advocate who has represented, among others, Carlos the Jackal, Slobodan Milosevic and Klaus Barbie. A DVD which "attempts to illuminate the mystery behind this enigmatic and controversial lawyer" was described by English reviewers as telling the story of a man who had polluted the principles of advocacy.

In the annual law reform lecture at Inner Temple (November 2010), Lord Justice Moses is reported to have made the following comments:

- The Court of Appeal do not sit and listen to the summing up: indeed, if they had to, few would remain awake for longer than 30 minutes, even with the aid of a flacon of Portuguese smelling salts.
- Trial judges are fearful of the expense and distress of a re-trial, and it is that which leads them to this endless exercise in composing a defensive summing up, a summing-up crafted to defend the trial from appeal.
- In trials lasting more than a week, the judge should provide regular written and oral summaries.
- A criminal trial costs about £4,300 a day and £7,000 a day at the Old Bailey. Summing-ups regularly last a day in trials lasting more than two weeks.
- There were 389 such trials in the year to April 2010. £4,000 or even £7,000 is an expensive ticket to listen to a replay of the drama delivered in monotone.
- The judge's summing up is a frequent source of appeals against conviction.
- Conviction appeals cost about £14,000 a day.

The boredom of law

Most law is dull. As noted above, Kafka likened reading a law book to eating sawdust. For anyone with a spark of individuality or creative genius, the following are examples which can kill the drive to originality and provide an effective cure for insomnia:

- The endless tedium of the detail of the law of trusts.
- The mind-numbing aridity of the law of intestate succession.
- The excruciating dullness of conveyancing procedure.
- The incomprehensibility of the more arcane aspects of the law of contract.
- Administrative law in all its deadening detail.
- Tax law with its endless sections and subsections of Finance Acts.
- European commercial law in all its abstract splendour.
- The grinding complexity of the Civil Procedure Rules, even after reform.

The Ogden Tables

These Tables took their name from Michael Ogden QC who was the chair of the working party which first drew them up. They involve the calculation of multipliers for future financial loss in personal injury cases based on actuarial principles. They are of crucial significance in personal injury cases.

The multiplier takes a claimant's life expectancy and multiplies it by a rate of annual loss. The age of the claimant is a key factor. The Tables do not refer at all to

a claimant who does not know his or her age.
The assessment of compensation is a highly-paid branch of law on its own. It is practically impossible for a successful claimant to accurately calculate his amount of compensation himself. Money can thus be made by lawyers from deciding on an amount of money.
The assessment of amounts of compensation for civil wrongs depends, as a starting point, on the age of the claimant. Legal textbooks dealing with civil procedure state, without further explanation, that formulas for future loss of earnings and other aspects of compensation depend upon the claimant's age. The assumption of knowledge of age is the basis of the entire system of assessing amounts of compensation. Did the compilers of the Ogden Tables realise that some citizens have no birth certificates? Those of us who have worked with deprived persons from the Afro-Caribbean community know that, for a number of the middle aged and elderly, their date of birth is unknown. They know that they were born in the Caribbean fifty or sixty years ago but they have no record of their date of birth. The absence of proper certification systems in the colonial or post-colonial territories, with the implications of a legacy of slavery, means that such persons are at a huge disadvantage in their dealings with the legal system. On top of their weakness on financial and educational grounds, they face the added disadvantage of a third-world registration system up against a first-world legal system. How can you assess compensation if the client does not know his or her age? The unthinking assumption that all potential claimants know their dates of birth can be characterised as a form of unintentional

racism in that it places certain ethnic groups at a disadvantage.

The issue of those who do not know, or cannot prove their age, is significant in the context of asylum and immigration cases, where "age dispute" is a recognised area of law. The Ogden Tables are untouched by this reality.

Mediation

It may appear to outsiders to be bizarre that the main aim of English civil procedure is to avoid litigation. A legal system has become so complex and expensive that those in charge of it advise users to avoid it if at all possible. Alternative dispute resolution (ADR) is highly recommended by the drafters of the reformed civil procedure rules. It is expressly stated that litigation should be a last resort. A refusal to consider ADR may have costs implications – once again, money is the key.

Mediation is one form of ADR. It consists of a sort of shuttle diplomacy between the parties and their legal advisers with the aim of settling disputes out of court.

Some clients have concluded that mediation has developed into yet another money-making quasi-legal racket. Its aim is to avoid litigation and it is said to be cheaper than litigation, which gives plenty of scope for high charges.

There is an absurdity about a system of civil procedure which is so expensive to operate that claimants are urged to use it as a last resort and to seek alternative means of dispute resolution. This means, in effect, that the massively sophisticated machinery for civil claims is available only to the very rich.

There is every chance that we are witnessing the development of another layer of legal procedure which, although not expensive to the crippling extent of full-tilt litigation, still costs more than most people can afford. Alternative dispute resolution is now, effectively, compulsory because a refusal to mediate carries costs implications.

The potentially rich pickings of mediation are illustrated by a circular advertising a commercial mediator training course at a cost of £2950 plus VAT. A worthwhile investment in another layer of law for the rich.

Gifts to solicitors

The English Bar has recently been concerned about hospitality, entertainment and gifts offered to solicitors by sets of barristers' chambers. Barristers' marketing budgets, apparently, now include sums for dinners, sporting and social events to which solicitors are invited. It was commented that there was no doubt that if there was evidence that barristers were receiving instructions in return for entertainment that would bring the Bar into serious disrepute.

It is well-known that many barristers who keep to the mainstream system of acting as consultants, and receiving work only through solicitors, offer their solicitor contacts hospitality and entertainment. In the view of the Bar's governing body:

The indirect use of legal fees for entertainment purposes tarnishes the image and reputation of the profession, particularly if the entertainment offered is on a scale beyond the means of many consumers.

It was suggested that the "blush" test should be applied. This means:
Whether the individual entertained would be embarrassed to disclose it to his or her colleagues, clients or the regulating authorities. Or where the host would be embarrassed if the fact, or extent, of the entertainment were to become widely known. Of course, this test does not deal with the problem of those who find nothing to be embarrassed about.
Reports have been received of solicitors requiring payments to be made to them by barristers in return for work to be referred to barristers in criminal cases. This is forbidden by the Bar Code of Conduct. It is not clear how such payments are made. If cash is surreptitiously handed over, this may involve tax evasion or even moneylaundering issues.

Alternative practice

The practice of law in an alternative way attempts to address the fact that the poor are denied justice and to resist the fact that law is used by many lawyers as a means of making large sums of money – in some cases, obscenely large.
Alternative practice challenges the absurdly unbalanced relationship between the most highly-paid lawyers and poor people who cannot afford their services.
It resists the deliberate obscurity of legal rules, interpreted and explained by the legal priesthood, which mean that even the most articulate and highly educated non-lawyer finds it practically impossible to penetrate the curtain of incomprehensibility.

The following are suggested ideas for the development of a legal practice outside the mainstream. In this context it is important to note that all aspects of legal practice in England have changed significantly during the last decade, and are likely to develop further. Most of these changes have followed a neoliberal agenda and reflect movement towards the free market, for example the permitting of mixed legal businesses and direct access to barristers.

The following proposals have nothing to do with the often-quoted and accepted supremacy of the market. Rather, they defy market forces and aim to develop legal practice, not in the interests of an elite profession, but in the interests of deprived groups, for example the poor, the homeless, the unemployed, the disabled and victims of discrimination.

Campbell's view (*The Left and Rights*) is that the radical lawyer is both tolerated and ignored. Tolerated because his existence seems somehow "good" for the profession at large – making it representative of all opinion – and ignored because what he does in the affluent liberal hour threatens no-one. The radical lawyer is entangled in a situation where he is committed to undermining the very structure which provides his own power base.

The theoretical basis of alternative practice involves the following principles:

- Resistance to war, racism, discrimination and exploitation
- Opposition to money fetishism
- A commitment to demystification
- The pursuit of social justice

- Opposition to traditional formalities and conventions which hinder access to justice.

Many English lawyers with a social conscience are so involved with making money or with the daily pressures of court work that alternatives to the current system are never considered. The great majority of lawyers, being essentially conservative, practise according to traditional conventions. The time demands of practice can offer few opportunities for lawyers to stand back and think about alternatives to mainstream practice. There is an almost unbridgeable gap between critical academic lawyers on the one hand, and coal-face practitioners on the other (although it is unrealistic to compare the daily work of the lawyer with that of the miner). The dynamics of daily practice can result in lawyers submerging their ideals to economic considerations and pragmatic results.

Traditional practice as a barrister confirms, and indeed encourages, remoteness from the client. Barristers have traditionally kept clients at arms length through the rule that a solicitor must act as an intermediary. This principle has been eroded by the introduction of public access rights, but it is important to be aware that this relaxation was forced upon the profession in the teeth of determined opposition. The profession has always emphasised objectivity, detachment and the application of legal skills as a technical exercise.

An American commentator has stated the view that many of the left-wing lawyers who preached revolution thirty years ago are now well-paid members of the legal establishment. Some use their power and status to help poor people: others do not. The experiences and day-to-day practice of American radical lawyers is very different from their English counterparts: the Americanisation of the English legal system has not extended to the adoption of radical US techniques.

Everyone knows that poor people find it difficult to have effective access to justice. This is accepted as if it were as inevitable as English weather. The mainstream discussion of alternatives to this state of affairs generally involves a tinkering with financial elements of the system, for example franchising or marginally increased money for Law Centres. As these arcane discussions continue, poor people continue to suffer. Are there serious alternatives to traditional practice? This question is seldom raised.

For largely tactical reasons, alternative practice must come within the scope of the detailed practice rules laid down by the Bar Code of Conduct, and in full compliance with the overriding duty of a barrister to promote and protect fearlessly and by all proper and lawful means the client's best interests and to do so without regard to his own interests or to any consequences to himself or any other person.

Practice as a lawyer can be "alternative" in the following ways:

- **Money.** By not treating money as the primary consideration when dealing with a new client. This is the key basic principle. It contradicts mainstream practices and values, and defies the free market. If a client of an alternative practice has no money (which would almost certainly rule him out from the mainstream) it is crucially important that his case is handled with as much care as a paying client. There are a number of ways in which money fetishism can be dealt with. These include charging according to the means of the client, not submitting a bill if the claim is unsuccessful, accepting payment in instalments, and bartering. Bartering can be a radical alternative to charitable work. Legal services can be exchanged for whatever the client can offer, or has a surplus of. The Bar Code of Conduct does not deal with bartering, but the most relevant provision of the Code states that a self-employed barrister may charge for any work undertaken by him on any basis or by any method he thinks fit, provided that such basis or method is permitted by law. The lawyer in alternative practice can help to deal with one layer of anxiety afflicting clients: by not taking all their money.

- **Direct access.** Dealing directly with the client, within the scope of the public access rules, rather than by using the traditional client-solicitor-barrister relationship to keep the client at arms length, directly contradicts traditionally accepted principles of detachment.

- **Demystification.** The explanation of procedural and legal points clearly and in plain English so that the client understands exactly what is happening at every stage of the case. Alternative practice necessarily implies a commitment to demystification and education. The law should be explained to clients, as far as possible, in understandable terms. This follows the Benthamite tradition and undermines the normal practice of preservation of the mysteries of the craft. This is more fully examined in Chapter 6 (Mystery).

- **Education.** Sources of law and procedure should be available to the client. Textbooks and articles in journals should be made available for reference or loan. Library facilities and Internet sources should be identified. Handbooks and guides to law and procedure can be published and distributed at a fair price. Education should also include an element of scepticism as to the effectiveness of the legal system in solving people's problems. The analysis and identification of the non-legal aspects of the problem may be more significant than a legal analysis. The limitations of law should be accepted and explained.

- **Professional standards.** Practising law in an alternative way should involve setting standards higher than those of mainstream practitioners. The running of an alternative practice necessarily involves conflict with the principles and practice of the mainstream, especially with its obsession with money. One way of dealing with this conflict, and of asserting the principles of an alternative practice against the traditionalists, is to do everything better than them. Thus, administration should be as efficient as possible, with support staff highly trained and motivated. Standards of literacy, research, timekeeping and communication should be of the highest. The result of this should be that mainstream practitioners cannot criticise the alternative practice on grounds of poor standards or inefficiency. Disadvantaged clients should receive better service than if they had bankrupted themselves in the mainstream. Academic excellence should be one aspect of an alternative practice.

- **Professional codes of conduct** should be strictly adhered to, although this may cause difficulties where the aims of an alternative practice conflict with those of the traditional profession. But if an alternative practice falls foul of professional rules, for example by refusing to represent fascists, it is in a far stronger position to defend itself against charges of professional misconduct if it has an unblemished record of efficiency and good administration. The general test should be that every document which goes out from an alternative practice should be considered, in theory, as if it were to be examined and analysed by the most reactionary judge. If the documents are beyond criticism from the viewpoint of efficiency, literacy and administration, then problems with the *content* of documentation can far more easily be dealt with.

- **Equal opportunities**. The Bar Code of Conduct states that a self-employed barrister must have regard to any relevant guidance issued by the Bar Council including guidance as to good equal opportunities practice in chambers in the form of the Equality and Diversity Code for the Bar. The Code and the Guidance deal, generally, with discrimination on the grounds of race, colour, ethnic or national origin, nationality, citizenship, sex, sexual orientation, marital status, disability, age, religion or belief. An alternative practice can go further than this and deal with the issue of discrimination for social and economic reasons.

- **Seminars.** Practitioners must comply with continuing professional development requirements, involving a set number of hours. These can be fulfilled by holding seminars. There is no reason why clients cannot be invited to seminars where the topic under discussion relates to their own problems. Unfortunately, the authorities now charge for accreditation of seminars, whether or not an entry charge is made, and this makes holding free seminars problematic. Again, the free market dominates. Since compulsory continuing legal education was introduced for all barristers, we have seen a scramble to turn this into a money-making opportunity. All kinds of individuals and institutions offer training courses to comply with the new regulations, at a high price. The progressive lawyer should, in any event, have kept up to date with his speciality, so that he can take on traditional lawyers on equal or better terms. Seminars, which count towards the continuing education requirements, can be offered free of charge and open to the public. In this way, free advice and information can be offered without any element of the patronising charitable ethic.

- **Recruitment.** The difficulties of running an alternative practice show themselves when attempts are made to recruit new members. Many lawyers are so immersed in a professional culture which has the unchallenged characteristic of an obsession with money, arrogance, formality and authoritarianism that they simply cannot cope with a practice which puts these factors at the bottom of its list of priorities. A practice which is determined to function according to broad principles of co-operation, justice and accessibility faces huge problems when it attempts to recruit from the mainstream.

- **Website.** My free employment advice website – www.freeemploymentadvice.co.uk – operated to provide free or low cost advice for people with employment law problems. It contained information on a number of areas of employment law and offered advice by telephone or email. The initial telephone or email advice, if brief, was free. Further advice was available for a small fee. A standard charge of £100 was made for an initial conference, regardless of its length. The website received, on average, 10 requests a week. Many of the enquiries were clients driven into mental illness by their workplace experiences and by the cost, delays and complexity of the legal system. They had started down the civil procedure road confident that they would obtain justice. As the case proceeded, their optimism changed to bewilderment and disillusion. Their savings disappeared. These were people with a partial grasp of the details of law and procedure, obsessed with the fine detail of their case, doomed to wander the obscure byways of English law and procedure until their money was gone, their spirit broken and their illusions as to English justice shattered. Their initial naïve belief that they would get justice or have their day in court soon disappeared.

Typically, the enquirers were unemployed, poor and desperate. Many of them had been dismissed or made redundant. They might complain of discrimination, bullying and harassment. They might have been made ill by workplace conditions. One thing which almost all of them had in common was that they could not afford advice and/or representation through the mainstream legal profession. Most were not members of a trade union, nor did they have legal expenses insurance. Many had approached the Citizens' Advice Bureau for help and some had contacted Law Centres, only to be told that the Centres were fully occupied and could not take on any more cases.

The majority of enquirers had some idea of their employment rights but most became lost in a fog of incomprehension and despair as they discovered how complex and opaque the law is, and how difficult it is to deal with procedural points. In almost every case, the root of the problem was money.

Working with these clients for free or for a small fee is difficult. The facts are often complex and may involve detailed allegations of bullying or harassment over long periods of time. Medical evidence is normally crucial and expensive to obtain.

An alternative practice may also prepare templates for unrepresented litigants to use in courts and tribunals, particularly where they cannot afford representation. The following is an example of this:

Specimen opening statement for an unrepresented client

- Ask the court or tribunal for permission to make a brief opening statement.
- Explain one's own position so far as any or all of the following apply: limited financial means, no legal training or background, inability to obtain representation because of lack of money. Employment, medical and family status. Legal aid not available. No legal expenses insurance. Not a member of a trade union. Unable to obtain conditional fee. Have approached local Law Centre and charitable bodies for example the Bar Pro Bono Unit, without success.
- Draw the attention of the court or tribunal to the overriding objective of the Civil Procedure Rules. The overriding objective of the Rules is to enable the court to deal with cases justly. This includes ensuring that the parties are on an equal footing.
- Submit that the parties are not on an equal footing because the defendant has legal representation which he can afford, whereas the claimant does not.
- Draw the attention of the court or tribunal to Article 6 of the European Convention on Human Rights: in summary, everyone is entitled to a fair trial. Submit that there is a danger of this principle being breached

where one party can afford representation and the other side cannot.

- Draw the attention of the court or tribunal to the decision of the European Court of Human Rights in the case of *Airey v Ireland (1979) 2 E.H.R.R. 305*, where that court ruled that there had been violations of Article 6 because Mrs Airey did not enjoy an effective right of access to the Ireland High Court to seek a decree of judicial separation. Legal aid was not available for the purpose of seeking judicial separation and Mrs Airey had insufficient means to pay the cost of proceedings herself. The court made the following points:
  - The European Convention on Human Rights was intended to guarantee not theoretical or illusory but practical and effective rights. Having regard to the complexity of the procedure and points of law involved, to the evidential questions arising and to the emotional involvement entailed by marital disputes, the possibility open to Mrs Airey of conducting her case herself did not provide her with an effective right of access.
  - The fact that the alleged right of access stemmed solely from Mrs Airey's personal circumstances was not decisive. Hindrance in fact could constitute a violation of the Convention just like a legal impediment and certain Convention obligations, such as that to secure an effective right of access to the courts, could on occasion necessitate positive State action.

    - It was most improbable that a person in Mrs Airey's position could effectively present his or her own case.
- Draw the attention of court or tribunal to the decision of the European Court of Human Rights in the case of *Steel and Morris v United Kingdom (2005) The Times, February 16*, where that court ruled that the denial of legal aid to the applicants deprived them of the opportunity to present their case effectively before the court and contributed to an unacceptable inequality of arms.

- Point out to the court or tribunal the decision in *Bertuzzi v France (2003)*. In June 1995 B obtained full legal aid to start proceedings against a lawyer. The lawyers assigned to the case applied to withdraw because they had personal links with the defendant. Later in 1995 B asked the president of the legal aid office and the president of the bar council to assign another lawyer. B received no reply until March 1997 when he was told that the grant of legal aid had lapsed.

  The European Court of Human Rights ruled that there had been a breach of Article 6 of the European Convention on Human Rights – B had not had effective access to a court. The court made the following points:
    - The relevant authorities should have arranged for a replacement who would provide B with proper assistance.
    - Permitting B to represent himself in proceedings against a legal practitioner did not afford him

access to a court under conditions which would secure him the effective enjoyment of equality of arms which was inherent in the concept of a fair trial.

  - The Convention is intended to guarantee not rights which are theoretical or illusory but which are practical and effective. This is particularly so of the right of access to the courts in view of the prominent place held in a democratic society by the right to a fair trial.
- State that one appreciates that the court or tribunal may regard this submission as not relevant to current proceedings: advise the court or tribunal that the issues raised in the submission may also be raised in future appeal proceedings and/or in an application to the European Court of Human Rights.

The reality of alternative practice

In the summer of 2007 I received an email from a young Slovakian woman telling me, in acceptable English, that she had recently returned home after working in England for a month. She had been working night shifts as an office cleaner and had not been paid by her temporary employer. Her sister was working in England and would contact me to see if I could help.

This was a case where the client was abroad, had no money, and there was no documentation. For the mainstream, it was a non-starter.

For an alternative practice, the case was difficult but not impossible. Starting with the theoretical view that this could be described as a case of modern day slavery, and as such must be fought with the utmost determination, the first step was to identify the migrant worker's employer. This was achieved after lengthy inquiries at the Job Centre which had found work for the young woman. Details of the company involved were found via the Internet.

A grievance letter sent to the employing company on behalf of the young woman did not succeed in recovering the wages due. With the help of the woman's sister we lodged a claim for unlawful deduction from wages in the employment tribunal. Shortly after this, the money was paid into the client's sister's English bank account. No fee was charged.

Unusually, justice was done and was seen to be done – mainstream issues of hourly billing and cost analysis were wholly irrelevant.

I was invited to visit Slovakia where the woman's family treated me as an honoured guest.

It seemed to me, and to others with whom I discussed the case (lawyers and non-lawyers) that we were indeed looking at a form of modern-day slavery. This was a young woman, highly intelligent and well-educated, who had come to England to earn money because wages were low and jobs were few in her own country. She also wanted to improve her English. She had worked hard in a menial job, for long hours, and had not been paid. There was a suspicion that she had been treated in this way because she was a migrant worker with a poor grasp of English.

Applying the traditional and dominant model of the English legal system, she had no chance whatever of recovering her unpaid wages. She would be denied justice because she was poor.

Through collective action, with the help of the Haldane Society, we were able to achieve some sort of justice. Money for us did not enter into the calculation. Justice was done without a financial incentive.

LIBEL: the board game

This was devised by William Roache after he sued the Sun newspaper for printing a defamatory article about his portrayal of Ken Barlow in Coronation Street. The Sun called him boring and unpopular. He won the case. He then sued his lawyers and reportedly faced debts of £300,000.

The game, described as a legal game for all the family, with some similarities to Monopoly, can be seen as a bitter analysis of English civil procedure.

As a plaintiff in a libel case, each player races to gather together a legal team and successfully win their case. The game involves wooden figures moving around a board through the throw of a dice. Players have to collect cards to complete their legal team. These are priced at, for example, £5000 for a barrister, £7000 for a QC and £3000 for a solicitor.

The game has two stages. The first involves lengthy preliminaries with the expenditure of large sums of money (supplied with the game). The second stage – trial – leads eventually to judgment at the centre of the board. Again, there are lengthy moves and expensive developments. When all these moves and financial transactions are completed, the result is reached by the simple throw of a dice. Roache seems to be making a game of the high cost of legal representation and the chance element of judicial decisions.

Welfare law in practice

Previously the poor were oppressed by the state, by landlords, by employers. Now they have to carry a powerful new burden on their already-straining backs, that of law, lawyers and all the attendant paraphernalia. (Bankowski & Mungham)

My own experience of working in an inner city Advice Centre was that my main function was to provide advice for poor people. An overwhelming need for advice and representation was met by mostly middle-class whites advising working-class Afro-Caribbeans and Asians.

The main problem was poverty. Most of the advice was in the area of welfare benefits, housing, debt and employment.

In summary, the work involved helping illiterate or semi-literate victims of colonialism through the maze of bureaucracy. This meant explanation, writing letters and making telephone calls.

The volume of individual casework was so great that there could be little or no theoretical discussion and no real attempt to help the local community to organise. The work was done under extreme pressure. The Centre operated an open door policy which meant that planning was an unattainable luxury.

The light-switch syndrome

Some welfare rights workers see all their clients' problems as "legal", that is, as capable of being solved only through formal structures and rules. At its most extreme, this can result in the "light-switch" syndrome.

A typical "light-switch" case would be that of a single female parent, malnourished, poorly educated and badly clothed, living in grinding poverty in very poor local authority housing. She perceives her local advice centre as having some sort of semi-official status and has faith in its ability to get something done. She visits the centre to complain that the light switch in her kitchen is broken. Without considering the long-term implications of the action, and because this may be the tenth housing problem of the morning, with a mass of urgent correspondence to be dealt with, a waiting room full of desperate clients and a funding meeting to be attended in half an hour, the welfare rights worker telephones the housing department. The line is engaged. After five or six unsuccessful attempts to contact housing officials by telephone, the worker writes to the housing department pointing out the defect.

A week later the housing department responds with a request for more information. The worker replies by letter. Two weeks afterwards, the switch is repaired by council workmen. In the meantime, the woman has had no light in her kitchen. Because the room is in a dark basement, she has been unable to cook meals for her children.

The victim of the light switch syndrome has become totally dependent on a state which gives her enough money to prevent her children from dying of starvation but which offers little else apart from long-term unemployment, poverty and an appallingly low quality of life.

Self-help community groups based on mutual aid and the free exchange of labour and materials could have fixed the light switch in half an hour. But an obsession with "legal" remedies for such an obviously non-legal problem creates its own delays, helps to perpetuate inequalities and confirms long-term dependence upon a welfare state which is on the verge of collapse.

In 1971 Stephen Wexler, an American lawyer, put forward the view that, in such cases, if the state cannot be exploited at every opportunity for the benefit of the claimant, then it should be bypassed altogether. Wexler argued that the role of the poverty lawyer should be either to seek to strengthen existing organisations of poor people or to help them to start organisations where none exist. Further:

"... if organising is the object of the practice, what are the methods for achieving that object? When an organisation exists, a lawyer must strengthen it: he should refuse to handle any matter for anyone who is not in the organisation".

This point of view is seldom aired in the welfare law industry. It offends against the largely white, middle class charitable ethic which dominates the voluntary sector.

Tribunal representation

Successful applications to tribunals by welfare rights workers are often welcomed in the same way that traditional lawyers get drunk over their first brief with a four-figure fee, or an unexpected not guilty verdict in the Crown Court. Some welfare rights workers ape their mainstream colleagues to the extent of pressing for duty representation at tribunals, effectively restricting the choice and discretion of their clients. Individual successes in tribunals are important for the winners, but they should be weighed against their long-term implications. These include cushioning people from the realities of a run-down welfare state, raising naïve expectations that English justice will somehow see them through, and emphasising the distinction between amateur claimants and professional representatives.

Positive proposals for welfare rights workers

Such workers should devote much more of their time and energy to organising self-help, community-based groups in the following areas:

- Tenants' associations, with the aim of developing tenants' ability to enforce their own rights and to improve their housing conditions through aggressive collective action.

- Claimants' unions, so that claimants themselves may fight to improve their position by informing themselves as to social security regulations and the development of tribunal expertise.

- Squatters' associations, formed to take over empty houses where the state and its agencies are unable or unwilling to provide decent accommodation. An important function of the trained welfare rights worker in this area should be to advise squatters of the risks of criminal prosecution.

- In relation to the huge problem of illiteracy, which is becoming ever more serious in a high-technology society, instead of advice workers reading out letters to their clients, or explaining over and over again the meaning of gas bills and incomprehensible application forms, moves should be made towards developing community-based programmes of adult education and English teaching. The state has patently failed to teach large numbers of people how to read and write. New community schemes should aim to help people to educate themselves and to resist the oppression of an obscurantist bureaucracy.

- A national boycott of all tribunals for a specified period with the express, publicised aim of exposing the inadequacies of the tribunal system.

Forty years ago, the discussion of such proposals was commonplace. Claimants' unions, tenants' associations and squatting groups were widespread and influential. Welfare rights work, then in its infancy, seemed to be moving in the direction of organising the poor to fight back for themselves, with the help of literate professionals. The Up Against the Law collective could state in Issue 2 of its magazine:

The law holds us in chains – if we can't begin to see the chains, how can we begin to free ourselves? But the struggle isn't limited to the courts. Up Against the Law is about more than defence – it is a part of people's "crime" – tenants' groups, strikes, squats, occupations - a class offensive against the people in power.

This is considered in more detail in Chapter 3 (Dissent).

Cuba

The following aspects of legal practice in Cuba have been reported:

- After the revolution, the prestige of lawyers declined and many left the country. Fidel Castro advised young Cubans to study medicine, science and engineering rather than law. This resulted in a dramatic decline in the number of lawyers, who were disparaged as corrupt and useless vestiges of the capitalist class.
- Independent legal practice is not permitted.
- Lawyers work in Bufetes Colectivos. These are collective law offices. They were established by the Ministry of Justice following the abolition of the private practice of law. Bufetos Colectivos are controlled by the National Organization of Bufetos Colectivos (ONBC). This body is responsible for professional conduct and ethics.
- In 2009 there were estimated to be 2000 lawyers in practice in 250 bufetos. They are reported to have large caseloads and to work in difficult conditions.
- Lawyers are expected to uphold the principles of socialist legality.
- Cuban law reflects the country's history. Influences on Cuban law include Spanish Codes, American law and Soviet bloc principles.

The Cuban legal system is fully examined in Chapter 2 (Class) and Chapter 4 (Rights).

GLOSSARY

The following is a provisional explanation of words and phrases which appear in this book (listed in Chapter 6) and which in my experience I have had to explain to students and clients or which have a technical legal meaning different from their normal usage.

Actus reus: Conduct of the accused: see *R v Miller (1983)*

Advocacy: Professional pleading in court

Advocate: Any person who represents another in legal proceedings

Attorney General: The principal law officer of the government, and head of the Bar

Bands: The development of a neckband into two hanging strips

Bear Garden: Rooms in the Law Courts where Masters hear short applications (see Chapter 6 for full description)

Bench wig: The wig worn by judges when they are sitting in court

Bencher: A senior member of an Inn of Court

Bibliography: A systematic list of books and articles used as source material

Black bag: The bag at the back of the barrister's gown is often called a fee bag. The origin of this is said to be that the barrister's fee was placed in the bag so that the barrister did not have to demean himself by handling money

Blue bag: The traditional bag used by junior barristers for carrying fancy dress

Bona fide: Genuine

Breach of statutory duty: Breaking a duty imposed by statute

Breeks: A Scottish term for trousers

Bundle: A collection of documents

Cab rank principle: A barrister has a public obligation, based on the paramount need for access to justice, to act for any client in cases within their field of practice. A barrister cannot refuse a case because of disapproval of what the client has done or is alleged to have done

Call: A formal ceremony, conducted at the Inns of Court, when a student barrister has completed vocational training and is qualified to act as an advocate under the supervision of another barrister

Case law: Law created by decisions of courts

Caveat emptor: Let the buyer beware. A disclaimer of responsibility

Chambers: A judge sitting in chambers does not mean that he is sitting in any particular room, but that he is not sitting in open court. Also, the traditional name for a group of barristers sharing office space

Chambers tea: A traditional gathering of barristers for light refreshments at a particular time

Champerty: The offence of assisting in a case with a view to receiving a share of the disputed property

Civil action/proceedings: Legal proceedings based on a civil right as opposed to a criminal prosecution

Civil Procedure Rules (CPR): Procedural rules prescribed for civil courts

Class justice: Justice which operates in favour of one class and against another

Clerk: An administrative assistant to judges, magistrates or barristers

Client: Customer

Collar stud: A device for attaching a collar to a tunic shirt. There are two types of collar stud. One is short and used at the back of the shirt. The other is long, hinged and is used at the front

Collarette: A female barrister's collar. It consists of a high, round, soft collar. The extra fabric forming the front sits over the shoulders and chest and hides clothing

Common law: Law which has been developed by the judiciary through the setting of precedents, as opposed to being created by the legislature through statutes and regulations

Conditional fee agreement: An agreement for the supply of legal services where a fee is payable only in certain circumstances, normally if the client wins

Conduct of litigation: Steps taken by a restricted group of lawyers to progress a case

Conspiracy: An agreement to carry out an unlawful act

Contingency fee: An agreement for the supply of legal services where a fee is payable only if the client wins

Conveyancing: The transfer of an interest in land.

Corporate manslaughter: Under the Corporate Manslaughter and Corporate Homicide Act 2007, a company is guilty of corporate manslaughter if the way in which its activities are managed or organised amounts to a gross breach of the duty of care which it owes to employees or the public and those failings have caused a death

Counsel: Barrister

Crown immunity: The ancient principle that the sovereign and many government departments are exempt from legal sanctions

Damages: Financial compensation

Devil: A barrister paid by another barrister to do the latter's work

Directives: European legislation which imposes a duty on member states to enact legislation

Director of Public Prosecutions: The head of the Crown Prosecution Service who has power to decide whether prosecutions should proceed

Disability: Under the Naturalisation Act 1870, "disability" meant "the status of being an infant lunatic, idiot or married woman". The most recent definition is now set out in the Equality Act 2010 as "a physical or mental impairment that has a substantial and long-term adverse effect on the ability to perform normal day-to-day activities"

Discovery: A civil procedure which enables a party to a case to obtain evidence before a trial by asking the other party questions or requiring the production of documents

Employment Appeal Tribunal: The appellate tribunal for decisions made by employment tribunals

Employment Tribunal: The tribunal with jurisdiction to hear employment disputes

Entail: A settlement of succession in land so that it cannot be bequeathed at pleasure

Eructation: Belching

Ex parte: In summary, legal proceedings brought by one party in the absence of other parties

Fee bag: See **Black bag**

First instance: The first decision made by a court or tribunal in a case which has subsequently been appealed

Folio: (Obsolete) The number of words (72 or 90) taken as a unit in reckoning the length of a document

Full bottomed wig: The wig worn by judges on ceremonial occasions

Green bag: A bag for exclusive use by judges.

Grievance procedure: Employers' procedure for complaints by employees

Guinea: 21 shillings. Replaced in 1816 as currency in Britain but retained in legal circles until decimalisation in 1971

Habeas corpus (Have your carcase): An ancient remedy requiring the production of a detained person to a court

Hearing: A formal session in a court or tribunal

Human rights: Fundamental rights and freedoms

In camera: Private hearing

Incorrigible rogue: A criminal offence of vagrancy under the Vagrancy Act 1824. Last known to be invoked in 2000 against a 19 year old

Inns of Court: Four legal societies having the exclusive right of admitting persons to practise at the Bar (Inner Temple, Middle Temple, Lincoln's Inn, Gray's Inn)

Intellectual property: Exclusive rights to a range of intangible assets, for example copyright, trademarks and patents

Judiciary: Professional judges in a legal system

Justice: Fairness and/or equality

Ladies' collar: Similar to a collarette but without the extra fabric front

Law Centre: In summary, an organisation providing free legal assistance

Legal aid: Financial assistance given by the state to those who cannot afford legal advice or representation. Now largely of historical interest

Legal expenses insurance: Insurance, often contained in a wider policy, which provides cover for the cost of legal assistance

Letters Patent (Literae patentes): Writings of the sovereign, sealed with the Great Seal, whereby a person or company is enabled to do acts or enjoy privileges which he or it could not do or enjoy without such authority

Libel: A statement in writing which attacks a person's reputation

Lightweight pincetta gown: A gown which is "ideally suited to warmer climates"

Litigant in person: A party to legal proceedings who is not represented by a lawyer

Litigation: The conduct and progression of a case

Lord: A member of the House of Lords

Manslaughter: In summary, killing without the intention required for murder

Master: A member of the judiciary who deals, generally, with procedural matters

Mediation: A type of alternative dispute resolution involving negotiation with an independent third party

Mens rea: Guilty mind

Miscarriage of justice: The conviction and punishment of an innocent person

Murder: In summary, killing with intent. May not be criminal if committed by the state

Natural justice: Based on innate moral sense; minimum standards of fairness in judging a dispute

Natural law: Belief in a system of justice common to all men, with vaguely mystical origins

Neckband shirt see **Tunic shirt**

Negligence: A civil wrong developed by the courts, involving a duty of care, breach of that duty and resulting loss

Novus actus interveniens: A new intervening act which breaks the chain of causation and avoids liability

Ogden Tables: Actuarial tables for use in personal injury and fatal accident cases, based on various factors

Parliamentary draftsman: Professional drafters of legislation

Party: A person involved in litigation

Pecunia non olet: Money does not smell. Reputedly originating from the Roman Emperor Vespasian's urine tax

Perpetuities: This property law concept is impossible to define concisely. See Chapter 6

Practice: Work as a lawyer

Pro bono: Pro bono publico, for the public good. Professional work done without charge

Pro hac vice. An appointment for a particular occasion only

Public access: Direct access for the public to a barrister without having to employ a solicitor as a go-between

Punter see **Client**

Pupil: A trainee barrister working under the supervision of another barrister

Pupilmaster: The barrister who supervises a pupil

QC tail: A coat worn by Queen's Counsel

Quantum: The amount of compensation

Quantum meruit: As much as has been earned; reasonable value

Queen's Counsel: An honour conferred on barristers of standing and experience

Red bag: A bag bestowed as a gift from a QC to a junior barrister for outstanding work. The bag carries the initials of the junior barrister and there is parchment in the bag for the QC to write a message

Refreshers: A barrister's additional fee when a case overruns its estimated length; effervescent confectionery

Res ipsa loquitur: A circumstantial rule of evidence based on the concept that, where an accident happens under circumstances where it is so improbable that it could have happened without negligence, the mere happening of the accident gives rise to an inference of negligence

Risk assessment: The assessment of potential hazards

Rogue and vagabond: "Every person pretending or professing to tell fortunes, or using any subtle craft, means, or device, by palmistry or otherwise, to deceive and impose on any of his Majesty's subjects; every person wandering abroad and lodging in nay barn or outhouse, or in any deserted or unoccupied building, or in the open air, or under a tent, or in any cart or waggon… and not giving a good account of himself or herself… every person, wilfully, openly, lewdly, and obscenely exposing his person … with intent to insult any female; every person wandering abroad, and endeavouring by the exposure of wounds or deformities to obtain or gather alms; every person going about as a gatherer or collector of alms, or endeavouring to procure charitable contributions of any nature or kind, under any false or fraudulent pretence … every person being found in or upon any dwelling house, warehouse, coach-house, stable or outhouse, or in any inclosed yard, garden or area, for any unlawful purpose … and every person apprehended as an idle and disorderly person, and violently resisting any constable, or other peace officer so apprehending him or her, and being subsequently convicted … shall be deemed a **rogue and vagabond.** (Vagrancy Act 1824, section 4, as amended).

Royal Bencher: A member of the Royal family who holds the office of Bencher in an Inn of Court without having to obtain legal qualifications

Rule of law: The subordination of all authorities to certain legal principles

Senior barrister: A proposal that a barrister with a number of years' experience should be described as a senior barrister was rejected by the Bar Council because it would confuse the public

Serious Fraud Office: An organisation responsible for the investigation and prosecution of serious criminal offences

Silk: King's Counsel or Queen's Counsel, so-called because they wear silk gowns

Supreme Court: The new name for the House of Lords, the highest appeal court

Table/Tabling: Lists of statutes and cases which appear in legal textbooks

Taxonomy: Principles of classification

Temple: Two Inns of Court – Inner and Middle – originally occupied by the Knights Templars. Part of London between the Strand and the Thames

Tippet: For those, like me, who have no idea what a tippet is, the Shorter Oxford English Dictionary gives the following guidance:

- A long narrow strip of cloth or hanging part of dress, either attached to and forming part of the hood, head-dress or sleeve, or loose, as a scarf or the like
- A garment, usually of fur or wool, covering the shoulders, or the neck and shoulders; a cape or short cloak
- A band of silk or other material worn round the neck, with the two ends pendent from the shoulders in front
- A hangman's rope

Touting: Soliciting custom

Trousering: Obsolete slang for stealing; pilfering

Tunic shirt: A collarless shirt worn by lawyers.

Vesting: Conferring an immediate right

Volenti non fit injuria: No injury is done to a person who consents to it. A largely obsolete defence of consent to a claim for compensation for a civil wrong

War crime: A violation of the laws of war

Welfare law: Generally, the law of social security

Wig: A horsehair wig is worn in most courts by barristers. Reputedly imported from France in the seventeenth century to indicate social standing and wealth

Work-related stress: Mental disorder caused by workplace conditions

FURTHER READING

Abel, Richard, *English Lawyers Between Market and State: the Politics of Professionalism*, Oxford 2003

Abel-Smith, Brian, and Stevens, Robert, *In Search of Justice*, Allen Lane The Penguin Press, 1968

Abel-Smith, Brian, and Stevens, Robert, *Lawyers and the Courts: a sociological study of the English Legal System*, Heinemann, 1967

Ackroyd, Carol; Margolis, Karen; Rosenhead, Jonathan; and Shallice, Tim, *The Technology of Political Control*, Penguin 1977

Bailey, S.H., Ching, J.P.L., Gunn, M.J. and Ormerod, D.C., Smith, *Bailey & Gunn on the Modern English Legal System*, 4th ed., Sweet & Maxwell 2002

Bankowski, Zenon, and Mungham, Geoff, *Images of Law*, Routledge & Kegan Paul, 1976

Barclay, Harold, *People Without Government*, Kahn & Averill 1982

Barrie, Peter, *Compensation for Personal Injuries*, OUP 2002

Becker, Theodore L., *Political Trials*, Bobbs-Merrill 1971

Begg, Moazzam, *Enemy Combatant*, Pocket Books 2007

Behr, Edward, *Prohibition: Thirteen years that changed America*, Arcade Publishing 1996

Bennion, F.A.R, *Statute Law*, Oyez Publishing Ltd 1980

Berlins, Marcel and Dyer, Clare, *The Law Machine*, Penguin 2000

Bingham, Tom, *The Rule of Law*, Allen Lane 2010

Bird, Roger, *Starting in Practice*, Sweet & Maxwell 1984

Black, Jonathan, ed., *Radical Lawyers: Their Role in the Movement and in the Courts*, Avon Books 1971

Boulton, W.W., *Conduct and Etiquette at the Bar*, Butterworths 1965

Bowring, Bill, *The Degradation of The International Legal Order?* Routledge Cavendish 2008

Boyle, Kevin; Hadden, Tom; and Hillyard, Paddy, *Law and State*, Martin Robertson 1975

Brailsford, H N, *The Levellers and the English Revolution*, Spokesman 1983

Broue, Pierre, and Temine, Emile, *The Revolution and the Civil War in Spain*, MIT 1970

Burke, John, ed., *Jowitt's Dictionary of English Law*, Sweet & Maxwell 1977

Cain, Maureen and Hunt, Alan, *Marx and Engels on Law*, Academic Press 1979

Campbell, Colm, *Emergency Law in Ireland 1918-1925*, Clarendon Press 1994

Campbell, Tom, *The Left and Rights*, Routledge Kegan Paul 1983

Camus, Albert, *The Fall*, Penguin 1963

Camus, Albert, *The Rebel*, Penguin 1984

Carlen, Pat (ed.) *The Sociology of Law*, University of Keele, 1976

Chambliss, W.J., and Seidmann, R.B., *Law, Order and Power*, Addison-Wesley 1971

Chesterman, Michael, *Charities, Trusts and Social Welfare*, Weidenfeld & Nicolson 1979

Clayton, Richard, and Tomlinson, Hugh, *The Law of Human Rights*, Oxford University Press 2000

Cordery on Solicitors, Butterworths 2009

Cotterrell, Roger, *The Politics of Jurisprudence*, 2nd ed, Lexis Nexis 2004

Cranston, M., *What are Human Rights*, Bodley Head 1973

Curzon, LB, *A Dictionary of Law*, Macdonald & Evans 1979

Dale, William, *Legislative Drafting: A New Approach*, Butterworths 1977

De Smith, Stanley, and Brazier, Rodney, *Constitutional and Administrative Law*, 7th ed., Penguin 1994

Denning, Lord, *What Next in the Law*, Butterworths 1982

Devlin, Patrick, *The Judge*, Oxford University Press, 1979

Dias, RWM, *Jurisprudence*, 5th ed., Butterworths 1985

Elliott, Catherine, & Quinn, Frances, *English Legal System*, 10th ed., Pearson Longman 2009

Engels, Frederick, *The Condition of the Working Class in England*, Panther 1974

Evans, Keith, *Advocacy at the Bar*, Financial Training 1983

Evanson, Debra, *Revolution in the Balance, Law and Society in Contemporary Cuba*, Westview Press 1994

Feldman, David, *Civil Liberties and Human Rights in England and Wales*, OUP 2002

Foot, Michael, *Aneurin Bevan Volume 2*, Paladin/Granada 1975

Friedmann, Wolfgang, *Law in a Changing Society*, Penguin 1972

Gifford, Tony, *Where's The Justice*, Penguin 1986

Gladstone, Francis, *Charity, Law and Social Justice*, Bedford Square Press/NCVO 1982

Glossary of Scottish and European Union Legal Terms and Latin Phrases, Law Society of Scotland, Lexis Nexis Butterworths 2003

Godwin, William, *Caleb Williams*, Penguin 1988

Goldman, Emma, *Living My Life*, Pluto Press 1988

Graham,M. (ed), *Man!* Cienfuegos Press 1974

Griffith, John, *The Politics of the Judiciary,* Fontana 1985

Grigg-Spall, Ian, and Ireland, Paddy (eds) *The Critical Lawyers' Handbook*, Pluto Press 1992

Haas, Jeffrey, *The Assassination of Fred Hampton*: How the FBI and the Chicago Police murdered a Balck

Panther, Lawrence Hill Books 2009

Hain, Peter, *Political Trials in Britain*, Pelican 1985

Harding, Alan, *A Social History of English Law*, Penguin 1966

Hart, H.L.A., *Bentham and the Demystification of Law* 1973 Modern Law Review p.2

Harvey on Industrial Relations and Employment Law, Butterworths/Lexis Nexis 2007

Haskell, Paul G., *Why Lawyers Behave As They Do*, Westview Press 1998

Hazard, John N., *Communists and their law*, University of Chicago Press 1969

Hazell, Robert, ed., *The Bar on Trial*, Quartet 1978

Head, Michael, *Evgeny Pashukanis, A critical reappraisal*, Routledge Cavendish 2007

Hewart, Lord, *The New Despotism*, Ernest Benn, 1929

Hill, Christopher, *The World Turned Upside Down: Radical Ideas during the English Revolution*, Penguin 1991

Hillyard, Paddy, *Suspect Community*, Pluto Press 1993

Hobsbawm, E.J., *Bandits*, Pelican 1972

Hopes, Thomas W, *The Rules Against Perpetuities*, Solicitors Law Stationery Ltd 1961

Jackson, R.M., *The Machinery of Justice*, Cambridge University Press 1972

Jaffe, Louis L., *English and American Judges as Lawmakers*, Oxford University Press 1969

Jowitt's Dictionary of English Law, 2nd ed., Sweet & Maxwell 1977

Kafka, Franz, *The Trial*, Picador 1977

Kierkegaard, Soren, *Either/Or*, Princeton University Press 1971

Kirchheimer, Otto, *Political Justice*, Princeton University Press, 1961

Kramer, Adam, *Bewigged and Bewildered? A Guide to Becoming a Barrister in England and Wales*, Hart Publishing 2007

Kropotkin, Peter, *In Russian and French Prisons*, Black Rose 1991

Kropotkin, Peter, *The Great French Revolution*, Black Rose 1981

Laski, Harold J., *Studies in Law and Politics*, Allen & Unwin, 1932

Levenson, Howard, *A Reply to Pessimism*, Haldane Society Bulletin, November 1977

Levenson, Howard, *The Price of Justice*, Cobden Trust 1981

Livingstone, Owen & Macdonald, *Prison Law*, Oxford University Press 2003

Lloyd: Introduction to Jurisprudence, 6th ed., M.D.A. Freeman, Sweet and Maxwell 1994

Lottmann, Herbert R., *Camus*, Picador 1981

Mandel, Michael, *How America Gets Away With Murder: Illegal Wars, Collateral Damage and Crimes Against Humanity*, Pluto Press 2004

Mandela, Nelson, *Long Walk to Freedom*, Little, Brown and Company 1994

Mansfield, Michael, *Memoirs of a Radical Lawyer*, Bloomsbury 2009

Mansfield, Michael, *Presumed Guilty*, Mandarin 1994

Marshall, Peter, *Demanding the Impossible: A History of Anarchism*, Harper Collins 1992

Marshall, Peter, *The Anarchist Writings of William Godwin*, Freedom Press 1986

Marx, Karl, *The Civil War in France*, Progress Publishers Moscow 1974

Matthias & Oulton on Legal Aid and Advice, Butterworths 1971

McGrath, Alister, *In the Beginning: The story of the King James Bible*, Hodder & Stoughton 2002

Mellows, *The Law of Succession* (5th ed, Clive V Margrave-Jones), Butterworths 1993

Miers, David R., and Page, Alan C., *Legislation*, Sweet & Maxwell 1990

Mitford, Jessica, *The American Prison Business*, Penguin 1977

Morgan, Kenneth O, Michael Foot, *A Life*, Harper Press 2007

Mortimer, John, *The Second Rumpole Omnibus*, Penguin 1982

Naughton, Michael, *Rethinking Miscarriages of Justice*, Palgrave Macmillan 2007

Orwell, George, *Collected Essays*, Journalism and Letters, Penguin 1970

Orwell, George, *Homage to Catalonia*, Penguin 1962

Orwell, George, *1984*, Penguin 2004

Osborn's Concise Law Dictionary, 10th ed., Mick Woodley, Sweet & Maxwell 2005

Palmer, Tony, *The Trials of Oz*, Blond & Briggs 1971

Parry, Richard, *The Bonnot Gang*, Rebel Press 1987

Pashukanis, E.B., *Selected Writings on Marxism and Law*, Academic Press 1980

Pogge, Thomas (ed), *Freedom from Poverty as a Human Right*, Oxford University Press 2007

Postema, Gerald J: *Bentham: Moral, Political and Legal Philosophy*, Ashgate 2002

Pritt, Denis Nowell, *Law, Class and Society: Book 1, The Apparatus of the Law*, Lawrence and Wishart 1970; *Book 2, Employers, Workers and Law in the Colonies,* Lawrence and Wishart *1971; Book 3, Law and Politics, Law in the Colonies,*Lawrence & Wishart 1971; *Book 4, the Substance of the Law*, Lawrence and Wishart 1972

Rai, Milan, *War Plan Iraq*, Arrow Publications 2002

Reeves, Peter, *Are Two Legal Professions Necessary*, Waterlow 1986

Robertson, Geoffrey, *The Justice Game*, Vintage 1998

Rosebaum, Alan S (ed), *The Philosophy of Human Rights*, Aldwych Press 1980

Russell on Crime, 12th ed., JW Cecil Turner, Stevens 1964

Sachs, Albie, *Justice in South Africa*, University of California Press, 1973

Sachs, Albie, *Protecting Human Rights in a new South Africa*, OUP 1990

Sachs, Albie, *The Jail Diary of Albie Sachs*, Paladin 1990

Sachs, Albie, *The Strange Alchemy of Life and Law*, Oxford University Press 2009

Sachs, Albie, and Wilson, Joan Hoff, *Sexism and the Law*, Martin Robertson, 1978

Serge, Victor, *Memoirs of a Revolutionary 1901-1941*, OUP 1978

Serge, Victor, *Men in Prison*, Writers and Readers 1977

Serge, Victor, *What Everyone Should Know About State Repression*, New Park Publications 1979

Shafer, David A., *The Paris Commune*, Palgrave Macmillan 2005

Shelden, Michael, *Orwell, The Authorised Biography*, Heinemann 1991

Sim, Joe, *Punishment and Prisons:Power and the Carceral State*, Sage 2009

Simor, Jessica, and Emmerson, Ben, *Human Rights Practice*, Sweet & Maxwell 2000

Soelle, Dorothee, *Against the wind*, Fortress Press 1999

Spicer, Robert, *Conspiracy Law, Class and Society*, Lawrence & Wishart 1981

Spicer, Robert, *Employment Tribunals: A Summary of Developments 1999*, Monitor Press 2000.

Spicer, Robert, *Workplace Stress: The Legal Essentials*, Running Heads 2002

Stafford Smith, Clive, *Bad Men: Guantanamo Bay and the Secret Prisons*, Phoenix 2008

Starmer, Keir, *European Human Rights Law*, Legal Action Group 1999

Stiglitz, Joseph, and Bilmes, Linda, *The Three Trillion Dollar War*, Allen Lane 2008

Stringer, Peter, *Practical Ethics*, Cambridge University Press 1999

Swift, Jonathan, and Chapman, Chris, *Employment Court Practice*, 2nd ed., Sweet & Maxwell 2008

Taylor, Ian, Walton, Paul, and Young, Jock (eds) *Critical Criminology*, Routledge & Kegan Paul 1975

Thomas, Gwyn, *The Dark Philosophers*, Library of Wales 2006

Thomas, Gwyn, *Sorrow for thy Sons*, Lawrence & Wishart 1986

Thompson, E.P., *The Making of the English Working Class*, Pelican 1979

Thompson, E.P., *The Rule of the Judges*, New Society 22 November 1979

Thompson, E.P., *The Rule of Law in English History*, 10 Haldane Society Bulletin, 7

Thompson, E.P., *The Secret State*, State Research Pamphlet No 1, May 1979

Thompson, E.P., *Whigs and Hunters: The Origin of the Black Act*, Penguin 1977
Thompson, E.P., *Writing by Candlelight*, Merlin 1980

Thurlow, Richard, *The Secret State*, Blackwell 1994

Tifft, L., and Sullivan, D., *The Struggle to be Human*, Cienfuegos Press, 1980

Tigar, Michael, and Levy, Madeleine, *Law and the Rise of Capitalism*, Monthly Review Press, 1979

Todd, Olivier, Albert Camus, *A Life*, Vintage 1998

Tolstoy, Leo, *Government is Violence, Essays on Anarchism and Pacifism*, Phoenix Press 1990

Tolstoy, Leo, *Resurrection*, Progress Publishers 1972

Vague, Tom, *Televisionaries*, AK Press 1994

Vonnegut, Kurt, *Timequake*, Jonathan Cape 1997

Walker, Clive, and Starmer, Keir, *Miscarriages of Justice: A Review of Justice in Error*, Blackstone 1999

Walker, D.M., *The Oxford Companion to Law*, Clarendon Press 1980

Walker, DM, *The Scottish Legal System*, W Green/Sweet & Maxwell 1992

Ward, Richard, and Akhtar, Amanda, *Walker & Walker's English Legal System*, OUP 2008

Weissman, Susan, ed., *The Ideas of Victor Serge: A Life as a Work of Art*, Merlin Press 1998

Wilde, Oscar, *The Soul of Man under Socialism* (Collected Works, Spring Books 1963

Wilson, AN, *Tolstoy*, Hamish Hamilton 1988

Woetzel, Robert K., *The Nuremburg Trials in International Law*, Stevens & Sons 1960

Woodley, Mick, *Osborn's Concise Law Dictionary*, 10th ed., Sweet & Maxwell 2005

Words and Phrases Legally Defined, 3rd ed., Butterworth 1987

Zander, Michael, *The Law-Making Process,* 6th ed., Cambridge University Press 2004

DVDs

La Commune (Paris 1871) 2000, DVD, Peter Watkins, First Run/Icarus Films, Brooklyn, New York

McLibel 2005, DVD Spanner Films, London, United Kingdom

New Street Law 2006-2007, DVD, BBC/Red Production Company/One-Eyed Dog Ltd, Wales

Terror's Advocate 2007, DVD, Artificial Eye, France

The Battle of Algiers 2003, DVD, Argent Films, United Kingdom

WEBSITES

BAILLI (British and Irish Legal Information Centre (free access to source materials): www.bailli.org

Bar pro bono unit: www.barprobono.org.uk

Citizens Advice Bureaux: www.adviceguide.org.uk

Cuba Solidarity Campaign: www.cuba-solidarity.org

Ede & Ravenscroft: www.edeandravenscroft.co.uk

Frederick Place Chambers:
www.frederickchambers.co.uk

Free Representation Unit: www.thefru.org.uk

George Monbiot: www.arrestblair.org

Haldane Society: www.haldane.org

Health and Safety Executive: www.hse.gov.uk

Justice (All-party law reform and human rights organisation): www.justice.org.uk

Law Centres Federation: www.lawcentres.org.uk

Law Works: www.lawworks.org

Legal Action Group: www.lag.org.uk

Legal Services Commission: www.legalservices.gov.uk

Liberty: www.liberty-humanrights.org.uk

Peace News: www.peacenews-info

Peacerights: www.peacerights.org

Rowntree Trust: www.jrct.org.uk

CASE LIST

A v X and others [2004] UKHL 56

A and Others v Secretary of State for the Home Department [2005] 2 AC 68, HL

Airey v Ireland (1979) 2 E.H.R.R. 305, ECHR

Al-Saadoon and Mufdhi v United Kingdom (2010) ECHR, The Times March 10

Bertuzzi v France (2003) ECHR February 13

Brown Quinn and Another v Equity Syndicate Management Limited and Another [2012] EWCA Civ 1633

Cowl and Others v Plymouth City Council (2002) The Times, January 8, CA

Cox v Ministry of Justice [2014] EWCA Civ 132

Customs and Excise Commissioners v Polok and Another [2002] EWHC 156, ChD

Davies v Global Strategies Group [2010] EWCA Civ 648, CA

Davy v Leeds Corporation [1965] 1 WLR 445, HL

Ferguson v Home Office (1977) The Times, October 8 , HL

Fryer v Pearson (2000) The Times, April 4, CA

Fytche v Wincanton Logistics plc [2004] ICR 975, HL
GE Capital Bank v Rushton & Jenkin [2006] EWCA Civ 1556, CA

Government of the RSA v Grootboom 2001 (1) SA 46 (CC)

Green & Sons v Minister of Health [1948] 1 KB 34

Harman v Home Office [1981] 2 WLR 310, CA

Hatton v Sutherland and Others (2002) ICR 613, CA

HM Advocate v Balmer and Others (2007) Scottish Court of Session, February 21

Hopps v Mott Macdonald Ltd & Ministry of Defence (2009) The Times, July 24, HC

ICI v Shatwell [1964] 2 All ER 999, HL

James v United Kingdom (1986) 8 EHRR 43, ECHR

JL (A Youth) v Director of Public Prosecutions (2007) The Times, October 8, CA

London Borough of Southwark v Williams [1971] 2 All ER 175

Matthews v Ministry of Defence [2003] UKHL 4, HL

McIlkenny v Chief Constable of West Midlands Police Force [1980] QB 283

Minister of Health v Treatment Action Campaign 2002 (5) SA 721 (CC)

Mogul Steamship Co v McGregor, Gow & Co (1889) 23 QBD 598

Napier v Scottish Ministers [2005] CSIH 16

Neary v Governing Body of St Albans Girls' School and Another (2009) the Times, November 23, CA

Ng v Director of Public Prosecutions (2007), The Times, February 7, HC

Niyazi's Will Trusts, Re [1978] 1 WLR 910

O'Hanlon v Commissioners for HM Revenue and Customs [2007] EWCA Civ 283, CA

Pullen v Prison Commissioners [1957] 3 All ER 470

R v Director of Public Prosecutions and Others ex parte Jones [2000] IRLR 373, HC

R v Kendall-Smith (2006) (unreported)

R v Miller [1983] 1 All ER 978, CA

R v Nottinghamshire Healthcare NHS Trust (2009) The Times, August 10, CA

R (On the application of Binyam Mohamed) v The Secretary of State for Commonweath and Foreign Affairs [2010] EWCA Civ 65

R (On the application of Corner House Research and Others) v Director of the Serious Fraud Office [2008] UKHL 60, HL

R (On the application of Gentle and Another) v The Prime Minister [2008] UKHL 20, HL

R (Corner House Research and Another) v Director of the Serious Fraud Office [2008] UKHL 60

R v Mary, Queen of Scots (1586) 1 St Tr 1161

Sanders Will Trusts, Re [1954] 1 Ch 265

Soobramoney v Minister of Health Kwazulu Natal 1998 (1) SA 765 (CC)

Steel and Morris v United Kingdom [2005] ECHR 103

Suffolk Mental Health Partnership NHS Trust v Hunt and Others (2009) The Times, April 28, CA

Williams v J. Walter Thompson Group Ltd (2005) The Times, April 5, CA

LIST OF ABBREVIATIONS

ABA: American Bar Association

AC: Appeal cases

ADR: Alternative dispute resolution

All ER: All England Law Reports

CA: Court of Appeal

CAB: Citizens' Advice Bureau

CFA: Conditional fee agreement

Ch: Chancery (Law Reports)

ChD: Chancery Division

CPD: Continuing professional development

CPR: Civil Procedure Rules

DDA: Disability Discrimination Act

DPP: Director of Public Prosecutions

EAT: Employment Appeal Tribunal

ECHR: European Court of Human Rights

EHRR: European Human Rights Reports

EWCA: England and Wales Court of Appeal

EWHC: High Court of England and Wales

FRU: Free Representation Unit

HC: High Court

HL: House of Lords

HSE: Health and Safety Executive

ICC: International Criminal Court

ICR: Industrial Cases Reports

ILO: International Labour Organization

KC: King's Counsel

LAG: Legal Action Group

MLR: Modern Law Review

OFT: Office of Fair Trading

ONBC: Organisacion Nacional de Bufetes Colectivos

QB: Queen's Bench (Law Reports)

QBD: Queen's Bench Division

QC: Queen's Counsel

RCJAB: Royal Courts of Justice Advice Bureau

SA: South Africa

SIAT: Special Immigration Appeals Tribunal

St Tr: State Trials

UKHL: United Kingdom House of Lords

UPAL: Up Against The Law

WLR: Weekly Law Report

INDEX

ND - #0187 - 110926 - C0 - 210/148/38 - PB - 9781784560881 - Gloss Lamination